MOTHERS
in Children's and
Young Adult Literature

Illustration by Sir R. Noel Paton from Charles Kingsley's *The Water Babies* (Macmillan, 1863)

MOTHERS
in Children's and Young Adult Literature

From the Eighteenth Century to Postfeminism

Edited by Lisa Rowe Fraustino and Karen Coats

University Press of Mississippi / Jackson

Children's Literature Association Series

www.upress.state.ms.us

The University Press of Mississippi is a member
of the Association of American University Presses.

Copyright © 2016 by University Press of Mississippi
All rights reserved

First printing 2016

∞

Library of Congress Cataloging-in-Publication Data

Names: Fraustino, Lisa Rowe, editor. | Coats, Karen, 1963–editor.
Title: Mothers in children's and young adult literature : from the eighteenth century to postfeminism / edited by Lisa Rowe Fraustino and Karen Coats.
Description: Jackson : University Press of Mississippi, [2016] | Series: Children's literature association series | Includes index.
Identifiers: LCCN 2015042374 | ISBN 9781496806994 (hardback)
Subjects: LCSH: Children's stories, English—History and criticism. | Children's stories, American—History and criticism. | Mothers in literature. | Motherhood in literature. | Mothers in popular culture. | Motherhood in popular cutlture. | Young adult fiction, English—History and criticism. | Young adult fiction, American—History and criticism. | Feminism and literature. | Women and literature. | BISAC: LITERARY CRITICISM / Children's Literature. | SOCIAL SCIENCE / Women's Studies. | SOCIAL SCIENCE / Popular Culture.
Classification: LCC PR990 .M69 2016 | DDC 820.9/9282—dc23 LC record available at http://lccn.loc.gov/2015042374

British Library Cataloging-in-Publication Data available

Contents

ix   Acknowledgments

3   Introduction: Mothers Wanted
    —Lisa Rowe Fraustino and Karen Coats

Part I—Historical Legacies: Maternal Instruction and Delight

27   **CHAPTER 1**   Barbauld and the Body-Part Game: Maternal Pedagogy in the Long Eighteenth Century
    —Donelle Ruwe

45   **CHAPTER 2**   Juliana Ewing's *Six to Sixteen*: Realizing and Rewriting Maternal Legacy
    —Koeun Kim

59   **CHAPTER 3**   The Romance of Othermothering in Nineteenth-Century *Backfisch* Books
    —Julie Pfeiffer

Part II—Mothering in Modernity: Shifting Cultures and Subjectivities

77   **CHAPTER 4**   The Women Who Sent Their Children Away: Mothers in Kindertransport Fiction
    —Adrienne Kertzer

96	**CHAPTER 5**	Minority Mama: Rejecting the Mainstream Mothering Model —Dorina K. Lazo Gilmore
113	**CHAPTER 6**	Cultural-Historical Activity Theory and the Expansive Cycle of Mothering while Black —Lauren Causey and Karen Coats
133	**CHAPTER 7**	"The hills were in her bones": Living in the Blend of Mothers and Environments —Anna Katrina Gutierrez

Part III—The Mother-Child Bond: Fantasy and Desire for the Real

153	**CHAPTER 8**	Animal Mothers and Animal Babies in Picture Books —Robin Calland
170	**CHAPTER 9**	A Daughter's Sacrifice: Saving the "Good-Enough Mother" from the Good Mother Fantasy —Alexandra Kotanko
182	**CHAPTER 10**	"The Mother Was the Mother, Even When She Wasn't": Maternal Care Ethics and Children's Fantasy —Mary Jeanette Moran

Part IV—Performing Postfeminist Motherhood

201	**CHAPTER 11**	"I Would Never Be Strong Enough": Sarah Dessen's Postfeminist Mothers —Sara K. Day
216	**CHAPTER 12**	Abandoning Mothers —Lisa Rowe Fraustino

| 233 | **CHAPTER 13** "A Mom-Shaped Hole": Psychoanalyisis and the Dystopian Maternal
—Jennifer Mitchell |

251 Contributors

255 Index

Acknowledgments

This is Lisa. First and foremost I must thank Karen Coats. If she had not visited my Mothers in Children's and Young Adult Literature class at Hollins University in the summer of 2013, this book idea would still be one of many projects filed away in the category of "one I really want to do when I have more time." She offered to coedit a collection, and being a long admirer of her work, I jumped at the opportunity. I have enjoyed every minute and learned a great deal from her, especially about the latest developments in cognitive studies and reading schemas. Karen and I think differently about things and have different editorial skill sets that complement each other nicely; of her many talents, the one that I think most benefited this book is her rare gift for climbing into someone else's complex theory and explaining it in ways that make it crystal clear on the page. A partnership like this has the potential to strain a friendship, but it only strengthened ours.

Next, I must thank the three institutions that have supported my scholarship. First is the Children's Literature Association, which has given me an academic home, introduced me to many scholarly friends (including Karen), and allowed me to test my ideas on mothers and other topics at annual conferences since 1994. At my first conference, in Missouri, I met Elizabeth Keyser, the ChLA foremother who is responsible for inviting me to propose a course to teach at the next institution I must thank: Hollins University. In the summer of 1995 I joined the visiting faculty in the Graduate Program in Children's Literature at Hollins and since then have had opportunities to teach a wide range of courses in my areas of interest, both in creative writing and critical approaches to texts. Amanda Cockrell, the director, has been my enabler, not only embracing the idea of offering a special topics course Mothers in Children's and Young Adult Literature in 2005 but then deeming the topic important enough to become a permanent course that generations of Hollins students may experience. Thank you, Amanda.

The third but not least institution I must thank is Eastern Connecticut State University, beginning with the English Department for providing its members the freedom to offer the two-semester senior seminar on any topic we propose. That was the format in which I first conceived my course Mothers in Children's and Young Adult Literature, and for which I received a curriculum development grant in 2003. Thank you, Eastern, for that and also for a research grant to support the editing of this book in 2013. This funding allowed me to set aside some time to concentrate on editing but even more importantly, to travel to Bloomington and work with Karen in person on the manuscript before submitting it to the press. Thanks also to Meena Roy and Laura Duquette, two outstanding undergraduate research assistants.

Your names are too numerous to list here, but I also send out a huge thank you to all of my students in every section of Mothers in Children's Literature that I have ever taught at Hollins and Eastern. I learned more from you than you did from me.

I thank the suffragettes.

I thank the second-wave feminists, especially those who wrote about mothers when I myself was still in the intended audience of children's and young adult literature—you changed the world in ways that allowed me to become a mother with my own subjectivity and a writer with a room of my own. Specifically I want to acknowledge my feminist foremothers whose thinking most influenced my own creative writing and scholarship: Donna Bassin, Jessica Benjamin, Nancy Chodorow, Patricia Hill Collins, Simone de Beauvoir, Moyra Davey, Dorothy Dinnerstein, Susan Faludi, Shulamith Firestone, Betty Friedan, Evelyn Nakano Glenn, Susan Griffin, Suzette Henke, Luce Irigaray, Julia Kristeva, Jane Lazarre, Ursula K. Le Guin, Andrea O'Reilly, Adrienne Rich, Sarah Ruddick, Susan Rubin Suleiman, Alice Walker, Virgina Woolf.

And Mary Wollstonecraft.

I thank my husband, Jeff Meunier, for his infinite patience as I spent countless hours working on this book instead of playing board games with him and singing karaoke. Also, I can't imagine myself becoming so interested in this topic if it weren't for my three children, Daisy, Dan, and Livvie.

Finally, and most importantly, I thank own my mother, Carole Linda Reardon Rowe, and her mother, Barbara Evangeline Ladd Reardon. Both of you were and still are good-enough mothers, which, as Coraline finds out and Alexandra Kotanko writes about in chapter 9, is the best possible kind to have.

This is Karen. As her acknowledgments demonstrate, Lisa is much too tough an act to follow, so I want to thank her for letting me come alongside her in this project. Her greatest gifts are her boundless energy, sterling diplomacy, and phenomenal close reading skills. But I think what I most want to thank her for is her openness: open heart, open mind, and open hand. Her generosity of thought, spirit, and commitment to the work carried this project forward from the overwhelming response to our paper call through the smart suggestions for revision to the meticulous process of editing. She has a splendid ear for how things should sound, and the essays are the better for it.

I also want to thank my colleagues and the institutions and organizations that support my work. I am humbled and blessed to have found places where my vocation, avocation, and career happily converge; Illinois State University, the Center for Children's Books at University of Illinois at Urbana-Champaign, ChLA, and Hollins University have each offered me community, inspiration, and encouragement to pursue and test ideas with students and like-minded colleagues. I also want to say a special thank you to our authors for their fantastic work and their willingness to so smartly attend to our suggestions; I hope they are as pleased with the way their essays turned out as we are.

I would also like to thank my terrific family: my parents, who continue to support me in so many large and small ways; Will, who is still listening after all these years, even when I don't say a word; Emily, who breaks my heart daily and remakes it at the same time; and Blair, who continues to amaze me with her wisdom and spirit. In the words of the psalmist: "The boundary lines have fallen for me in pleasant places; surely I have a delightful inheritance" (16:6).

MOTHERS
in Children's and
Young Adult Literature

Introduction

Mothers Wanted

Lisa Rowe Fraustino and Karen Coats

> But she took Tom in her arms, and laid him in the softest place of all, and kissed him, and patted him, and talked to him, tenderly and low, such things as he had never heard before in his life; and Tom looked up into her eyes, and loved her, and loved, till he fell fast asleep from pure love.
> —Charles Kingsley, *The Water-Babies* (1863)

Whether living or dead, present or absent, sadly dysfunctional or happily good enough, the figure of the mother carries an enormous amount of freight across the emotional and intellectual life of a child. In her materiality as well as in the child's imaginary landscape, she plays many roles and bears many burdens: a place from which to launch and a home to return to; a secure envelope that protects or one that hides and stifles; a voice that guides and chastises; a surface on which to project the quest for self-understanding.

Her guises in the literature written for children often seem almost cartoonish given the complexity of her position within a child's actual life. The discursive mother is often static if not flat, as authors enact a sort of pedagogy or wish for both adult and child readers regarding how an ideal mother should or should not act, revealing through plot and character arcs the consequences of her brand of nurturance. Often she is relegated to background noise as the focus understandably shifts to the development of the child character, but her influence remains significant and worthy of close consideration.

Much of the theoretical writing on motherhood is focused on gender studies, chastising the rigid gender stereotyping that is found in many portrayals of mothers in children's and young adult literature as well as fairy-tale representations of mothers and stepmothers, an important focus of early feminist readings. Given the vital role literary mothers play in books for young readers, as they of course do in actual children's lives, it is remarkable how little scholarly attention has been paid to other aspects of their representation. The range of critical approaches to mothers in children's and young adult literature in the published scholarship does not yet begin to approach the volume and quality of attention paid to mothers in other disciplines, including psychology, sociology, anthropology, history, women's studies, and of course, literature for adults.

Two Streams of Scholarship

At the turn of the millennium, sociologist Terry Arendell published a review of the previous decade's scholarship on mothering and motherhood in which she identified "two predominant streams" in "a rapidly expanding body of literature." The first stream, which she describes as "conceptual" and "theoretical" in nature, "can be characterized as interpretive, critical, hermeneutic, qualitative, and feminist." The second stream "adheres, more or less, to the classical conventions of positivist social science," focusing on lived experiences; this work, she reports, "is extensive and generally considered to be mainstream in the study of mothering." Arendell's lengthy bibliography, which numbers 170 sources from a range of disciplines, makes this conclusion visually evident with the predominance of books and articles "coming especially out of psychology, human development, and child and family studies."

In her discussion of "the conceptualizing of mothering," where most work in the humanities falls, Arendell identifies feminist constructionism as the dominant theory; that is, mothering practices are viewed as socially constructed and historically variable rather than universal and biologically determined. In this stream Arendell places feminist psychoanalytic revisitings (e.g., Chodorow, 1978; Bassin, 1994; Benjamin, 1994; Dinnerstein, 1976), philosophical attention to care relationships (Ruddick, 1989; Noddings, 1984), cultural studies of situational contexts (Collins, 1991; Glenn, 1994), and personal experience narratives (Rich, 1976; Walker, 1983). As one example, psychologist Shari L. Thurer's 1994 book, *The Myths of Motherhood: How Culture Reinvents the Good Mother*, traces the history of societal attitudes toward mothers from the revered "Old Stone Age Mom" (4) in the

Neolithic period to the "Fall from Grace: Twentieth-Century Mom" (225).[1] In this conceptual stream of scholarship, Arendell notes, dominant ideologies are problematized and deconstructed; thus the subject of mothering and motherhood offers the potential to "focus attention on the interrelated systems of gender, race, ethnicity, and class stratification." For these gaps to be closed, however, "we need more attention to the lives of particular mothers—to mothers' own voices—and to the lives and voices of diverse groups of mothers." The same need applies to mothers as literary characters, and this assumption underlies the aims of this volume.

Arendell urges scholars to work at bridging the gap between the streams of conceptual arts and empirical sciences. This gap even occurs in her own work, as her literature review, surprisingly, omits any reference to a mother-thinker whom Claudia Glenn Dowling has described as "the scientist who destroyed our quaint concept of what a mother ought to be," the sociobiologist-anthropologist Sarah Blaffer Hrdy. Hrdy's trilogy of pathbreaking works—*The Woman That Never Evolved* (1981), *Mother Nature: Maternal Instincts and How They Shape the Human Species* (1999), and *Mothers and Others: The Evolutionary Origins of Mutual Understanding* (2009)—radically challenged the historical primacy of masculine aggression in the narrative of evolutionary psychology by calling out the cultural construction of accepted scientific "truths" as coming from a patrilineal perspective. In an interview with Eric Michael Johnson in 2012, Hrdy explains how becoming a mother led her to research the female reproductive strategies of primates and her findings that human evolution was based on cooperative parenting and communal care:

> I needed to understand maternal ambivalence a lot better than I did and I made that a research priority. The resulting book *Mother Nature* is really about maternal love and ambivalence. Human maternal ambivalence I came to realize is completely natural. If, instead of evolving like chimpanzees where mothers are turning themselves over in a totally dedicated, single-minded way to their infants, we had evolved as cooperative breeders, it makes sense that I would feel the need for more social support. . . . This made me rethink how maternal emotions and infant needs are playing out in our own species. . . . I needed others around to help me provide the emotional security that [my] children required.

Hrdy's approach has been central to changing scientific assumptions that have a broad-ranging impact on thinkers in other disciplines and the potential for application to literary studies, as readers of this volume will find in Robin Calland's chapter, "Animal Mothers and Animal Babies in Picture Books."

Like ships passing in the night, sociologist Steph Lawler's *Mothering the Self: Mothers, Daughters, Subjects* came out the same year as Arendell's encyclopedic review of the literature and thus went unmentioned there even though in their preface, the Routledge Transformations series editors describe the book as "the first to reflect upon the radical changes that have taken place within, and around, the discourse of motherhood from the perspective of the 1990s" (n.p.). Lawler advances interdisciplinary scholarly discourse on the social construction of motherhood from a Foucauldian understanding about self-knowledge. She critiques predominant psychoanalytic narratives and situates subjectivity in social structures, finding that presumed "truths" about both motherhood and childhood "are produced in the context of social and political preoccupations. Furthermore, they are bound up with the mechanism of power and with the government of populations" (20). While her theoretical approach integrates the ideas of a wide range of thinkers on mothering, much of her analysis is rooted in the actual experiences of mothers she interviewed. Hence her book does blend the conceptual with the empirical.

More recently, book-length studies have appeared that focus on mothering experiences that challenge white, middle-class stereotypes of the nuclear, two-parent biological family, including ethnographic studies of teen mothers (see, for instance, Kaplan, 1997; Davis, 2004; Edin and Kefalas, 2005; Sidel 2006), working-class and poor mothers (Edin and Lein, 1997; Lareau, 2003; Gillies, 2006), adoptive mothers (Berebitsky, 2000; Dorow, 2006; Fessler, 2006; Jacobson, 2008), and lesbian mothers (Lewin, 1993; Mezey, 2008). Challenges to hegemonic views of mothering have also come from increased attention to globalization. Barbara Ehrenreich and Arlie Russell Hochschild refer, for instance, to a "care drain" (29) as women from poor countries are solicited to provide childcare for working mothers in rich countries, often leaving their own children behind. This transnational caregiving labor is one of a number of factors considered by the contributors in Wendy Chavkin and JaneMaree Maher's *The Globalization of Motherhood: Deconstructions and Reconstructions of Biology and Care* (2010), which looks at issues such as declining fertility rates, increasing female employment, the ability and expense of reproductive technologies, and changing family structures, all of which explode traditional myths of motherhood in Western culture. Andrea O'Reilly, a tireless promoter of motherhood studies, offers perhaps the most comprehensive collection of theoretical considerations of motherhood from different disciplines in her collection, *Maternal Theory: Essential Readings* (2007).

Of course, the turn of the millennium also ushered in an escalation in the media's "mommy wars" and a flood of popular books about mothers, mothering, and motherhood. The best of these did, indeed, integrate the conceptual and the empirical—albeit avoiding the jargon of academic discourse for the most part, while documenting scholarly research in endnotes. One of the first and most influential of these was financial reporter Ann Crittenden's 2001 national bestseller, *The Price of Motherhood: Why the Most Important Job in the World Is Still the Least Valued*, which "is based on more than five years of research in economics, sociology, history, child development, family law, public policy, demography, anthropology, and evolutionary psychology, as well as hundreds of interviews with mothers and fathers in the United States and Europe" (10). Crittenden begins with an anecdote about reading *The Giving Tree* to her son, using the picture book to illustrate her point that a mother's selfless service to her child is a labor of love, and one with costs that need to be understood for women to achieve equality. "Unpaid female caregiving is not only the life blood of families, it is the very heart of the economy" (8), she asserts, and in her concluding chapter, "How to Bring Children Up Without Putting Women Down," she offers proposals for reforms.[2]

Another widely read foray into the mommy wars was Judith Warner's *Perfect Madness: Motherhood in the Age of Anxiety* (2005), a *New York Times* best-seller that intertwines research and Warner's personal experiences to engage the following questions: "Why do so many smart, sensitive, sensible, and otherwise self-aware women get caught up in mindless and self-belittling pursuits once they become mothers? Why do anxiety, obsessive thinking, and self-doubt so often mar these women's experience of motherhood?" (xiv). Like Crittenden, Warner refers to Shel Silverstein's "Giving Tree Motherhood" (63) as a metaphor for the sacrificial mothering of many women who devote themselves "body, mind, and soul" (62) to their children.

Clearly, humanities scholarship in general, and children's literature scholarship in particular, has the potential to flow in with both streams of scholarly thought about mothers.

In Search of Maternal Thinking

Why, with so much attention given to mothers elsewhere, is there a relative dearth of attention to mothers in the humanities? We think there are several reasons. One may be the suspicion and derision accorded by many to Freudian theory, which remains, for better or worse, the basis for much scholarly discourse concerning mothering. Certainly, Freud's views on penis envy, castration anxiety, and Oedipus complexes are so often caricatured in their dissemination and reception that they become fodder for jokes, but insofar as he was one of the first thinkers to take childhood experience, and in particular a child's relationship with his or her parents, seriously as a prelude to adult personality, his theories founded a discourse for motherhood studies to inhabit, push against, and innovate as society's attitudes toward femininity, women, and mothering have evolved. Specifically, Freud posited that the quality of a child's relationship to his or her biological mother was a defining developmental factor. The mother is the first "other" that a child encounters, and thus she is extremely powerful; she quite literally holds the power of life and death over the child, so she is experienced psychically not only as the firmest existential support but also a potential existential threat. What has grown out of that paradox has been a continuing refinement of theoretical perspectives that explore the importance of the mother in terms of her presence in the child's life and the relative quality of her care. Many of these perspectives have sought to offer important correctives to Freud's physiologically based model, but the invocation of Freud and mothers in the same sentence is more likely to evoke eye rolling than genuine inquiry.

Nonetheless, several scholars continue to investigate the representation of mothering in literature from a psychoanalytic perspective; for instance, Karen Coats (2004, 2008) argues that Lacan's take on Freud is particularly relevant to discussing literary representation because it emphasizes the role of language and image in the child's understanding of the mother in relation to himself; once the child has undergone the mirror stage, representations matter more than lived experience. But other psychoanalytic paradigms, such as D. W. Winnicott's, Bruno Bettelheim's, and Nancy Chodorow's, are also relevant to theorizing the representation of motherhood and have been taken up by scholars such as Lucy Rollin (1992, 1999) and Margaret and Michael Rustin (1987). Nonetheless, since psychoanalysis tends toward the positing of universal structures, it is regarded with skepticism by many who fear that it is essentializing and dismissive of cultural variations. (Karen Coats would not agree with this assessment, but that is a discussion for another venue.)

Perhaps the most significant reason for the paucity of discussion of mothering in children's and young adult literature scholarship, however, is the vexed relationship between feminism and motherhood studies. One might assume that since mothering is a primary concern for women, it would be front and center in feminist scholarly discourse. And indeed, for a time, it looked like that would be the case. Lauri Umansky asserts that during the 1970s and 80s, "Feminist psychoanalytic theory, ecofeminism, feminist peace activism, feminist spirituality, and feminist antipornography theory all explored differences between men and women, and similarities among women, each foregrounding in some way women's functions as mothers, actual or symbolic, as the key to enhanced human relations and the building of authentic community" (158). However, popular and right-wing political culture absorbed traditional views of motherhood as part of the "family values" movement in the aftermath of the Murphy Brown era, making it somewhat anathema to broader feminist goals, so that by the late 1990s, Lisa D. Brush was led to conclude: "I suspect that maternalism is feminism for hard times" (430). But while mainstream academic feminism drifted away from motherhood studies during the 1990s and early 2000s, a path has opened up for scholars to explore motherhood in its material situatedness; motherhood studies became liberated from an essentialist position into poststructuralist discourses of the diversity and intersectionality of experience. Still, uptake of motherhood studies has been limited by this ambivalence within feminism with regard to gender difference, which focuses on motherhood as the special province of women, versus gender equity, which advocates for motherhood as part of the more inclusive performance of caregiving. Such ambivalence has real effects in terms of the institutional presence of motherhood studies; despite the efforts of activist scholar Andrea O'Reilly,[3] motherhood studies has not yet become a "thing" in the humanities wing of the academy.

This became evident to Lisa Rowe Fraustino in 2002 when she began preparing to teach Mothers in Children's and Young Adult Literature for the first time as a senior seminar at Eastern Connecticut State University, a course that she later developed as a regular offering in the Graduate Program in Children's Literature at Hollins University. Though mothers do of course appear in book-length discussions of various genres, authors, or critical approaches to children's and young adult literature, Lisa's initial search for relevant scholarship brought up only two book titles focused *directly* on mothers: Adrienne Kertzer's *My Mother's Voice: Children, Literature, and the Holocaust* (2002) and Hilary S. Crew's *Is It Really Mommie Dearest?: Daughter-Mother Narratives in Young Adult Fiction* (2000). Both provided starting points for examining a narrow swath of a much larger topic. As Karen concluded in her 2001 *Children's Literature Association Quarterly* review, Crew's book "marks a significant entry into the analysis of the conventions of Young Adult fiction as well as offering a feminist intervention into the potentially damaging effects of following the traditional daughter-mother script too closely" (109).

With no broader textbook available on the topic, Lisa embarked on a quest to collect articles, chapters, and book excerpts using theoretical lenses to look at mothers. For that first class being developed in 2002, she was able to compile only a one-inch binder full of critical articles that moved beyond gender role stereotypes and fairy tales to analyze mothering in children's literature. First in the binder came Lois Rauch Gibson's 1988 *Children's Literature Association Quarterly* article, "Beyond the Apron: Archetypes, Stereotypes, and Alternative Portrayals of Mothers in Children's Literature," which used an archetypal approach. Next, and more helpful in growing beyond a study of gender role stereotypes, were Lucy Rollin's contributions to her 1999 book coauthored with Mark West, *Psychoanalytic Responses to Children's Literature*. Rollin's chapters "The Good-Enough Mother Hubbard" and "The Reproduction of Mothering in *Charlotte's Web*" applied the psychoanalytic approaches of D. W. Winnicott and Nancy Chodorow, respectively, and presented a simple model for further investigation in Lisa's classes, namely: to learn how theorists in other disciplines are approaching mothers and then apply those theories to a deeper understanding of mothers in particular texts or subgenres of children's literature.

Interdisciplinary anthologies and academic essay collections, despite their lack of focus on children's literature, provided Lisa and her classes with the broad introduction they sought for thinking with and about mothers. Primary source journals, memoirs, creative nonfiction essays, and stories were conveniently gathered in one place by Moyra Davey in *Mother Reader: Essential Writings on Motherhood* (2001), which aims "to bring together examples of the best writing on motherhood of the last sixty years, writing that tells firsthand of the mother's experience" (xiv). Many of these readings—classics in women's studies but not as widely known within the discourse of children's literature scholarship—offer beginning scholars important historical background as well as direction for further study.[4] Extremely helpful in adding interdisciplinary scholarly perspectives were two earlier collections of essays: *Mothering: Ideology, Experience, and Agency*, edited by Evelyn Nakano Glenn, Grace Chang, and Linda Rennie Forcey (1994); and *Representations of Motherhood*, edited by Donna Bassin, Margaret Honey, and Meryle Mahrer Kaplan (1994).[5]

Expanding the Conversation

Picking up maternal thinking in other disciplines and transporting it to the reading of mothers in children's literature led Lisa to the publication of essays such as "The Berenstain Bears and the Reproduction of Mothering" (2007) and "The Apple of Her Eye: Ideology Fed by Best-Selling Trade Picture Books" (2009). Two students from her 2005 Hollins class continued to develop their final projects into published works: Meredith R. Ackroyd's "Mothers of Misselthwaite: Mothering Work and Space in *The Secret Garden*" appeared in the centennial volume on the children's classic edited by Jackie C. Horne and Joe Sutliff Sanders (2011); and Claudia H. Pearson expanded her thesis into a monograph, *Have a Carrot: Hidden Messages in Margaret Wise Brown's Runaway Bunny Trilogy and Other Popular Picture Books* (2012). This volume contains two chapters that began as papers for Hollins classes: Dorina K. Lazo Gilmore's "Minority Mama: Rejecting the Mainstream Mothering Model" (2005) and Alexandra Kotanko's "A Daughter's Sacrifice: Saving the 'Good-Enough Mother' from the Good Mother Fantasy" (2013).

The work on mothers in children's and young adult literature is slowly growing; however, it is scattered and lacks cohesion. Some of the best conversations regarding mothers and children's literature take place outside of academic audiences. Scholar Elizabeth Rose Gruner, a founding editor and columnist blogging as Libby Gruner, has reflected that her "columns and essays [for *Literary Mama*] . . . got the kind of attention that my academic writing hadn't always received." Creative writers have also weighed in with theories on mothers in children's books, for example, Catherine Gilbert Murdock's 2009 post "The Adventures of Mommy Buzzkill" at *The Horn Book* website, where she claims that "we mothers cannot be present in any story in which the child needs protection, because the reader needs to believe without question that we would instantly overwhelm any quest." Julie Just, in her 2010 *New York Times* essay "The Parent Problem in Young Adult Lit," finds it "striking . . . that some of the most sharply written and critically praised works reliably feature a mopey, inept, distracted, or ready-for-rehab parent, suggesting that this has become a particularly resonant figure." This also suggests that fathers are overdue some scholarly attention.

Over the past decade, Lisa has graduated to a three-inch binder with several additions to readings used in her courses, including such articles as "Nancy's Ancestors: The Mystery of Imaginative Female Power in *The Secret Garden* and *A Little Princess*," by Mary Jeanette Moran; "The Sow in the House: The Unfulfilled Promises of Feminism in Ian Falconer's *Olivia Books*," by Daniel Greenstone; "The Other Mother: Neil Gaiman's Postfeminist Fairytales," by Elizabeth Parsons, Naarah Sawers, and Kate McInally; and "A Womb with a Political View: Barbara Park's MA! There's Nothing to Do Here!: Prenatal Parenting, and the Battle over Personhood," by Michelle Abate. But those who wish to study and teach the subject need more than a binder and an Internet search engine: we need books. We also need to explore the ramifications of the representations we find. As Karen noted in her review of Crew's *Is It Really Mommie Dearest?*, even though Crew attempted to find the mother's own voice in these narratives, "it seems that in most of the books included in her study, the story is told through the daughter, with the result that the mom is often vilified and the daughter emerges as strong, independent, and capable, filling in the gaps left by incompetent parenting in almost miraculous ways" (108). Shouldn't scholars interrogate that trend, shed light on it, and perhaps recommend a path correction? Thus upon visiting Lisa's Mothers in Children's and Young Adult Literature class at Hollins in the summer of 2013, Karen posed the question: "You and your students have been doing all this important work on mothers for years. When are you going to publish the book?" Lisa saw the ideal coeditor in Karen, who has addressed the important structural roles mothers play in children's and adolescent subjectivity in her psychoanalytic study *Looking Glasses and Neverlands: Lacan, Desire, and Subjectivity in Children's Literature* (2004). We agreed to collaborate on the current volume with the goal of charting a course to fill this significant scholarly gap—with this text as a starting point.

We posted our call for papers in August. By our November 15 deadline, we had received well over eighty submissions from all over the world, as well as a number of inquiries and notes of appreciation. With this excess of riches, we took advantage of the opportunity to expand the conversation with new perspectives and coedited the June 2015 edition of *Children's Literature in Education* (46.2) as a special issue devoted to representations of motherhood. The essays within coalesce around the idea that motherhood is best understood as a performative act. The scripts that inform the performance of mothering change throughout history and across texts aimed at various ages. Images embedded in and reinforced through book-related toys, TV series, films, and picture books establish scripts and schemas for mothering that children come to expect and mothers strive to enact, while middle-grade and young adult novels more often seek to disrupt or extend those roles by challenging gender stereotypes as well as nurturing mother schemas.

In this book we share the same aims brought to *Representations of Motherhood* by editors Bassin, Honey, and Kaplan: "By bringing together a multiplicity of theoretical perspectives, we are attempting to broaden the ground on which motherhood is constructed," they explain in their introduction, continuing: "The potentially subversive character of mother-as-subject is a theme that runs implicitly through this volume with attention both to how mothers are perceived in the political arena and to how listening to the maternal voice disrupts deeply held views of women and motherhood" (8, 10). If the character of mother-as-subject is subversive, and if listening to the maternal voice is disruptive of deeply held views in society overall, then such theoretical perspectives on children's literature—ground on which motherhood is undeniably constructed from a child's viewpoint—are bound to shake up unexamined assumptions in our field. According to Bassin and colleagues, "Even in our attempts to focus directly on maternal subjectivity we frequently found ourselves and our contributors shifting to the vantage point of the child seeking the need-satisfying mother and then struggling to construct a full vision of the mother herself" (8). The contributors to the current volume have found this pattern securely in place across children's and young adult literature.

From Historical Legacies to Postfeminist Subjectivities

In the essays we have chosen to include here, we have sought to expand the theoretical paradigms within which representations of mothering can be understood and applied to a range of topics. We have divided the book into four parts that put the text sets and critical approaches to mothering into conversations that are both historical and theoretical.

Part 1 focuses on the pedagogical roots of maternal influence in early children's literature, beginning with Donelle Ruwe's chapter "Barbauld and the Body-Part Game: Maternal Pedagogy in the Long Eighteenth Century." *Lessons for Children* (1778–79), inspired by actual parent-child interactions between Anna Letitia Barbauld and her adopted nursery-age son Charles Aikin, initiated a new children's literature style of familiar, informal conversation that by the end of the eighteenth century was a distinguishing characteristic of prose for children. However, Barbauld's *Lessons* was also revolutionary for content that reveals the eighteenth-century roots of modern pedagogical practice. Barbauld demonstrates the use of manipulatives, motherese, and response priming, techniques linked to rationalist pedagogical approaches that reach a high point with Maria and Richard Lovell Edgeworth's *Practical Education* (1801). After examining Barbauld's maternal pedagogy in *Lessons* and its link to contemporary discussions about mother-child interactions and pedagogical techniques, this chapter tracks Barbauld's influence on two major children's literature texts of the long eighteenth century: Sarah Trimmer's *Easy Introduction* and Ann and Jane Taylor's *Rhymes for the Nursery*.

Next, in "Juliana Ewing's *Six to Sixteen*: Realizing and Rewriting Maternal Legacy," Koeun Kim explores how Juliana Ewing both establishes and interrogates the maternal legacy of her mother, Margaret Gatty, through the intertextual relationship of her novel *Six to Sixteen* (1875) with Gatty's allegorical story "The Fairy Godmothers" (1851). By realizing and rewriting her mother's artistic vision, Ewing points to the restrictions of the Victorian domestic ideology that limit the fulfillment of her mother's legacy, namely, "love of employment." Although Ewing idealizes Gatty as the model mother, she also reverses Gatty's use of an omniscient, motherlike narrator by employing a young girl as the narrator, demonstrating thus that the female writer eventually has to go beyond the literary mother to gain artistic freedom. Considering that the nineteenth-century domestic story itself served as a literary mother for successive female writers, Ewing's new narrative technique can be read as an attempt to move beyond maternal legacy and point to a wider field of activity for the female genre.

Part 1 concludes with "The Romance of Othermothering in Nineteenth-Century *Backfisch* Books," by Julie Pfeiffer. The German *Backfisch* book for adolescent girls follows a standard plot: the girl in need of an education leaves home to be mentored by an unmarried, childless woman, and her successful transformation results in engagement or marriage. Pfeiffer explores the uneasy balance in these novels between what Nancy Chodorow calls "the reproduction of mothering" and what Patricia Hill Collins calls "othermothering," arguing that while these heroines appear to be reinforcing a gendered expectation that the happy end to a girl's adolescence is marriage, they actually allow their readers to explore self-knowledge rather than maternal intimacy. The books contribute to nostalgia for the idealized mother of childhood as well as an implicit critique of childbearing. "Ultimately," as Pfeiffer demonstrates, "the 'romance' that illuminates these novels is not a heterosexual or a Christian romance, but a romance of othermothering, as girls learn to mother one another without the distractions of husbands or children."

While the representations of mothers and mothering in children's literature of the eighteenth and nineteenth centuries had explicit didactic aims for primarily white and middle-class readers, the twentieth century brought shifting cultural perspectives that tie together the chapters in part 2 of this collection. First comes Adrienne Kertzer's chapter "The Women Who Sent Their Children Away: Mothers in Kindertransport Fiction." Kertzer compares Lore Segal's *Other People's Houses* with recent young adult fiction such as Mona Golabek and Lee Cohen's *The Children of Willesden Lane: Beyond the Kindertransport: A Memoir of Music, Love, and Survival*; Linda Newbery's *Sisterland*; and Alison Pick's adult novel *Far to Go* to highlight the evolving shape of Holocaust memory. Finding in contemporary Kindertransport fiction that mothers are routinely mythologized, misrecognized, and misunderstood, she links this pattern and its dependence on tropes of maternal abandonment and the fantasy of maternal recognition to a shift in focalization. The shift to granddaughters, rather than daughters, as the primary writers and focalizations has major implications for the representation of the mothers who sent their children away.

Dorina K. Lazo Gilmore extends the conversation on othermothering introduced by Pfeiffer in the next chapter, "Minority Mama: Rejecting the Mainstream Mothering Model." She argues that mothers from ethnic minority backgrounds operate under different cultural imperatives than those idealized through mainstream mothering models and emerge more multidimensional as a result. In preparing their children to deal with racial oppression, they demonstrate personal resilience, encourage independence, and promote education. But they also embrace their own sexuality, serve their wider communities, and express a full range of emotions. By contrasting ideals established in *The Giving Tree* and *Love You Forever* with those found in Barbara M. Joosse's *Mama, Do You Love Me?*, Katherine Leiner's *Mama Does the Mambo*, Pat Mora's *The Desert Is My Mother/ El Desierto Es Mi Madre*, Juan Felipe Herrera's *Calling the Doves*, JaNay Brown-Wood's *Imani's Moon*, and Katheryn Russell-Brown's *Little Melba and Her Big Trombone*, Gilmore highlights the vibrant portrayal of minority mothers as a template for developing a more complex model of mothering.

The ramifications of how mothers of color mother in a racist world are further theorized by Lauren Causey and Karen Coats in "Cultural-Historical Activity Theory and the Expansive Cycle of Mothering While Black." Mothering is a historically and culturally rooted phenomenon that occupies ideological gyres, or what Yrjö Engeström calls "expansive cycles," within well-loved African American children's and young adult literature. Cultural-historical activity theory, or CHAT—which itself exists within multiple iterations since Lev Vygotsky—frames this chapter's discussion. Causey and Coats analyze CHAT in the portrayal of African American mothering through texts of various genres, including Eloise Greenfield's *Childtimes: A Three-Generation Memoir* (1979), Angela Johnson's *Toning the Sweep* (1993), Jacqueline Woodson's *Show Way* (2005), Marilyn Nelson's *A Wreath for Emmett Till* (2005), and Reneé Watson's *This Side of Home* (2015). Tracing the cycles of motherhood (old and new) within the literature mirrors the functions of the theory, making CHAT a uniquely appropriate theoretical methodology for understanding the communitarian values of the texts.

Just as CHAT helps us to understand the convergence of history and story structure in many African American texts, so do modern cognitive approaches help us to understand how young readers acquire and adapt myths of motherhood across cultures. Thus this section of the book wraps up with a chapter by Anna Katrina Gutierrez, "'The hills were in her bones': Living in the Blend of Mothers and Environments." From the viewpoint of conceptual blending, a theory developed by Gilles Fauconnier and Mark Turner to describe the way humans automatically form vital connections between two distinct conceptual spaces through the identification of sameness, the recognition of similar elements between mother schemas and the protagonist's environment transforms the mother figure into an ideological representation of both motherhood and the system of beliefs that underpins the protagonist's world. Mother, then, is a third concept that greatly affects the movements of the protagonist and gives him or her the power to negotiate with and interrogate his or her domain. This chapter focuses on texts featuring protagonists who are affected by oppositional mother-world blends, including Banana Yoshimoto's *Kitchen* (1988), Gennifer Choldenko's *Al Capone Does My Shirts* (2004), and Terry Pratchett's *The Wee Free Men* (2003).

Because such cultural schemas of mothering become so pervasive as cognitive furniture, it is increasingly important to parse the distinctions between fantasy and reality, particularly when it comes to the mother-child bond and the ethical dimensions of the constructs of mothering found in educational texts and popular fiction. Part 3 begins with Robin Calland's chapter "Animal Mothers and Animal Babies in Picture Books," which traces the representations of animal mothers in the text and images of nineteen nonfiction and fiction picture books about baby animals, exploring whether recent naturalist books' representations of animal mothers disseminate what Lisa Jean Moore calls "biological fairy tales" about the process of birthing and nurturing children (281). Biological fairy tales are accounts of reproduction that have been "scrubbed, washed, massaged, and homogenized for consumption by the young" and that work to reinforce prescribed social roles by naturalizing them (278). Calland surveys naturalist children's books published between 1980 and 2013 to assess the degree to which they naturalize mothers as virtuous nurturers as opposed to apprehending motherhood through the new biological paradigm of active strategist, as articulated by evolutionary biologists such as Sarah Blaffer Hrdy. Her close readings find that prevailing ideologies about human mothers may be naturalized, inscribed, and, perhaps, sometimes disrupted by quasiscientific children's picture books.

The same anthropomorphic assumptions about human mothering communicated by nonfiction picture books about "real" animals reveal themselves as well in fantasy fiction for older children, as discussed in the next two chapters, starting with "A Daughter's Sacrifice: Saving the 'Good-Enough Mother' from the Good Mother Fantasy," by Alexandra Kotanko. D. W. Winnicott's conceptualization of the "good-enough" mother challenged ideals of Victorian motherhood by acknowledging the ambivalence mothers feel toward their children and positing that children are better served by mothers who step back from providing for all of their child's needs on the child's terms. *Peter and Wendy* and *Coraline*, while written one hundred years apart, both interrogate the fantasy of the ideal mother, albeit from different directions: in *Peter and Wendy*, it is the mother's need to consume her children in self-sacrificial love, while in *Coraline*, it is the child's belief that she should be the recipient of that love. This tension causes the destruction of the mother within the children's minds and an immersion into fantasy. Through their respective escapes, however, the girls work through the inevitable trauma of loss and are able ultimately to distinguish successfully between and hold in tension the fantasy of the ideal mother and the reality of the good-enough mother.

How can the dynamic of the mother-child relationship, with its inherent power imbalance, serve as a model for relationships between adults or communities in which some level of parity is a desired goal, if not a present reality? That is the question addressed in the conclusion of part 3 of the book with Mary Jeanette Moran's chapter "'The Mother Was the Mother, Even When She Wasn't': Maternal Care Ethics and Children's Fantasy." Scholars such as Carol Gilligan, Nel Noddings, Sara Ruddick, Virginia Held, and Fiona Robinson seek to articulate an ethics that takes the maternal relationship as an exemplar of the kind of care that should inform our public as well as our private ethical decisions. Children's fantasy, with its imaginative reinterpretations of subjectivity and interpersonal relationships, offers new ways to consider a maternal basis for care ethics. This chapter considers the variations on maternal relationships found in Philip Pullman's His Dark Materials series primarily, with briefer examples drawn from Madeleine L'Engle's *A Swiftly Tilting Planet* and Robin McKinley's *Spindle's End* offered to illustrate how ideas of motherhood contribute to feminist ethics of care in children's fantasy.

Finally, in part 4, we turn to readings of postfeminist motherhood in children's fiction, from contemporary realism to dystopian fantasy. Sara K. Day introduces the section's discussion of postfeminist theory with her chapter "'I Would Never Be Strong Enough': Sarah Dessen's Postfeminist Mothers." Day argues that Dessen consistently undermines the seemingly empowering messages embodied by her adolescent women protagonists by pairing them with the implicit suggestion, exemplified by these young women's mothers and stepmothers, that women really *cannot* "have it all." By emphasizing the struggles these women face while navigating—to various degrees—their careers, their home lives, and their social lives, Dessen offers a distinctly postfeminist view of contemporary motherhood as fraught and foreboding. Her teen protagonists' ostensibly happy endings ultimately depend on an acceptance of simple, straightforward goals that stand in stark contrast with the complicated lives of their largely unhappy mothers. In the process, Dessen's novels contribute to a systemic assumption that, rather than attempting to juggle work, family, and personal lives, young women should lower their ambitions for their own future womanhood.

Next, in "Abandoning Mothers," Lisa Rowe Fraustino examines the significant pattern of missing mothers that has emerged since the 1970s in a literary field predominated by women as authors, editors, critics, librarians, and teachers. Unlike traditional orphan stories, where mothers abandoned their children by accidental death, today's maternal characters increasingly leave the family out of choice and for selfish reasons. Fraustino contextualizes her discussion through the real-life public complaints from Rebecca Walker regarding the feminist commitments of her prominent mother, Alice Walker, which she felt irrevocably damaged their relationship. Drawing, then, on the work of Susan Faludi, she examines patterns of backlash to feminism in two novels from the second wave (Katherine Paterson's 1979 National Book Award winner, *The Great Gilly Hopkins*, and Cynthia Voigt's 1983 Newbery Award winner, *Dicey's Song*); and one from the third wave (Kimberly Willis Holt's 2000 National Book Award winner, *When Zachary Beaver Came to Town*), these three serving as examples of a much wider trend. Though the implicit demonizing of these selfish mothers could be deconstructed—their liberation privileged, that is—their absence combined with their depiction from the viewpoint of the abandoned child negates the possibility of a sympathetic reading.

In the final chapter of the book, "'A Mom-Shaped Hole': Psychoanalysis and the Dystopian Maternal," Jennifer Mitchell uses the synthesis of psychoanalytic models of motherhood and queer theory's conceptions of gender performativity to suggest that the framing of the dystopian heroine is contingent upon a great maternal lack. By examining Katniss's disavowal of her mother's failed parenting in Suzanne Collins's The Hunger Games trilogy and the recovery of a lost maternal legacy in Patrick Ness's Chaos Walking books, Mitchell explores how the "mom-shaped hole," as Violet Durn terms it in M. T. Anderson's *Feed*, acts as a specific catalyst for the development of the heroine and hero in these dystopic worlds. Specifically, their missing mothers compromise their negotiation of the Oedipus complex, and it is their different responses to that failure that provide the key to their eventual successes.

Ultimately, we hope that the range of critical approaches to mothers in children's and young adult literature in this volume will continue to provide the maternal thinking and ethics of care for more scholars to investigate these and other approaches to mothers. We hope ours will be the first book of many because even within this book conceived to fill a gap, there are gaps. For instance, we would like to see further research on the portrayal of lesbian mothers, adoptive mothers, and mothers from underrepresented groups and non-Western cultures. And we know the ideas are out there and ripe to be developed, shared, and discussed. The enthusiastic response to our call for submissions leads us to believe our project is tapping into a very deep well.

Notes

1. Susan J. Douglas (a scholar of communication studies) and Meredith W. Michaels (a philosopher) extend Thurer's approach in their 2004 book, *The Mommy Myth: The Idealization of Motherhood and How It Has Undermined Women*, which analyzes "how the images of motherhood in TV shows, movies, advertising, women's magazines, and the news have evolved since 1970, raising the bar, year by year, of the standards of good

motherhood while singling out and condemning those we were supposed to see as dreadful mothers" (14).

2. Similarly, Miriam Peskowitz in *The Truth Behind the Mommy Wars: Who Decides What Makes a Good Mother?* (2005) deconstructs the "mommy wars" and identifies the reality as "not a working-mom problem or a stay-at-home-problem" but a "parent problem" (8) in which a diversity of mothers and fathers are "caught between a rock and a hard place, as they used to say, of work and family, paychecks and parenting, living in a society that takes more and more hours from its workers" (17). Peskowitz's work was followed the next year by Joan Blades and Kristin Rowe-Finkbeiner's *The Motherhood Manifesto: What America's Moms Want—and What to Do about It*, which covers issues such as paid family leave, flexible work options, after-school programs, universal healthcare for children, childcare for working parents, and realistic wages necessary to support a family.

3. O'Reilly, an associate professor in the School of Women's Studies at York University, founded the Association for Research on Mothering, which evolved into the Motherhood Initiative for Research and Community Involvement; founded and edited the *Journal for the Association of Research on Mothering*, which began publication in 1999 and ceased publication in 2010; established Demeter Press; organizes conferences on motherhood; and publishes widely on the topic.

4. See especially Susan Griffin's "Feminism and Motherhood" (1974); Jane Lazarre's *The Mother Knot* (1976); Adrienne Rich's "Anger and Tenderness" from *Of Woman Born* (1976); Alice Walker's "A Writer Because of, Not in Spite of, Her Children" and *"One* Child of One's Own: A Meaningful Digression within the Work(s)," both from *In Search of Our Mothers' Gardens* (1983); Tillie Olsen's "Writer-Mothers: The Fundamental Situation" from *Silences* (1978); Susan Rubin Suleiman's "Writing and Motherhood" (1979); Ursula K. Le Guin's "The Fisherwoman's Daughter" (1988); and Sara Ruddick's "Talking About Mothers" from *Maternal Thinking: Toward a Politics of Peace* (1989).

5. In *Mothering: Ideology, Experience, and Agency*, see especially Glenn's chapter, "Social Constructions of Mothering: A Thematic Overview," and "Shifting the Center: Race, Class, and Feminist Theorizing about Motherhood," by Patricia Hill Collins. Other chapters will also be of interest to scholars with a narrower focus (e.g., mothering under slavery or negotiating lesbian motherhood). In *Representations of Motherhood*, see especially the following chapters: "Thinking Mothers/Conceiving Birth," by Sara Ruddick; "The Omnipotent Mother: A Psychoanalytic Study of Fantasy and Reality," by Jessica Benjamin; "Mothering, Hate, and Winnicott," by Elsa First; and "Maternal Subjectivity in the Culture of Nostalgia: Mourning and Memory," by Donna Bassin.

Works Cited

Abate, Michelle. "A Womb with a Political View: Barbara Park's MA! There's Nothing to Do Here!: Prenatal Parenting, and the Battle over Personhood." *Children's Literature in Education* 44 (2013): 326–43. Print.

Ackroyd, Meredith R. "Mothers of Misselthwaite: Mothering Work and Space in *The Secret Garden.*" *Frances Hodgson Burnett's The Secret Garden: A Children's Classic at 100.* Ed. Jackie C. Horne and Joe Sutliff Sanders. Lanham, MD: Scarecrow, 2011. 45–62. Print.

Arendell, Terry. "Conceiving and Investigating Motherhood: The Decade's Scholarship." *Journal of Marriage and Family* 62.4 (2000): 1192–1207. Wiley Online Library. Web. 30 Apr. 2015.

Bassin, Donna, Margaret Honey, and Meryle Mahrer Kaplan, eds. *Representations of Motherhood.* New Haven: Yale UP, 1994. Print.

Benjamin, Jessica. "The Omnipotent Mother: A Psychoanalytic Study of Fantasy and Reality." *Representations of Motherhood.* Ed. Donna Bassin, Margaret Honey, and Meryle Mahrer Kaplan. New Haven: Yale UP, 1994. Print.

Berebitsky, Julie. *Like Our Very Own: Adoption and the Changing Culture of Motherhood, 1851–1950.* Lawrence: U of Kansas P, 2000. Print.

Blades, Joan and Kristen Rowe-Finkbeiner. *The Motherhood Manifesto: What America's Moms Want—and What to Do about It.* New York: Nation Books, 2006. Print.

Brush, Lisa D. "Love, Toil, and Trouble: Motherhood and Feminist Politics." *Signs* 21.2 (1996): 429–54.

Chavkin, Wendy, and JaneMaree Maher, eds. *The Globalization of Motherhood: Deconstructions and Reconstructions of Biology and Care.* Abingdon: Routledge, 2010. Print.

Chodorow, Nancy J. *The Reproduction of Motherhood: Psychoanalysis and the Sociology of Gender with a New Preface.* 1978. Los Angeles: U of California P, 1999. Print.

Coats, Karen. "Between Horror, Humour, and Hope: Neil Gaiman and the Psychic Work of the Gothic." *The Gothic in Children's Literature: Haunting the Borders.* Ed. Anna Jackson, Karen Coats, and Roderick McGillis. New York: Routledge, 2008. 77–92. Print.

———. *Looking Glasses and Neverlands: Lacan, Desire, and Subjectivity in Children's Literature.* Iowa City: University of Iowa Press, 2004. Print.

———. Rev. of *Is It Really Mommie Dearest?: Daughter-Mother Narratives in Young Adult Fiction*, by Hilary S. Crew. *Children's Literature Association Quarterly* 26.2 (2001): 107–9. Print.

Collins, Patricia Hill. *Black Feminist Thought: Knowledge, Consciousness, and the Politics of Empowerment.* New York: Routledge, 1991. Print.

Crew, Hilary S. *Is It Really Mommie Dearest?: Daughter-Mother Narratives in Young Adult Fiction.* Lanham, MD: Scarecrow, 2000. Print.

Crittenden, Ann. *The Price of Motherhood: Why the Most Important Job in the World Is Still the Least Valued.* New York: Holt, 2001. Print.

Davey, Moyra, ed. *Mother Reader: Essential Writings on Motherhood.* New York: Seven Stories, 2001. Print.

Davis, Deborah. *You Look Too Young to Be a Mom: Teen Moms Speak Out on Love, Learning, and Success.* New York: Perigree, 2004.

Dinnerstein, Dorothy. *The Mermaid and the Minotaur.* 1976. New York: Other, 1999.

Dorow, Sara K. *Transnational Adoption: A Cultural Economy of Race, Gender, and Kinship.* New York: New York UP, 2006. Print.

Douglas, Susan J., and Meredith W. Michaels. *The Mommy Myth: The Idealization of Motherhood and How It Has Undermined Women*. New York: Free, 2004.

Dowling, Claudia Glenn. "Maternal Instincts: From Infidelity to Infanticide." *Discover* 1 Mar. 2003. Web. 19 Apr. 2015.

Edin, Kathryn, and Maria Kefalas. *Promises I Can Keep: Why Poor Women Put Motherhood before Marriage*. Berkeley: U of California P, 2005. Print.

Edin, Kathryn, and Laura Lein. *Making Ends Meet: How Single Mothers Survive Welfare and Low-Wage Work*. New York: Sage, 1997. Print.

Ehrenreich, Barbara, and Arlie Russell Hochschild. *Global Woman: Nannies, Maids, and Sex Workers in the New Economy*. New York: Metropolitan, 2003. Print.

Epp Buller. "Andrea O'Reilly: Motherhood Is NOT a Liability." *Literary Mama: Reading for the Maternally Inclined*. 1 June 2014. Web. 17 Jan. 2015.

Fessler, Ann. *The Girls Who Went Away: The Hidden History of Women Who Surrendered Children for Adoption in the Decades before* Roe v. Wade. New York: Penguin, 2006.

Fraustino, Lisa Rowe. "The Apple of Her Eye: The Mothering Ideology Fed by Bestselling Trade Picture Books." *Critical Approaches to Food in Children's Literature*. Ed. Kara K. Keeling and Scott T. Pollard. Children's Literature and Culture 59. New York: Routledge, 2009. 57–72. Print.

———. "The Berenstain Bears and the Reproduction of Mothering." *The Lion and the Unicorn* 31.3 (2007): 250–63. Print.

Gibson, Lois Rauch. "Beyond the Apron: Archetypes, Stereotypes, and Alternative Portrayals of Mothers in Children's Literature." *Children's Literature Association Quarterly* 13.4 (1988): 177–81. Print.

Gillies, Val. *Marginalised Mothers: Exploring Working-Class Experiences of Parenting*. Abingdon: Routledge, 2006.

Glenn, Evelyn Nakano, Grace Chang, and Linda Rennie Forcey, eds. *Mothering: Ideology, Experience, and Agency*. New York: Routledge, 1994. Print.

Greenstone, Daniel. "The Sow in the House: The Unfulfilled Promises of Feminism in Ian Falconer's *Olivia* Books." *Children's Literature Association Quarterly* 33.1 (2008): 26–40. Print.

Gruner, Libby. "Celebrating Ten Years of Literary Mama: Libby Gruner." *Literary Mama: Reading for the Maternally Inclined*. 15 Jan. 2014. Web. 29 Jan. 2015.

Hrdy, Sarah Blaffer. *Mother Nature: Maternal Instincts and How They Shape the Human Species*. Harvard UP, 1999. Print.

———. *Mothers and Others: The Evolutionary Origins of Mutual Understanding*. Cambridge: Harvard UP, 2009. Print.

———. *The Woman That Never Evolved*. Cambridge: Harvard UP, 1981. Print.

Jacobson, Heather. *Culture Keeping: White Mothers, International Adoption, and the Negotiation of Family Difference*. Nashville: Vanderbilt University Press, 2008. Print.

Johnson, Eric Michael. "Raising Darwin's Consciousness, Part One: An Interview with Sarah Blaffer Hrdy on Mother Nature." *Scientific American* 16 Mar. 2012. Web. 19 Apr. 2015.

Just, Julie. "The Parent Problem in Young Adult Lit." *New York Times*. New York Times, 4 Apr. 2010. Web. 4 Apr. 2010.

Kaplan, Elaine Bell. *Not Our Kind of Girl: Unraveling the Myths of Black Teenage Motherhood*. Berkeley: U of California P, 1997. Print.

Kertzer, Adrienne. *My Mother's Voice: Children, Literature, and the Holocaust*. Peterborough, ON: Broadview, 2002. Print.

Kingsley, Charles. *The Water-Babies, A Fairy Tale for a Land Baby*. 1863. London: Macmillan, 1863. *Project Gutenberg*. Web. 9 Feb. 2015.

Lareau, Annette. *Unequal Childhoods: Race, Class, and Family Life*. Berkeley: U of California P, 2003. Print.

Lawler, Steph. *Mothering the Self: Mothers, Daughters, Subjects*. New York: Routledge, 2000. Print.

Lewin, Ellen. *Lesbian Mothers: Accounts of Gender in American Culture*. Ithaca, NY: Cornell UP, 1993. Print.

Mezey, Nancy J. *New Choices, New Families: How Lesbians Decide about Motherhood*. Baltimore: Johns Hopkins UP, 2008. Print.

Moore, Lisa Jean. "Billy, the Sad Sperm with No Tail: Representations of Sperm in Children's Books." *Sexualities* 6.3-4 (2003): 277-300. Print.

Moran, Mary Jeanette. "Nancy's Ancestors: The Mystery of Imaginative Female Power in *The Secret Garden* and *A Little Princess*." *Mystery in Children's Literature: From the Rational to the Supernatural*. Ed. Adrienne E. Gavin and Christopher Routledge. New York: Palgrave Macmillan, 2001. 32-45. Print.

Murdock, Catherine Gilbert. "The Adventures of Mommy Buzzkill." *The Horn Book*. 13 Mar. 2009. Web. 9 Jan. 2013.

Noddings, Nel. *The Maternal Factor: Two Paths to Morality*. Berkeley: U of California P, 1984. Print.

O'Reilly, Andrea, ed. *Maternal Theory: Essential Readings*. Toronto: Demeter, 2007. Print.

Parsons, Elizabeth, Naarah Sawers, and Kate McInally. "The Other Mother: Neil Gaiman's Postfeminist Fairytales." *Children's Literature Association Quarterly* 33.4 (2008): 371-89. Print.

Pearson, Claudia H. *Have a Carrot: Hidden Messages in Margaret Wise Brown's* Runaway Bunny *Trilogy and Other Popular Picture Books*. City: Look Again, 2012. Print.

Peskowitz, Miriam. *The Truth behind the Mommy Wars: Who Decides What Makes a Good Mother?* Emoryville, CA: Seal, 2005. Print.

Rich, Adrienne. *Of Woman Born: Motherhood as Experience and Institution*. 1976. New York: Norton, 1986. Print.

Rollin, Lucy. "The Good-Enough Mother Hubbard." *Psychoanalytic Responses to Children's Literature*. By Lucy Rollin and Mark I. West. Jefferson, NC: McFarland, 1999. 97-110. Print.

———. "The Reproduction of Mothering in *Charlotte's Web*." *Psychoanalytic Responses to Children's Literature*. By Lucy Rollin and Mark I. West. Jefferson, NC: McFarland, 1999. 53-63. Print.

Ruddick, Sara. *Maternal Thinking: Toward a Politics of Peace*. 1989. Boston: Beacon, 1995. Print.

Sidel, Ruth. *Unsung Heroines: Single Mothers and the American Dream*. Berkeley: U of California P, 2006. Print.

Silverstein, Shel. *The Giving Tree*. 1964. New York: HarperCollins, 1992.

Thurer, Shari L. *The Myths of Motherhood: How Culture Reinvents the Good Mother*. New York: Houghton Mifflin, 1994. Print.

Umansky, Lauri. *Motherhood Reconceived: Feminism and the Legacies of the Sixties*. New York: New York UP, 1996.

Walker, Alice. *In Search of Our Mothers' Gardens*. New York: HBJ, 1983. Print.

Warner, Judith. *Perfect Madness: Motherhood in the Age of Anxiety*. 2005. New York: Riverhead, 2006. Print.

PART I

Historical Legacies: Maternal Instruction and Delight

Chapter 1

Barbauld and the Body-Part Game: Maternal Pedagogy in the Long Eighteenth Century

Donelle Ruwe

In her landmark 1986 essay, "Impeccable Governesses, Rational Dames, and Moral Mothers: Mary Wollstonecraft and the Female Tradition in Georgian Children's Books," Mitzi Myers argues that a new type of protagonist had arisen at the end of the Enlightenment: the mother as an educating heroine. This moral mother was "a dream of strength and power," and she represented "the heroic potential available in ordinary female life" (43, 50). These educating heroines are piercingly intelligent, benevolent, stern, and emotionally distant figures of authority, and they appear in a wide range of genres, from poetry and epistolary fiction to novels and didactic drama. A typical rational-dame text (such as Maria Edgeworth's "The Purple Jar" from *The Parent's Assistant*, 1796) depicts a mother and a daughter who take a walk together, and the mother uses the child's interest in the world around her as an opportunity for teaching. These texts as a body of literature are united by the shared characteristics of their mother figures as well as by a certain mode of female authority. Indeed, Anne Mellor suggests that this speaking mode—the voice of the mature, didactic, benevolent, and confident maternal figure—that began in children's books soon extended into a wider political arena, and rational dames such as Hannah More and Anna Letitia Barbauld adopted the powerful position of a moral mother who addresses the nation.[1]

The rise of the moral mother as a literary hero type was a reflection of the increasing visibility of parenting in the long eighteenth century. In *Some Thoughts Concerning Education* (1693), Locke explains that parents have the responsibility of establishing a child's lifelong habits of behavior and attitudes by vigilantly structuring their child's environment. Rousseau contends in *Émile* (1762) that "we begin to learn when we begin to live" (10) and that mothers have an essential role to play in early childhood. For example, a mother must breastfeed her children lest their link to their fathers, siblings, mothers, and, by extension, motherland be lost: when women "deign to nurse their own children, then will be a reform of morals, natural feeling will revive in every heart; there will be no lack of citizens for the state" (15). For Rousseau, writes Mary Trouille in *Sexual Politics in the Enlightenment*, "the refusal of motherhood was both a symptom and a primary source of the moral corruption and egoism of society in eighteenth-century France" (24). Madame de Genlis, in *Adèle et Théodore, ou Lettres sur l'éducation* (originally published in French in 1782), reminds her readers that "the fixing of our first principles and turn of mind depends greatly on the impressions we receive in infancy" (1.58), and Elizabeth Hamilton, in *Letters on the Elementary Principles of Education* (1801), excoriates mothers who have never assisted their children "in the acquirement of a single idea during infancy" and who assume that active teaching begins only after children are ready to learn to read (1.41). By contrast, writes Hamilton, as soon as a child is old enough to see, touch, taste, or smell, learning happens—and active teaching should begin.

These foundational figures of eighteenth-century rational pedagogy, despite having profound political, religious, and national differences, all share a basic assumption: children are physical creatures whose habits and sensibilities develop through interactions with their environment, and the best way to shape a child's development is by manipulating and carefully structuring this environment. The importance of the mother as an inculcator of the child's first sense impressions is undeniable. The sociopolitical power of rational education, as with all forms of education, is that it imprints the ideologies of society on an individual's consciousness.[2] Eighteenth-century mothers as the primary teachers of young children had authority over the child and his or her world, and their abilities to shape a child's environment and manipulate his or her responses shaped the child's "habitus," a term that refers to an individual's internalized set of responses and behaviors that allow an individual to function in the world and that reflect a personalized version of a society's ideology.[3]

Despite a broadly shared understanding in the eighteenth century that early childhood experiences lay the foundation for the child's development and that the mother has a vital role in the earliest stages of education, most pedagogical fiction from the Enlightenment depicts mother figures and female educators interacting with school-aged children, not infants and toddlers. At Mrs. Teachum's school for girls in *The Governess, or Little Female Academy* (1749), pupils range in age from eight to fourteen. Mary Wollstonecraft's Mrs. Mason from *Original Stories from Real Life* (1788) teaches a twelve- and a fourteen-year-old. The educating heroines in other rational dame texts—Charlotte Smith's mothers and aunts from *Rural Walks* (1795), *Rambles Further* (1796), *Minor Morals* (1798), and *Conversations, Introducing Poetry* (1804); the schoolmistress in Maria Edgeworth's "The Bracelets" (1787); the benevolent aunt in Adelaide O'Keeffe's *Dudley* (1819); and the moral mother in Mary Belson Elliott's *Precept and Example, or a Midsummer's Holiday* (1812)—teach children who have already learned to read and are primed to receive more complex lessons. These children have settled habits, and often the role of the mother-teacher is to "cure those faults by reason, which ought never to have taken root in the infant mind" (Wollstonecraft iii).

Most scholarly attention has understandably focused on this particular strand of the educating heroine, the mother figure who well knows the faults of her school-age charges and takes steps to address them. However, a different mode of interaction is necessary when the mother and child dynamic involves a toddler. The mother-teacher cannot instruct a toddler through lectures and abstractions. Her tools are more tactile and direct: educational games, repetitive practice, and physical objects. Instead of teaching complex social behaviors like humility, conversational skills, benevolence, or a neat simplicity in dress, the mother-educator of a toddler has a rather different educational agenda. Toddlers are being taught to be ready to learn. They practice their letters, count to ten, mimic animal noises, grip a crayon, and identify body parts.

In Anna Letitia Barbauld's groundbreaking *Lessons for Children* (1778–79), mothering is intimate and immediate. Barbauld captures the language of real-life mothers and their toddlers, and her simple, lucid prose in a natural idiom is compelling. As Sarah Trimmer would later write of Barbauld's *Lessons*, before its publication everything for little children had been written in diminutive font and too often in miniature books. By contrast, Barbauld insisted that "the eye of a child cannot catch, as ours can, a small, obscure, ill-formed word, amidst a number of others all equally unknown to him" (*Lessons* 1: 4). Trimmer praised her "stile of familiar conversation… free from all formality" (*Easy* xii), and Frances Burney described Barbauld's anecdotal dialogue between mother and child as "the new walk" of children's books (5: 419).[4]

Unlike other primers and spelling books of the period, *Lessons* does not supply word or syllable lists. It simply depicts the intimate conversations between a mother and her child from their intermingled points of view. *Lessons* was inspired by actual parent-child interactions between Barbauld and her adopted son, Charles Aikin. Volume 1 of *Lessons*, which was titled *Lessons for Children of Two to Three Years Old* and published by the important radical publisher Joseph Johnson in 1778, recounts the events of a single day, from morning to evening as Barbauld and two-year-old Charles explore the small world of home, farm, and field. Barbauld as the mother in the text is nothing like earlier educating heroines such as Sarah Fielding's Mrs. Teachum. Mrs. Teachum observes her charges from a distance lest her presence disrupt their group dynamic, and she requests regular reports about her pupils' progress from her acolyte and stand-in, Jenny Peace. Barbauld, by contrast, plays baby games, word games, and body-part games. She teaches math through counting and eating raisins. She demonstrates the proper way to pet the family cat.

The toddler-appropriate approach to mothering in *Lessons for Children of Two to Three Years Old* anticipates modern pedagogical practices in its use of manipulatives, motherese, response priming, and, in particular, the co-opting of child's play for pedagogical purposes. Play is an important teaching strategy when one is working with a toddler, and it was recognized as such in works of education throughout the long eighteenth century. In *Thoughts Concerning Education*, Locke famously advocated for the use of play as a pedagogical tool so as to make learning a "play and a recreation to children" (114). He offered several suggestions for using play as a teaching strategy, including the use of alphabet dice to teach letters and syllables (115). Over the course of the eighteenth century, his insight—that play can be used to enhance learning—is reiterated in children's texts and in the writings of various rational education proponents. In *The History of Little Goody Two-Shoes* (1765), Margery Meanwell teaches reading to children by having them play a game in which they create words out of wooden alphabet blocks. Adam Smith, in *The Theory of Moral Sentiments* (1759), explains that childhood play is a profoundly important element in the growth of moral sensibility, for it is through our early interactions with others that we learn how our actions impact others and how to act altruistically in order to satisfy our own self-interests. One of the first fully developed books of original poems for children, Dorothy and Mary Ann Kilner's *Poems on Various Subjects, for the Amusement of Youth* (circa 1783), opens with a long poem depicting children who amuse themselves by playing a word game.

In Barbauld's *Lessons for Children of Two to Three Years Old*, we see how a particular mother maintains a level of tension between parent as play-companion and parent as adult-teacher so as to maximize learning. Barbauld takes play and directs it toward a productive, instrumental, and purposeful pedagogical goal. Some twenty-first-century game theorists, following the lead of Johan Huizinga, define play as an act of autotelicity, activity for its own sake, unproductive, noninstrumental, and purposeless.[5] However, as Peter Hopsicker and Chad Carlson suggest, a parent's participation in a child's game fundamentally alters the nature of play. If parenting is the top priority, parents might use play to teach life skills or even how to better play the game, but they run the risk of taking away the fun. Even parents who attempt to play without obvious instrumental purposes still cannot merely play—for example, they must think beyond the game so as to see ways to sustain play or to keep the game at the child's level. Hopsicker and Carlson argue that creative adults are the best parent-teachers: they maintain a stretched and tenuous point between the two poles of parent-play (parent as play-companion, and parent as adult-teacher) so as to keep a high quality of play and a high level of skill learning.

In *Lessons for Children of Two to Three Years Old*, Barbauld as mother keeps the tension between the two poles of parent play and, in doing so, maximizes play as fun as well as learning. Charles is demanding and egoistic, and the mother constantly engages in a subtle flanking action in which the child's own self-centered desires are redirected into learning activities—both learning about the world as well as learning how to play effectively and keep a game going. For example, in the following passage, Barbauld initiates a body-part game:

> Charles, what are eyes for?
> To see with.
> What are ears for?
> To hear with.
> What is tongue for?
> To talk with.
> What are teeth for?
> To eat with.
> What is nose for?
> To smell with.
> What are legs for?
> To walk with.

> Then do not make mamma
> carry you. Walk yourself.
> Here are two good legs.
> Will you go abroad?
> Fetch your hat.
> Come, let us go into the fields,
>   and see the sheep, and the
>   lambs, and the cows, and
>   trees, and birds, and water. (1: 37–39)

Barbauld simplifies diction by omitting articles and speaks in short sentences that communicate in direct and uncomplicated ways. Little Charles answers each question with the same sentence phrase, changing only the verb: to see, to hear, to talk. Charles is learning not only body parts, but how to play interactive games that require give and take between two players. The sudden snap from the body-part game to parental exasperation is instantly recognizable by any parent of a toddler, and it functions as both closure and transition. One element of creative play is the ability to have self-perpetuating script writing and the improvisation of good lines that perpetuate the game—as Barbauld does by asking a repetitive question that Charles can successfully answer. However, Barbauld destroys the game's pattern by inserting a "bad line" (a line that ends the game). Her bad line is both an ending and a beginning. The shift to the mother's perspective, "Then do not make mamma carry you," ends the game, but it also readies the child for a new activity, the walk.

The linguistic simplicity of this passage has multiple functions: it helps Charles learn body parts, develop cognitive and linguistic patterns, and develop affectively and socially. These intimate scenes of learning show how Barbauld as mother adapts her teaching approach to a child's earliest level of language use: drawing attention to the self (as when Charles thinks about his own body), identifying objects, offering objects, and requesting objects.

This passage is also an ingenious display of parenting techniques. The question-and-answer format coaxes the little boy into appropriate behavior (standing on his own instead of clinging to his mother) by getting the child to participate in playful interactions that culminate in a desired behavior. Behavioral psychologist Alan Kazden calls this parenting technique "response priming." Children are more likely to engage in a desired behavior if they participate in an activity that is an initial step in a chain of activities leading to a desired outcome. Charles willingly plays the body-part game, and it leads to his own acknowledgment of what legs are for—standing up and walking. A second response priming in this passage is the mother's command to Charles, "Fetch your hat," which is the first step in the chain of actions that lead to taking a walk. Rather than tell a toddler to "go and get ready," a vague command to give a two-year-old and one that is fraught with potential false starts, Barbauld gives a specific command, that of fetching a hat, and links following the command to a treat: seeing sheep, lambs, cows, birds, and water.

Barbauld applies a second parenting technique in this passage, the "reinforcement of opposite, positive behaviors" (Kazden 265–66). Barbauld encourages the opposite positive behavior to clinging—standing and walking—by making it part of a treat, a little trip to see animals. Barbauld does not scold Charles for sitting, which would have rewarded the child's negative behavior by giving him her full attention during a scold. Instead, she primes positive behavior through the body-part game, initiates the first response in a positive chain of behavior by telling Charles to fetch his hat, and then reinforces an opposite positive behavior. What child would not run to fetch his hat if offered the promise of seeing lambs?

The tight focus of action and the simplicity of Barbauld's toddler-accessible language make it easy to overlook the sophisticated intertextuality of her prose. Barbauld's repeated phrases about body parts by an interrogator and a respondent echo archetypal texts such as "Little Red Riding Hood" ("What big eyes you have, Grandma!"; "The better to see you with"), but the most significant hypotext for this passage is the King James Bible (Song of Solomon 7:11, "Come, my beloved, let us go forth into the field"). The same Song of Solomon verse was Barbauld's source text for "Hymn II" in *Hymns in Prose for Children*. For Barbauld, as for other classical humanists of the eighteenth century, the power of language distinguishes humans from animals, and thus Barbauld's focus on language is an important epistemological statement. So, although Barbauld's book teaches children how to identify objects, it also teaches them how to use language for analytical and poetic thought. For instance, little Charles is taught the rudiments of poetic language during an al fresco picnic: the mother tells Charles that the tree stump will be their table and explains how the grass can be compared to a carpet. This lesson in metaphoric language is tailored to a two-year-old—the descriptions are of ordinary objects, and neither the vehicle nor the tenor of the comparison is abstract. Rather, the mother selects as objects of comparison two physical items that are connected to Charles's daily world—grass and carpets.[6]

Barbauld's pedagogical use of mother-child play continues throughout *Lessons*. In the following passage Barbauld plays an improvised counting game with Charles and uses raisins as manipulatives, that is, physical objects that make abstract concepts concrete, and thus cognitively accessible to a toddler:

> Pray give me a raisin.
> Here is one.
> I want another.
> Here is another. One, two.
> I want a great many; I
>   want ten.
> Here are ten. One, two
>   three, four, five, six, seven,
>   eight, nine, ten. (1: 42–43)

The numbers might be spoken by the mother, or by Charles, or by both together. The two voices are almost indistinguishable from each other, for the mother speaks in a child's register of simple words and sentences. The moment is psychologically real, for, if we apply psychoanalytic terms of child development to this moment, the child's consciousness has not yet separated from the mother's, and the oral satisfaction of sweet raisins entices the child from the oral stage and into the symbolic order of numerals.

Barbauld's text never strays from the ordinary linguistic world of a toddler, and this passage contains multiple elements of motherese, or infant-directed speech, such as exaggerated intonation and rhythms, brevity, simplicity, a melodic singsong quality, repetition, and parallelism.[7] Barbauld repeats her sentence structure, setting up a rhythmical syntax through parallel phrasings—"Here is one," "Here is another," "Here are ten." Each "here" statement is followed by a numbered list beginning with "one." Charles's demand statements are also syntactically parallel: "I want another," "I want a great many," "I want ten." Motherese is intensely intimate, for it responds to the child's verbal expressions and bodily movements. Words are often used not for their semantic value but for affect, and the mother's affection shows as she offers more and more raisins.

Barbauld's *Lessons*, by replicating the actual interaction of mother and child, established a particular kind of simplified, intimate, conversational diction that is still used in teaching young children in the learning-to-read stage. By the end of the eighteenth century, titles and title pages of

Robinson Crusoe in Words of One Syllable, by Lucy Aikin (1882)

children's early readers boasted their use of one-syllable words, as in Sarah Trimmer's *The Ladder to Learning, Step the First: Being a Collection of Select Fables, Consisting of Words of Only One Syllable* (1789), Elizabeth Semple's *Short Stories, in Words of One Syllable* (1803), and the anonymous *Walks with Mamma, or, Stories in Words of One Syllable* (1824). Barbauld's niece, Lucy Aikin (under the pseudonym Mary Godolphin), is credited with multiple one-syllable adaptations of classic works: *Aesop's Fables, in Words of One Syllable*; *Evenings at Home, in Words of One Syllable*; *The Pilgrim's Progress, in Words of One Syllable*; *Sandford and Merton, in Words of One Syllable*; *The Swiss Family Robinson, in Words of One Syllable*; and *Robinson Crusoe, in Words of One Syllable*.

Today, single-syllabled early readers are a staple of the publishing industry. For example, *Bob Books Set 1* (1976, 2006), a popular set of first-book readers by Bobby Lynn Maslen and John Maslen, features monosyllabic texts that use limited sounds: the first *Bob* book, *Mat*, uses only four letters—M, A, T, and S.

Barbauld's revolutionary approach to pedagogy as depicted in *Lessons for Children*—individualized lessons that evolve organically out of a mother and child's interactions—exerted enormous influence over children's literature in England and America. Indeed, as Sarah Robbins notes, *Lessons for Children* in its original form was pirated extensively and constantly recirculated in the United States, but many publishers adapted the text so as to focus on a specifically Americanized version of Barbauld's maternal pedagogy: *Lessons* set the stage for nineteenth-century America's "strongly interconnected appeals for improved female education, for feminine control of young children's at-home and in-school teaching, and, eventually, for an ennobling social role for women as the guardians of middle-class family values" (158). *Lessons for Children* inspired Honora Sneyd Edgeworth, the second wife of Richard Lovell Edgeworth, to develop pedagogical approaches which were drawn from her real-life interactions with her children. Her journals of anecdotes about these children formed the basis of Maria and Richard Lovell Edgeworth's *Practical Education* (Myers, "Anecdotes").

Lessons for Children had such a profound effect on the traditions of writing for children that echoes of Barbauld's work crossed genres and appeared in children's verse collections throughout the nineteenth century. For example, Jane Taylor's "Charles and Animals" from *Rhymes for the Nursery* (1806) is a rewriting of Barbauld's body-part game. Taylor's poem begins like a traditional children's animal-identification verse and ends by reminding Charles of his superior qualities as a human:

> The cow has a horn, and the fish has a gill;
> The horse has a hoof, and the duck has a bill;
> The bird has a wing, that on high he may sail;
> And the lion a mane, and the monkey a tail;
> And they swim, or they fly, or they walk, or they eat,
> With fin, or with wing, or with bill, or with feet.
>
> And Charles has two hands, with five fingers to each,
> On purpose to work with, to hold and to reach;
> No birds, beasts, or fishes, for work or for play,
> Have anything half so convenient as they:
> But if he don't use them, and *keep* them in use,
> He'd better have had but two legs, like a goose. (italics original 19–20)

Taylor's poem was reprinted in children's primers and spelling books throughout the nineteenth century, appearing in British, Irish, Scottish, American, and French volumes such as *The Glasgow Infant School Magazine*

Jane Taylor, ["The Cow Has a Horn"], *The New National Spelling Book and Pronouncing Tutor*, ed. B. D. Emerson (Boston: Hammett, 1833), 65.

Like Jane Taylor's "The Star," ("Twinkle, Twinkle, Little Star"), "Charles and Animals" entered into the folkloric tradition of children's nursery rhymes and has multiple variants. The final verse, "Charles has two hands," with its greater complexity of syllables, sounds, and ideas, is frequently dropped from early readers. When it is included, as it is here, the final two lines might be dropped, or Charles's name changed to John. Additionally, words of more than two syllables might be changed or, as here, separated with a hyphen.

(1832), *The New National Spelling Book, and Pronouncing Tutor* (1833), *Book of Lessons for the Use of Schools* (1836), *The Primary Reader* (1844), *The Excelsior Reading Made Easy, or the Child's First Book* (1855), *Illustrated Series of Technical Reading Books* (1871), *Langue Anglaise: Rhymes ad Rimes; Textes en verse avec* (1873), *Manchester Reader* (1875), and *American Childhood* (1925). Almost without fail, these works reproduce Taylor's poem without citing her authorship, and they present her poem as a learning-to-read activity. The poem jettisons Barbauld's free-flowing conversational style and motherese, and it is often preceded by abecedary and syllabary pages and printed on the same page as a word list.

So, although the body-part game in Barbauld's original text celebrates the playful interactions of a mother and her child and adopts an innovative, interactive, hands-on mode of literacy training, as soon as her work is coopted by conservative writers (such as Taylor) and adapted for use within traditional primers, the text is surrounded by the apparatus of rote memorization, and the voice of the mother is buried beneath lines of anapest and lists of sounds and syllables.

Sarah Trimmer's 1780 *An Easy Introduction to the Knowledge of Nature, and Reading the Holy Scriptures (Adapted to the Capacities of Children)* follows close on the heels of Barbauld's *Lessons*, and Trimmer keeps the voice of the educating mother fully intact while adopting Barbauld's conversational style, use of play, and parenting techniques such as response priming. The plot of *Easy Introduction* is straightforward. A mother decides to take walks through the countryside with her daughter, Charlotte, and her much younger son, Henry, who has just gone into breeches. The entire 250-page work is a running monologue in the mother's voice as she speaks to her two children about the different objects and scenes before them. Trimmer's mother gently plays along with Henry's pride in his new breeches. She sets up pedagogical activities, but rather than simply dictate to her children, she shows them the reasons behind each activity:

> I have been thinking, my dear Charlotte, that you and I might take some very profitable Walks together, and at the same time that we are benefitting our Health, by Air and Exercise, might improve our Minds; for every object in Nature, when carefully examined, will fill us with Admiration, and afford us both Instruction and Amusement. . . .—Tho' Henry is so young, he is a sensible little Boy, and . . . therefore I think to take him with us: I long to see him, as I suppose he is greatly pleased with his Change of Dress!—oh! here he comes.—Your Servant, Sir; you are very smart, indeed; I could not imagine what little Beau it was, strutting along;—I suppose now you are dressed like a Man, you begin to fancy that you are one; but tho' you can read and spell, spin a Top, and catch a Ball, I do assure you there are a great many Things for you to learn yet, and I shall be happy to teach you what I know.—Your Sister and I are going to take a Walk; we shall have many pretty Things to look at, and talk about, therefore, I dare say, you will be happy to be of our Party; will you not? . . . Fetch your Hat, Henry, and let us go into the Meadows, where I am sure we shall soon find Something worth examining. (1–4)

Eighteenth-century readers would have recognized the style of Trimmer's text, for it was inspired by Barbauld's *Lessons for Children* as Trimmer states in her preface to *Easy Introduction*. Trimmer praises *Lessons* for its informal, conversational style, recommends that her readers purchase Barbauld's book, and includes the exact address at which it can be found (xii). Trimmer adopts the same parenting techniques as Barbauld, such as response priming and play. As with Barbauld's Charles, little Henry is asked to fetch his hat in preparation for a walk. Further, the mother turns the walk into a game, for Henry will have "many pretty things to look at" and will learn new things to add to his already mastered skills of spinning a top and catching a ball. Thus, the mother encourages the positive behavior of learning by associating it with play.

Barbauld's maternal approach to education—her emphasis on intimate play, sensory descriptions, hands-on lessons, and conversational language drawn from real-life interactions—predates by over a century the radical education innovations associated with the early twentieth-century American socialist and progressive educator Lucy Sprague Mitchell. Mitchell's philosophy of education emphasized process and teaching children to understand relationships within and among social, ecological, and physical elements of the world.[8] Like Barbauld's multivolume *Lessons for Children*, in which the title of each volume includes the age of its intended readers, Mitchell's *Here and Now Story Book* (first published in 1921) was subdivided into sections by age groups: two-year-olds, three-year-olds, and so forth. As with Barbauld's approach, Mitchell emphasized the importance of drawing content from a child's world: "anything to which a child gives his spontaneous attention, anything which he questions as he moves around the world" (2). As with Barbauld's "new walk" of simplified, conversational diction, Mitchell emphasizes the necessity of repetition and diction composed of brief sentence units that are simple and "close together" (48). For example, in *Another Here and Now Story Book* (1937), Mitchell offers a two-year-old's animal-name, body-part game that is so evocative of Barbauld's style that it seems lifted wholesale from *Lessons*:

Remember the goldfish?
   Has no hands!
Remember the goldfish?
   Has no hands. (3)

However, the piece that most strikingly demonstrates a direct line of influence from Barbauld's *Lessons for Children* to Jane Taylor's "Charles and Animals" to Mitchell's *Here and Now Story Book* is Mitchell's poem "How the Animals Move" for four- and five-year-olds. As in Taylor's piece, Mitchell transitions from animal movements in the first stanza to depictions of the child's body in the final stanza:

> The lion, he has paws with claws,
> The horse, he walks on hooves,
> The worm, he lies right on the ground
>   And wriggles when he moves!
>
> The seal, he moves with swimming feet,
>   The moth, has wings like a sail,
> The fly he clings; the bird he wings,
>   The monkey swings by his tail!
>
>   But boys and girls
>   With feet and hands
>   Can walk and run
>   And swim and stand! (*Here and Now* 191)

The closing stanza, as with Barbauld's body-part game and Taylor's poem, shifts from a neutral description of animals to something that feels more like an adult's direct address, if not to a specific child, then to all children generally.

Like Barbauld, who based volume 1 of *Lessons* on her interactions with her two-year-old child, Mitchell's *Here and Now Story Book: Two- to Seven-Year-Olds* is based on the words, stories, questions, and interests of the young pupils who attended her school and teacher-training academy in New York City, which is today called the Bank Street School. Whereas Mitchell is responding to the principles of a leftist education practice that borrows from an early twentieth-century Communist perspective in its emphasis on training children to take the tools of production and industrial process into their own hands, Barbauld is responding to a rational pedagogical emphasis on physical experience as well as to a new Enlightenment emphasis on the importance of the mother as the first inculcator of a child's foundational sense impressions and, thus, the child's life-long habitus. Both twentieth-century radical and eighteenth-century rational educators emphasized the importance of sensible objects in child learning and recognized that the circumstances of everyday life afforded the parent with endless educational opportunities. Despite their very different historical and sociopolitical origins, Lucy Sprague Mitchell and Anna Letitia Barbauld arrived at the same point: an embodied maternal pedagogy that aims to make young children fully engaged and active participants in the world.

Notes

1. Mary Hilton's *Women and the Shaping of the Nation's Young* provides an in-depth discussion of the importance of the maternal mode of writing as a powerful form of public speech for British women writers of the Romantic era. Lissa Paul's *The Children's Book Business: Lessons from the Long Eighteenth Century* (especially 95–130) discusses the importance of mothers to Enlightenment education and identifies how mothers such as Mary Wollstonecraft and Eliza Fenwick created pedagogical works with strong maternal figures and shared a supportive London network of female friends. In *British Children's Poetry in the Romantic Era*, I examine how the idealized educating heroine was gradually superseded by sentimental mother figures. This transition is epitomized by the reception history of Ann Taylor's "My Mother" (Ruwe, *British* 84–107). Rebecca Davies, in *Written Maternal Authority and Eighteenth-Century Education in Britain*, has explored the "trope of maternity" as a way in which women writers, by embracing an authoritative voice as mothers through their accepted function as the educators of children, gained social and cultural status as women (1).

2. I refer to Louis Althusser's important insights regarding education as the primary mode by which society imprints ideologies onto an individual's consciousness. Education, as an ideological state apparatus, creates subjects who share the received values, desires, and cultural preferences of a given society. See "Ideology and Ideological State Apparatuses" in Althusser's *Lenin and Philosophy and other Essays*, 121–76.

3. In *Plots of Enlightenment*, Richard A. Barney argues that in eighteenth-century fictive texts, the habitus is inculcated through a "soft" pedagogy of nondirective methods like dialogue, or a "strong arm" approach of heavy-handed didacticism. Either method results in the "improvisational disposition" of the habitus, a durable selfhood that constantly adapts to specific circumstances (14). The links between associationist philosophies and children's books is explored in Samuel F. Pickering, Jr.'s *John Locke and Children's Books in Eighteenth-Century England*.

4. See Michele Cohen for a brief history of conversational or "familiar" modes in the eighteenth century. Aileen Fyfe discusses the use of dialogue and conversation in pedagogical texts by dissenters such as Barbauld and her brother John Aikin. Donelle Ruwe's *British Children's Poetry in the Romantic Era* traces the influence of Barbauld's conversational style on children's verse (especially 6–8).

5. Huizinga sums up play as "a free activity standing quite consciously outside 'ordinary' life as being 'not serious,' but at the same time absorbing the player intensely and utterly" (13). It is "connected to no material interest, and no profit can be gained by it," and it is a "voluntary activity . . . having an aim in itself" (13, 26).

6. William McCarthy links Barbauld's preference for a whole-language experience to the dissenting preference for concepts over rote memorization ("Mother" 92). Likewise,

Joanna Wharton sees Barbauld's dissenting perspective as the force behind *Lessons's* sensory imagery. Samuel Pickering suggests that Barbauld takes her approach, which moves from external objects to internal sense, from Locke (146–47). Mitzi Myers's "Of Mice and Mothers" places Barbauld's approach to literacy and education within a feminist and liberatory pedagogical context.

7. Motherese is variously known as baby talk, infant-directed speech, or child-directed speech. For a general introduction to child-directed speech, see Gleason and Ratner, especially 311–13. For an early definition of motherese, see Elissa L. Newport's 1975 dissertation, "Motherese: The Speech of Mothers to Young Children." In "Mother, I'd Rather Do It Myself," Newport, Henry Gleitman, and Lila R. Gleitman define motherese as speech that is personal and individualized, focused on the mother's needs to get the child to do something, brief, well-formed, highly intelligible, and "topical" in that it deals with the here and now and the constraints of the child's limited vocabulary and knowledge of the world. See 121–26.

8. For discussion of Lucy Sprague Mitchell's *Here and Now Story Book* and her progressive education philosophies, see Julia L. Mickenberg's *Learning from the Left: Children's Literature, the Cold War, and Radical Politics in the United States* (especially 40–45).

Works Cited

Althusser, Louis. *Lenin and Philosophy and Other Essays*. New York: Monthly Review, 1972.

Barbauld, Anna Letitia. *Hymns in Prose for Children*. London: Johnson, 1781.

———. *Lessons for Children*. 4 parts. London: Johnson, 1778–79.

Barney, Richard A. *Plots of Enlightenment: Education and the Novel in Eighteenth-Century England*. Stanford: Stanford UP, 1999.

Burney [D'Arblay], Frances. *Diary and Letters of Madame D'Arblay (1778–1840)*. Ed. Charlotte Barrett. 6 vols. London: Macmillan, 1905.

Cohen, Michele. "'Familiar Conversation': The Role of the 'Familiar Format' in Education in Eighteenth- and Nineteenth-Century England." *Educating the Child in Enlightenment Britain: Beliefs, Cultures, Practices*. Ed. Mary Hilton and Jill Shefrin. Surrey: Ashgate, 2009. 99–116.

Davies, Rebecca. *Written Maternal Authority and Eighteenth-Century Education in Britain: Educating by the Book*. Burlington: Ashgate, 2014.

Edgeworth, Maria, and Richard Lovell Edgeworth. *Practical Education* (1798). *Novels and Selected Works of Maria Edgeworth*, vol. 11. Ed. Susan Manly. London: Pickering, 2003.

Fielding, Sarah. *The Governess; or, the Little Female Academy*. Ed. Candace Ward. Ontario: Broadview, 2005.

Fyfe, Aileen. "Reading Children's Books in Late Eighteenth-Century Dissenting Families." *The Historical Journal* 43.2 (2000): 453–73.

Genlis, Madame la Contesse de. *Adelaide and Theodore; or Letters on Education*. Trans. anon. 2nd ed. London: Bathurst, 1784.

Gleason, Jean Berko, and Nan Bernstein Ratner. *Psycholinguistics*. Fort Worth: Harcourt, 1998.
Godolphin, Mary. [attr. to Lucy Aikin]. *Robinson Crusoe: In Words of One Syllable*. New York: McLoughlin, 1882.
Hamilton, Elizabeth. *Letters on the Elementary Principles of Education*. 1801. 3rd ed. 3 vols. London: Robinson, 1803.
Hilton, Mary. *Women and the Shaping of the Nation's Young: Education and Public Doctrine in Britain 1750–1850*. Aldershot: Ashgate, 2007.
Hopsicker, Peter, and Chad Carlson. "To Play or to Parent?: An Analysis of the Adult-Child Interaction in Make-Believe Play." *The Philosophy of Play*. Ed. Emily Ryall, Wendy Russell, and Malcolm MacLean. London: Routledge, 2014. 175–84.
Huizinga, Johan. *Homo Ludens: A Study of the Play-Element in Culture*. Boston: Beacon, 1950.
Kazdan, Alan E. *Parent Management Training: Treatment for Oppositional, Aggressive, and Antisocial Behavior in Children and Adolescents*. Oxford: Oxford UP, 2005.
Locke, John. *Some Thoughts Concerning Education and of the Conduct of the Understanding*. Ed. Ruth W. Grant and Nathan Tarcov. Indianapolis: Hackett, 1996.
Maslin, Bobby Lynn, and John Maslen. *Bob Books Set 1* (1976). New York: Scholastic, 2006.
Mellor, Anne K. *Mothers of the Nation: Women's Political Writing in England, 1780–1830*. Bloomington: Indiana UP, 2000.
Mickenberg, Julia L. *Learning from the Left: Children's Literature, the Cold War, and Radical Politics in the United States*. Oxford: Oxford UP, 2006.
Mitchell, Lucy Sprague. *Another Here and Now Story Book*. New York: Dutton, 1937.
———. *Here and Now Story Book: Two- to Seven-Year-Olds*. New York: Dutton, 1921.
McCarthy, William. *Anna Letitia Barbauld: Voice of the Enlightenment*. Baltimore: Johns Hopkins UP, 2008.
———. "Mother of All Discourses: Anna Barbauld's *Lessons for Children*." *Princeton Library Chronicle* 60.2 (Winter 1999): 196–219.
Myers, Mitzi. "'Anecdotes from the Nursery' in Maria Edgeworth's *Practical Education* (1798): Learning from Children 'Abroad and at Home.'" *Princeton University Library Chronicle* 60.2 (Winter 1999): 220–50.
———. "Impeccable Governesses, Rational Dames, and Moral Mothers: Mary Wollstonecraft and the Female Tradition in Georgian Children's Books." *Children's Literature* 14 (1986): 31–58.
———. "Of Mice and Mothers: Mrs. Barbauld's 'New Walk' and Gendered Codes in Children's Literature." *Feminine Principles and Women's Experience in American Composition and Rhetoric*. Ed. Louise Wetherbee Phelps and Janet Emig. Pittsburg: U of Pittsburg P, 1995. 225–88.
Newport, Elissa L. "Motherese: The Speech of Mothers to Young Children." Diss. University of Pennsylvania, 1975.
Newport, Elissa L., Henry Gleitman, and Lila R. Gleitman. "'Mother, I'd Rather Do It Myself': Some Effects and Non-Effects of Maternal Speech Style." *Talking to Children:*

Language Input and Acquisition. Ed. Catherine E. Snow and Charles A. Ferguson. Cambridge: Cambridge UP, 1977. 109–49.

Paul, Lissa. *The Children's Book Business: Lessons from the Long Eighteenth Century*. New York: Routledge, 2011.

Pickering, Jr., Samuel F. *John Locke and Children's Books in Eighteenth-Century England*. Knoxville: U of Tennessee P, 1981.

Robbins, Sarah. "Re-Making Barbauld's Primers: A Case Study in the Americanization of British Literary Pedagogy. *Children's Literature Association Quarterly* 21.4 (1996–97): 158–69.

Rousseau, Jean-Jacques. *Émile*. Trans. Barbara Foxley. London: Dent, 1993.

Ruwe, Donelle. *British Children's Poetry in the Romantic Era: Verse, Riddle, and Rhyme*. Houndmills, UK: Palgrave, 2014.

Taylor, Ann, and Jane Taylor. *Rhymes for the Nursery*. London: Darton, 1806.

Taylor, Jane. ["The Cow Has a Horn."] *The New National Spelling Book and Pronouncing Tutor*. Ed. B. D. Emerson. Boston: Hammett, 1833. 65.

Trimmer, Sarah. *An Easy Introduction to the Knowledge of Nature, and Reading the Holy Scriptures*. London: Dodsley, 1780.

———. *The Guardian of Education. A Periodical Work*. 5 vols. London, 1802–6.

Trouille, Mary Seidman. *Sexual Politics in the Enlightenment: Women Writers Read Rousseau*. New York: SUNY P, 1997.

Smith, Adam. *The Theory of Moral Sentiments*. Ed. D. D. Raphael and A. L. Macfie. Oxford: Clarendon, 1976.

Wharton, Joanna. "'The Things Themselves': Sensible Images in *Lessons for Children* and *Hymns in Prose*." *Anna Letitia Barbauld: New Perspectives*. Ed. William McCarthy and Olivia Murphy. Lewisburg: Bucknell UP, 2014. 107–26.

Wollstonecraft, Mary. *Original Stories from Real Life*. London: Johnson, 1791.

Chapter 2

Juliana Ewing's *Six to Sixteen*: Realizing and Rewriting Maternal Legacy

Koeun Kim

This story was written before her death: it has been revised without her help.
—Juliana Ewing, Dedication to *Six to Sixteen*

When Juliana Ewing's *Six to Sixteen* was published in 1875, it was her first work that had not been revised by her mother and fellow writer, Margaret Gatty, who had died in 1872. At the same time, however, it was also one of the first novels in which Ewing returned to her native literary realm, the domestic sphere, after her short venture into the realm of fantasy. The years between 1868 and 1871 had been a phase of literary experiments for Ewing in which she had tried her pen at fantasy stories, a genre dominated at that time by male writers such as Lewis Carroll and George MacDonald. In 1869, in a letter to her mother, Ewing talks about her secret experiments with fairy tales: "I do not in the least mean to give up my own style and take to fairy tale-telling, but I would like to try this experiment" (Eden 182). The results of this experiment were anonymously published fairy-tale imitations and the domestic fantasies such as "Amelia and the Dwarfs" (1870), "Benjy in Beastland" (1870), and "Timothy's Shoes" (1871). She did not, however, attract a larger readership as she had hoped. In 1872, Ewing went back to what she herself called her "own style" of story writing, the realistic domestic story, a genre that had become throughout the nineteenth century the specialty of the female children's writer.

Thus, mother and daughter Gatty and Ewing shared not only the occupation of a children's writer but also the genre in which they wrote, namely the female domestic story. Having its roots in the moral tales of eighteenth- and early nineteenth-century women writers, the domestic story was the prevalent female mode of children's writing from the mid-nineteenth century, exhibiting, as Shirley Foster and Judy Simons observe, "pervasive motifs in their narrative and representational patterns" (24). The stories took domestic realism as their generic model, emphasized "emotional or psychological development in the private sphere of home and family, and portrayed the heroine's growth to ideal womanhood" (Foster and Simons 5). Their common purpose was "to explain and justify the feminine position in society" and to persuade their readers to conform to ideal gender roles, and tended therefore to be read more by girls (Rowbotham 7). Consequently, the conventional domestic story displayed a mother-narrator and child-narratee relationship in which the narrator took on the role of the experienced adult and assumed a morally superior position over the young reader.

Not only did these female writers and their domestic stories function as literary mothers for their (primarily) girl readers, but they also served as literary mothers for subsequent women writers of children's fiction, influencing significantly the content and writing style of their works. As the real-life daughter of her literary mother, Ewing provides a particularly appropriate example to explore the significant question of how literary daughters define themselves in relation to their literary mothers and their works. Thus, by analyzing Ewing's *Six to Sixteen*'s intertextual relationship with her mother's tale "The Fairy Godmothers" (1851), this chapter will explore how Ewing in *Six to Sixteen* continues the legacy of her literary foremothers while also questioning its nature and validity. Indeed, if one views Ewing's experimental phase in which she ventured into the male-dominated genre of fantasy as an attempt to break away from a female literary realm that restricted her literary ambition, her return to domestic stories with *Six to Sixteen* after her mother's death is clearly a gesture of recognizing, but also of reassessing, the literary legacy of a long line of female children's writers. Examining the various ways Ewing revises and rewrites the conventional domestic story in *Six to Sixteen*, I will show how Ewing points to the limitation of this maternal literary legacy in her effort to overcome the social conventions that confine women writers and how she suggests ways to widen the scope of female activity.

Realizing Maternal Legacy

When looking at Juliana Ewing's development as a female children's writer, it is difficult to ignore Margaret Gatty's influence on this process. Gatty herself was a famous children's writer renowned for her children's books *Aunt Judy's Tales* (1859) and *Aunt Judy's Letters* (1862). The popularity of these books was considerable enough that Gatty named her children's magazine, begun in 1866, *Aunt Judy's Magazine*. Considering the fact that "Aunt Judy" was the nickname of Juliana Ewing, who was the designated storyteller in the Gatty nursery, the intimate professional relationship between mother and daughter can be easily conjectured. Indeed, Gatty actively promoted and fostered Ewing's career as a children's author. She initiated Ewing into the literary world by introducing her daughter's first stories to Charlotte Yonge's magazine, *Monthly Packet*, for which Gatty herself was a regular contributor. Ewing's first published book, *Melchior's Dream and Other Tales* (1862), had a preface written by Gatty, who expressed her "feelings of pride and pleasure" (7) at introducing a daughter into the literary world. Later, Gatty would make Ewing the main contributor of her *Aunt Judy's Magazine*.

As Gatty and Ewing's collaborative writing relationship might indicate, Ewing's *Six to Sixteen* plainly displays influences of the female literary tradition Gatty helped to develop. The story takes place mainly within the domestic realm and charts the psychological development of Margery, the heroine. In terms of readership, Ewing's novel explicitly identifies its target audience through its subtitle, *A Story for Girls*. Furthermore, by exposing Margery to various value systems concerning significant issues such as education, domesticity, and gender differences throughout the story, the book aims to show the most ideal environment for instilling the virtues deemed desirable in a girl. Thus, by following these essential features that constituted and defined the conventional domestic story, Ewing firmly aligns *Six to Sixteen* with this female literary tradition. Above all, however, in *Six to Sixteen*, Ewing adheres to the genre of her literary foremothers in two important ways that reveal her own personal and familial circumstances. First, Ewing makes direct references to the intellectual influence of Gatty by modeling the story's ideal mother after her. And second, by adopting the moral "love of employment" (*Fairy* 58) from Gatty's story "The Fairy Godmothers" (1851) as her own novel's main message, Ewing appreciates and realizes Gatty's spiritual influence.

Furthermore, it is not only through her novel's main moral message that Ewing alludes to her mother's literary influence but also through *Six to Sixteen*'s essential structure. Gatty's story follows the conventional fairy-tale formula in which fairy godmothers endow various gifts to their goddaughters in order to discover the perfect gift that makes human beings most content. The gifts the fairy godmothers in Gatty's story present to their goddaughters range from beauty and riches to limitless power. The goddaughter who turns out to be the model of human happiness in the end is Hermione, who has been dowered with "love of employment" (*Fairy* 58). There are significant parallels between the fairy godmothers' search for the ideal gift for their goddaughters in Gatty's allegorical story and the heroine's search for the ideal mother in Ewing's realistic novel.

Ewing's *Six to Sixteen* is narrated by the heroine, Margery Vandaleur, who tells of her life from the ages of six to sixteen. Margery is an orphan, having lost her parents in India through an outbreak of cholera when she was six. She is brought back to England, where she is taken care of by a series of guardians and comes into contact with a variety of homes in which she encounters different mother figures who influence her in both bad and good ways. Just as the ideal gift in Gatty's story turns out to be "love of employment" (58), in Ewing's story the exemplary mother emerges as the one who is able to teach her daughters the pleasures of intellectual activities and constant occupation. Indeed, in Ewing's work the fortunate and significant impact of this maternal lesson is most conspicuously expressed at the end of the novel when Margery's friend Eleanor reveals to Margery the reason for the perfectly happy marriage she has with her husband:

> Oh, Margery dear, I do often feel so thankful to my mother for having given us plenty of rational interests. I could really imagine even *our* quarrelling or getting tired of each other, if we had nothing but ourselves in common. . . . As to social ups and downs, and not having much money or many fine dresses, a "collection" alone makes one almost too indifferent. Do you remember Mother's saying long ago, that intellectual pleasures have this in common with the consolations of religion, that they are such as the world can neither give nor take away? (296)

Eleanor eulogizes here her mother's teaching, namely, "rational interests" and "intellectual pleasures" that downplay worldly advantages like social status, "money," and "fine dresses." In this way, Ewing echoes not only the main lesson "love of employment" but also the examples of wrong fairy gifts, as it were, "beauty," "riches," and "power" in her mother's story. Thus, by appropriating elements of Gatty's fairy story into a realistic setting, Ewing is able to realize the moral of her mother's allegory in contemporary Victorian society and prove its validity.

As Ewing's novel follows the structure of Gatty's story, so do the various mother figures that are introduced in Six to Sixteen correspond to the fairy gifts of Gatty's fairy godmothers. While Gatty shows the untoward effects wrong fairy gifts can have on the girls, Ewing presents the unfortunate influences unwise mothers can have on their daughters. The first mother figure that makes her appearance in Ewing's novel is Margery's real mother. Without doubt, what distinguishes Margery's mother is her great beauty. Margery reports: "My mother was the prettiest woman on board the vessel she went out in, and the prettiest woman at the station when she got there. Some people have told me that she was the prettiest woman they ever saw" (20–21). According to Margery's description of her mother, who is "glittering with costly ornaments, beautiful and scented, like a fairy dream" (22), she could easily have been Aurora or Julia, the girls in Gatty's story who were bestowed the fairy gifts of beauty and riches. That beauty alone is insufficient, however, is pointed out in both stories. As Margery narrates, she would forego all this vision of her mother's dazzling beauty "for one—only one—memory of her praying by my bedside, or teaching me at her knee" (22). Since beauty and appearances are the only legacy Margery's mother left her daughter, in the first few years after her mother's death, Margery recalls how, as a little girl, her mind was solely engaged "with the question whether I did or did not inherit my mother's graces" (66). Just as her mother, who—rather than caring for her daughter—sought the pleasure of gentlemen friends to flaunt her beauty and fashionable clothes, Margery narrates how her imagination at that time was intensely preoccupied with making herself the center of attention in which she "always took care to fancy some circumstances that led to my being in my best dress on the occasion" (64).

Ewing presents a more serious case of an obsession with beauty through the girl Matilda, Mr. and Mrs. Buller's daughter. Mrs. Buller, or rather Aunt Theresa as she is called by Margery, is the mother figure in the novel after the death of Margery's mother. Aunt Theresa is not a self-centered beauty like Margery's mother, but she thinks of appearances as the decisive factor in the future happiness of her daughter. Ewing points out how Aunt Theresa's wrong criterion for happiness causes Matilda's heightened consciousness about her own appearance and her eventual social awkwardness.

Matilda's paralyzing self-consciousness, therefore, parallels Aurora's self-centeredness in Gatty's story in which the unlucky fairy gift of beauty gets in the way of everything Aurora does, "for it took away her interest in every thing but herself" (*Fairy* 20).

The last mother figure portrayed in the novel is Mrs. Arkwright, who is the ideal mother. Indeed, Ewing models Mrs. Arkwright closely after her own mother. When Mrs. Arkwright is first introduced, she is laden with tin cans full of sea creatures that she promptly examines through a magnifying glass—a clear allusion to Gatty's obsession with seaweeds.[1] Like her real-life counterpart, Mrs. Arkwright etches on copper, has a collection of old etchings, and is a naturalist. Moreover, just as Gatty's scientist friends Dr. Harvey and Dr. Johnston named their separate discoveries of a new genus of algae and sea serpent after her in 1855 (Maxwell 99), in *Six to Sixteen* the water weed discovered in the Arkwright household is "described and figured in the *Phycological Quarterly*, and received the specific name of *Arkwrightii*" (254). Mrs. Arkwright *is* effectually Margaret Gatty.

Naturally, Eleanor Arkwright, daughter of Mrs. Arkwright and the direct successor of the perfectly happy Hermione of Gatty's "The Fairy Godmothers," is the model outcome of perfect mothering. Being the daughter of an intellectual mother, Eleanor Arkwright is, however, also a mixture of Ewing herself and the family friend Eleanor Lloyd from whom she inherited her name. Like Margery, Lloyd, during the visits she paid the Gatty household, shared "with the zest of a sister" the "somewhat desultory, if intellectual, home education" (Eden 52, 53) of Gatty. Notable is that all four women, fictional and real, would be writers at some point. Ewing and Lloyd were both children's writers, while Eleanor Arkwright and Margery Vandaleur would narrate their fictional autobiographies. Ewing pays tribute in this way to the literary legacy of mother figures who—progressive and liberal such as Gatty—paved the way for the literary careers of successive daughter writers.

Rewriting Maternal Legacy

While *Six to Sixteen* displays Ewing's attempt to pay homage to her mother's literary and spiritual legacy, the work also expresses Ewing's resolution to overcome the restraints the female domestic story puts on the woman writer, and thus, to differentiate herself from her mother's work.

Ewing's most notable revision of the traditional female domestic story is the employment of Margery, a girl of sixteen, as the narrator of her novel, in contrast to the conventional mother-narrator and child-narratee relationship of the domestic story in which the mother-narrator possessed the moral superiority. Gatty states in the dedication of *The Fairy Godmothers* that she offers her book to her children to illustrate to them her "long cherished convictions" (Dedication) on life, establishing a mother-child relationship from the very beginning of her book. Indeed, the narrator of Gatty's story constantly addresses "dear little readers" (1) and "my dear children" (88), signaling in this way an intimate but also essentially hierarchical relationship with the audience. Ewing's *Six to Sixteen*, however, has a very different premise. Ewing declares in the dedication that her novel "contains no attempt to paint a model girl or a model education, and was originally written as a sketch of domestic life, and not as a vehicle for theories" (v). Different from Gatty, Ewing consciously keeps herself apart from a superior maternal role of offering child readers positive moral advice. Also, although the novel is implicitly a eulogy to Gatty, Ewing dedicates the work to Eleanor Lloyd, a fellow female writer of children's fiction. Thus, the novel's dedication to a friend writer and its withdrawal from a superior authorial position reveals Ewing's intention to distance her work from certain conventions of her mother's genre.

Indeed, employing a young girl as the narrator of her novel enables Ewing to convey her criticism of Victorian domestic ideology in a safer way than it would have been through a mother-narrator. Margery's not-always-orthodox opinions on the various English homes she goes through are, owing to her youth, not expressed in the authoritative voice of the mother-like narrator who is burdened with the responsibility to offer child readers positive precepts. Rather, Margery is allowed the freedom to articulate her thoughts as such, and not as absolute truths, often using verbs such as "believe" and "think" when she expresses her opinions. Ewing's most conspicuous use of Margery's young voice is when she aims to criticize the Victorian separate-spheres ideology that renders women uninformed outside their designated field of domesticity and thus narrow minded in their conception of the world. For instance, in regard to Matilda's increasing social awkwardness, Margery is of the opinion that her psychological instability is partly a natural consequence of the mentally cramped atmosphere of home life: "As she [Matilda] had heard Aunt Theresa and her friends discuss, approve, and condemn their friends by the standard of appearances alone, ever since she was old enough to overhear company conversation, I hardly think she was much to blame on this point" (124). Moreover, Margery notices how Aunt Theresa and her lady friends use speculative and sensational anecdotes from fashionable domestic magazines instead of scientific facts to deal with Matilda's deteriorating mental health, observing: "when Aunt Theresa took counsel with her friends about poor Matilda, they hardly kept to Matilda's case long enough even to master the facts, and on this particular occasion Mrs. St. John plunged at once into a series of illustrative anecdotes of the most terrible kind" (132). Indeed, after her observations on the mismanaged upbringing of Matilda within Aunt Theresa's home, Margery comes to the conclusion that the girls of the St. Quentin household are happier and healthier because "they always seemed to have plenty to do, which perhaps kept them from worrying about themselves" (126). Subsequently, Margery conjectures: "I *believe* that their greatest advantage over poor Matilda was that they had not been accustomed to hear dress and appearance talked about as matters of the first importance" (126; emphasis added). Not only does Margery illustrate here how the Victorian domestic ideology limits women's and girls' interests to the petty activities of the private domestic sphere and stifles the mind of the adolescent girl, but she also suggests how this might be prevented by keeping the girl occupied with work. When she states how Uncle Buller "seldom interfered" in domestic matters, particularly in the education of his daughters, Margery identifies the lack of communication between the domestic and public spheres as the fundamental reason for Matilda's poor upbringing. As Margery presumes: "I *think* Aunt Theresa would have been glad if he would have advised her oftener" (134; emphasis added). Focalizing from the still developing mind of Margery offers Ewing a liminal space to explore and also call into question the prevailing value systems.

The novel opens with an introduction in which sixteen-year-old Margery tells of her joint project with Eleanor to write their autobiographies. Therefore, in the main narrative of the novel, Margery discusses her life from the age of six up to the present. In the text that frames this autobiography, Margery reflects on the process of writing and the troubles involved in this. The act of writing a domestic story itself becomes a significant subject of Margery's narration, from narrative difficulties in keeping the story straight—"I must not allow myself to wander off" (14)—to serious doubts whether writing about one's own life might not be too vain an undertaking for a Victorian girl. "It seems an egotistical and perhaps silly thing to record the trivialities of our everyday lives," she says, "even for fun, and just to please ourselves" (12). In this way, Ewing uses Margery to take issue not only with the conventional features of the domestic story but also with the common criticism that was leveled against this genre. Listing the domestic story's limited readership, its supposedly petty and narrow subject matter, and its explicit moralism, Margery expresses her lack of confidence in regard to the authority and validity of her chosen genre. Indeed, Margery questions the value of writing a story that takes place entirely within the homely sphere and merely deals with everyday "trivialities" (11). In response to Margery's complaint, Eleanor reassures her by arguing "that the simple and truthful history of a single mind from childhood would be as valuable . . . as the whole of Mr. Pepys' Diary from the first volume to the last" (12). Margery, however, not convinced of Eleanor's arguments, asserts that her own "biography will not be the history of a mind, but only a record of small facts important to no one but myself" (12). In fact, just as the domestic story was dominantly written by *female* writers for young *female* readers, Margery's and Eleanor's records of their lives are to be read only by themselves as they promise to exchange them when they are finished. Eleanor, however, is depicted to be enthusiastic about this exchange: "If ever we are separated in life, how I shall enjoy looking over it again and again" (19). Thus, Ewing presents in *Six to Sixteen* two contrasting opinions on the female domestic story, as it were, noting on the one hand its triviality in subject matter and the smallness and fixedness of its readership, but on the other hand the valuable insights one might derive from its simple record of domestic life. These two opposing perspectives reflect Ewing's own divided view on her and her mother's genre: first, its supposed insignificance as a literary genre, and second, its crucial function of satisfying the specific needs of a tight-knit group of young female readers and future female writers.

Presenting a young girl's perspective on the domestic realm and the domestic story is only one way in which Ewing addresses the insufficiency of her maternal legacy. In addition, these two female writers differ significantly in how they deploy the guiding principle "love of employment." In contrast to Gatty's story, which implies that any kind of constant labor will keep a girl fulfilled as long as she is doing her best, Ewing's novel clearly means intellectual labor. In Gatty's story, Hermione's love of employment is illustrated by her finding pleasure in various activities, from simple tasks such as winding up the worsted to more sophisticated ones such as "French and music and drawing" (39). Although the latter activities seem intellectual, they represent ideal feminine accomplishments that were appreciated within the Victorian drawing room and would eventually "attract a good husband" (Poovey 128). There is a great difference between Hermione's aimless love for any kind of labor that lies in front of her and Eleanor's methodical and determined "fervour against 'the great war of ignorance'" (177).

From this point of view, Gatty's teaching of an uncritical love of employment can almost be read as conservative in that it encourages girls to be content with whatever duties they are burdened with. In contrast, Ewing seems to suggest that Hermione's indiscriminate love for any kind of labor as depicted in Gatty's work will not develop her intellect and expand her perspective.

Ewing also discloses the shortfalls of Gatty's life principle "love of labour" by applying it to a range of mother figures in *Six to Sixteen*. Despite Aunt Theresa's wrong educational methods, for example, Margery depicts her as a caring mother and very industrious housewife. Aunt Theresa's busyness is underlined when Uncle Buller, sick of wasting his time in social obligations, accuses his wife of not being able to know his feelings and complains to her: "If you had any one occupation, you'd know how maddening it is" (53). Whereupon Aunt Theresa angrily retorts:

> I'm sure, Edward, I'm always busy. I never have a quiet moment from morning to night. . . . But it is so like you men! You can stick to one thing all along, and your meals come to you as if they dropped out of the skies . . . and when one is ordering dinner and luncheon, . . . and looking after the children and the servants,. . . from week's end to week's end—you say one has no occupation. (53–54)

While Uncle Buller pursues his intellectual hobbies in his own room and does not assist his wife in domestic affairs, Aunt Theresa is absorbed in managing them, having time for nothing else. What Ewing calls attention to here is that Aunt Theresa cannot help but be narrow in her worldview; being overwhelmed with domestic chores, she simply does not have the time to educate her mind. Aunt Theresa abides by Gatty's motto of love of employment in a way that Ewing calls into question by suggesting that these domestic occupations fail to bring fulfillment. The domestic duties that dull Aunt Theresa's mind and make her a less than ideal mother are the direct causes of her Matilda's unknown illness, nervousness, and paralysing self-consciousness.

Margery's great-grandmother is another mother-character who is modeled after Ewing's mother. While Mrs. Arkwright echoes with her scientific pursuits the progressive aspects of Gatty's legacy, Margery's great-grandmother represents the ineffectiveness of Gatty's guiding principle "love of labour" within the confining mores of Victorian society. Just as Gatty, the wife of a poor clergyman, worked to make ends meet, Margery's great-grandmother, having a hopelessly impractical husband, is the one who holds the household together financially.[2] Gatty contributed to the household income by writing—one of the few socially acceptable occupations for a lady—despite the fact that her inclination was natural history.[3] For Margery's great-grandmother, who is described as a clever and energetic woman like Gatty, the only way to economize within social propriety is to secretly do the lowly housework herself. In showing how Gatty's and Margery's great-grandmother's love for labor essentially functions to keep the household financially afloat—after all, the very duty the Victorian man had to fulfill—Ewing disputes the common Victorian assumption that women's work should be domestic in nature. Significantly, however, by illustrating how these women had to limit their work within the home despite their abilities that reached beyond it, Ewing also points out that an indiscriminate following of her mother's life motto "love of employment" is ineffective in widening the working sphere of women.

It is not only Gatty who is split into two characters in the novel (Mrs. Arkwright and Margery's great-grandmother). Ewing also divides herself into two characters, Margery and Eleanor. Margery Vandaleur is simultaneously the object and observer of Ewing's experiment about the ideal upbringing of girls. Being an orphan, Margery is able to form her own opinions of the world from scratch without the intrusion of a mother-educator. Margery as the young narrator of the novel is therefore the part of Ewing who wants to free herself from the narrative restrictions of her mother's literary legacy.[4] Eleanor Arkwright, daughter of the model mother, Mrs. Arkwright, is the product of perfect mothering and represents Ewing's deepest respect for her mother's spiritual legacy. That not Eleanor but Margery, the motherless girl, acts as the narrator of the story marks *Six to Sixteen* as Ewing's first step of artistic separation from her mother's literary influence.

Six to Sixteen surprisingly ends with the marriage of Eleanor Arkwright. This ending seems to be on first sight a rather conservative move—after all, Margery and Eleanor promised each other to stay old maids. Within the context of the novel's overarching message that urges girl readers to widen their point of view and realm of activity, Eleanor's moving out of her intellectual but isolated home on the Yorkshire moors into the world outside is only appropriate. For Eleanor, following in the footsteps of her creator, Ewing—who married an army officer—marries a Captain of the British army, expanding her sphere from home to that of the regiment. Indeed, Ewing herself, the wife of a military officer who was often stationed abroad, led a nomadic life, coming into contact with various army camps, households, and countries, which naturally contributed to the diversity of style, subjects, and themes of her stories. Ewing's horizon of experience and activity, therefore, differed from that of her mother, who spent the majority of her life at her Yorkshire home; she "never travelled beyond the British Isles, and the holidays she took away from 'home' and 'the children' were only too rare," even though she "longed at times for foreign travel" ("Margaret Gatty" xxi). Thus, like herself, Ewing endows Eleanor with the opportunity to broaden her outlook on the world and the realm of her influence. It is also significant that through Eleanor's marriage, the domestic narrative of the girls finds a larger audience, for the story that was destined to be read only by a girl comes into the hands of Eleanor's husband, who is eager to read of his bride's girlhood. In this way, a girl's view on the world is communicated to a male audience. This communication between what is commonly regarded as two separate spheres can therefore be considered as Ewing's call for an expansion of vision on both parts, men's and women's.

It almost seems that through the death of Gatty, Ewing is finally able to gain enough distance from this traditionally female genre—one she attempted to break away from in her experimental phase—to evaluate it, perceive its drawbacks, and create her own version of the domestic story that transcends its limitations. As a matter of fact, Ewing's experiments with the children's domestic story did reach far. Frances Hodgson Burnett's *The Secret Garden* (1911), which begins in India during an epidemic of cholera that orphans the heroine Mary Lennox, exactly replicates the beginning of *Six to Sixteen*. Indeed, Burnett's heroine, Mary, even follows her predecessor, Margery Vandaleur, to the wide moors of Yorkshire, a place Ewing represents as the ideal surrounding in which to free and expand the mind of the growing girl. Like Ewing's, Burnett's story will chart how Mary—also the daughter of a beautiful but self-centered mother like Margery—gradually frees herself from the constraints of maternal legacy by creating her very own sphere, the secret garden. Additionally, glimpses of the questioning voice of Margery can be found again in the more irreverent child narrators of E. Nesbit's stories.[5] *Six to Sixteen*, Ewing's nod to the legacy of her literary foremothers, would, therefore, in turn, become a significant literary influence on subsequent female children's writers.

Notes

1. As Ewing herself states, to a large circle of Gatty's friends, Gatty was—rather than a children's author—"best known as a naturalist in the special department of phycology" ("In Memoriam" 481). In 1862, Gatty completed her book *The History of British Seaweeds* which, as Ewing says, "was written out of fourteen years' experience, comprising the first struggles of a beginner, and no small amount of a scholar's learning" ("Margaret" xvi). This two-volume work was, as late as 1946, used as a reference book by the Scottish Marine Biological Association (Thwaite 179).

2. Ewing was aware of her mother's great efforts in keeping the household afloat, as she wrote "of the dear Mum's years and years of work and earnings, poured as a matter of course into the leaky bucket of a large family's expenses" (Maxwell 81).

3. Christabel Maxwell writes that "Margaret Gatty was by nature a scientist rather than a writer. . . . Had she been born two generations later she would have devoted her life to some form of science; but living when she did, writing books was the only outlet available to her" (91). Ewing herself states: "She did so keenly enjoy everything at which she worked that it is difficult to say in which of her hobbies she found most happiness; but I am disposed to give her natural history pursuits the palm" ("In Memoriam" 481).

4. Jackie C. Horne, who also discusses Ewing's *Six to Sixteen* in the context of the British imperial project, notices how Mrs. Arkwright, in contrast to the so-called mentoria figures of Georgian children's writers like Maria Edgeworth, "does not take center stage in Margery's narrative as she would have in earlier works" (266). Horne observes that the work "clearly values and espouses such direct maternal instruction" but states that Ewing as a novelist seems to prefer to filter maternal advice through Margery's voice (266).

5. Marah Gubar also points out the significant influence Ewing's use of young narrators had on subsequent children's writers, as she asserts: "Ewing in particular excelled at this kind of writing, and as I will demonstrate, her work exerted a major influence over Nesbit and thus, indirectly, on a vast array of contemporary authors" (40).

Works Cited

Briggs, Julia. "Woman Writers and Writing for Children: From Sarah Fielding to E. Nesbit." *Children and Their Books: A Celebration of the Work of Iona and Peter Opie.* Ed. Gillian Avery and Julia Briggs. Oxford: Clarendon, 1989. 221–51. Print.

Burnett, Frances Hodgson. *The Secret Garden*. New York: Stokes, 1911.

Eden, Horatia K. F. *Juliana Horatia Ewing and Her Books*. London: Society for Promoting Christian Knowledge, 1896. Print.

Ewing, Juliana. "In Memoriam, Margaret Gatty." *Aunt Judy's Magazine* 12 (1874): 3–7. Reprinted in Salway (1976), 479–83. Print.

———. "Margaret Gatty." *Parables from Nature. With a Memoir by Her Daughter, Juliana Horatia Ewing*. Vol. 1. By Margaret Gatty. London: Bell, 1885. ix-xxi. Print.

———. *Melchior's Dream, and Other Tales*. 1862. London: Society for Promoting Christian Knowledge, 1895. Print.

———. *Six to Sixteen. A Story for Girls*. London: Society for Promoting Christian Knowledge, 1875. Print.

Foster, Shirley, Judy Simons. *What Katy Read: Feminist Re-Readings of "Classic" Stories for Girls*. Basingstoke: Macmillan, 1995. Print.

Gatty, Margaret. Dedication. *The Fairy Godmothers and Other Tales*. By Gatty. London: Bell, 1851. Print.

———. "The Fairy Godmothers." In *The Fairy Godmothers and Other Tales*. London: George Bell, 1851. Print.

———. *Parables from Nature. With a Memoir by Her Daughter, Juliana Horatia Ewing*. Vol. 1. London: Bell, 1885. ix-xxi. Print.

Gubar, Marah. *Artful Dodgers: Reconceiving the Golden Age of Children's Literature*. Oxford: Oxford UP, 2009. Print.

Horne, J. C. "Empire, Hysteria, and the Healthy Girl: The Deployment of the Body in Juliana Horatia Ewing's *Six to Sixteen*." *Women's Studies* 33.3: 249–77. Print.

Knoepflmacher, U. C. *Ventures into Childlands: Victorians, Fairy Tales and Femininity*. Chicago: U of Chicago P, 1998. Print.

Maxwell, Christabel. *Mrs. Gatty and Mrs. Ewing*. London: Constable, 1949. Print.

Poovey, Mary. *Uneven Developments*. Chicago: U of Chicago P, 1988. Print.

Rowbotham, Judith. *Good Girls Make Good Wives: Guidance for Girls in Victorian Fiction*. Oxford: Blackwell, 1989. Print.

Salway, Lance, ed. *A Peculiar Gift: Nineteenth-Century Writings on Books for Children*. Harmondsworth, UK: Kestrel, 1976. Print.

Thwaite, M. F. *From Primer to Pleasure: An Introduction to the History of Children's Books in England, from the Invention of Printing to 1914*. Rev. ed. Boston: The Horn Book, 1972. Print.

Wall, Barbara. *The Narrator's Voice: The Dilemma of Children's Fiction*. Macmillan: London, 1991. Print.

Chapter 3

The Romance of Othermothering in Nineteenth-Century *Backfisch* Books

Julie Pfeiffer

As Patrice DiQuinzio writes in *The Impossibility of Motherhood*, feminist discussions of mothering are caught between ideologies of essential motherhood and those of individualism. In order to acknowledge that mothering is different for different women and varies over the course of a mother's life, DiQuinzio suggests that we not look to a single overarching theory of motherhood (the project of individualism) but begin with "specific instances of mothering in specific contexts" as a way of illustrating the complexity of mothering relationships (244). This chapter examines mothering in four best-selling nineteenth-century novels for girls in order to argue that mothering as a communal enterprise can provide an alternative to essentialist motherhood. In so doing, it demonstrates how the embodied intimacy of shared mothering challenges the assumption that heterosexual or spiritual romance will be the primary form of romance in a girl's life.

This chapter examines four novels: the American *The Flower of the Family* (1853; translated *Die Perle der Familie*, 1875) and *Faith Gartney's Girlhood* (1863; translated *Faith Gartney's Mädchenjahre*, 1878), and the German *Backfischens Leiden und Freuden* (1863; translated as *Gretchen's Joys and Sorrows*, 1877) and *Der Trotzkopf* (1885; translated as both *An Obstinate Maid* and *Taming a Tomboy*, 1898). All four of these novels (and many of the other novels written by these authors) share a set of qualities that identify them as belonging to a genre the Germans call *Backfischliteratur*. While the mid-nineteenth century saw the publication of dozens of these novels, the four chosen here were particularly popular and demonstrate how nineteenth-century images of mothering are more diverse than we might assume. The term *Backfisch* is slang for a girl between the ages of fourteen and seventeen; too old for school and too young for marriage, these girls are in an awkward place both physically and socially. While German *Backfischliteratur* has been studied extensively in German-language criticism, very little has been said about the *Backfisch* novel in English-language criticism, and the link between German and American *Backfisch* novels has yet to be made.

Directed at adolescent girls, the *Backfisch* novel focuses on an individual protagonist rather than on her family more generally and describes the heroine's transformation through education, which takes places when she goes to live for a time with another woman, usually a single aunt or teacher. Also called *Wandlungsgeschichte* (transformation stories), these novels describe girls in a liminal space that simultaneously enables change and produces anxiety. Unlike the *Bildungsroman*, with its epic descriptions of a life, the *Backfisch* novel focuses on a year or two in the life of an adolescent girl and highlights the importance of the choices she makes in this crucial, transformative time of life. *Backfisch* books follow a standard plot: the girl is identified as in need of an education, she leaves home to be transformed, and her successful transformation is marked and rewarded when she becomes engaged or married. No longer an awkward adolescent, she is now fully mature, and her success is given the stamp of approval by the men in her life, particularly her new husband.

Within the framework of the girl's pursuit of a husband (and the children who will almost certainly follow), mothering could be assumed to be simply a consequence of marriage, and mothers could be seen as reinforcing patriarchal systems as they raise their daughters to replicate their own life journeys. Yet despite the conservative plot and its reliance on heterosexual marriage as the marker of a girl's successful maturation, the story of the *Backfisch* pushes us to rethink essentialist notions of mothering and the options available to women in two ways. First, the focus of these stories is not the courtship that leads to marriage, but a world of women supervised by single, adult women who are financially, socially, and intellectually independent. Though the heroine's explicit goal may be a husband, she spends most of the novel with adult women who have happy lives without a husband or children. Second, the heroine's journey away from home and her mother's care allows her and the reader to see that mothering, a form of physical and emotional care linked to preparation for the future, can be provided by women who are not biological mothers. The concept of othermothering, the need to share the nurturing and mentoring of children, extends biologically rooted notions of motherhood and decenters heterosexual models of power in favor of community mothering and mentoring.

As Evelyn Nakano Glenn observes in her essay, "Social Constructions of Mothering," "mothering—more than any other aspect of gender—has been subject to essentialist interpretation: seen as natural, universal, and unchanging" (3). Further, mothering is often seen as synonymous with motherhood, and the relationship of a biological mother with her child, taken from the experiences of twentieth-century white women, has been used as a standard (3–4). Glenn asks that we move alternate perspectives of mothering from the margins to the center and suggests that looking at the mothering practices of women of color is one way to do this (5). Patricia Hill Collins develops one such alternate model, the practice of "othermothering," which describes the experience of many black communities in which children are mothered by a number of community members, only some of whom are biologically related.[1] I argue that the nineteenth-century authors whose work I examine here—Elizabeth Prentiss, A. D. T. Whitney, Clementine Helm, and Emmy von Rhoden—are other sources of alternate models. These authors describe the lives of white, middle-class girls and women but do not center their stories on biological motherhood. Instead, the fictional worlds they create, like the communities of color Glenn and Collins describe, rely on communities of girls and women to mother children and each other.

Othermothering functions in three ways in the *Backfisch* novel, all of which suggest the relational and communal nature of identity: at a meta-level, as the authors take on a mentoring role with their readers; at a formal level, when the protagonist is sent away to another woman who takes on the responsibility of mothering her; and at an informal level, as girls learn to nurture and care for one another through physical care and storytelling. At all three levels, the implicit assumption is that girls need more and different mothering than they receive from their biological mothers and that mothering, the practice of providing physical and emotional care, is available to women who are not themselves biological mothers.

Authors as Othermothers

As Roger Clark, Joel McCoy, and Pamela J. Keller explain, "we can think of adolescent fiction about adolescent girls as a way in which women authors 'othermother' adolescent readers with stories about crises that other adolescents, their central characters, have experienced" (225). Unlike earlier novels, which were certainly read by adolescent girls, the *Backfisch* book is directly addressed, either in the preface or by a first-person narrator, to an audience of girls approaching womanhood. Presuming that the girl reader will benefit from or at least enjoy the mentorship of another woman—in this case the author/narrator—these stories allow the girl to focus on herself and to see herself as worthy of the attention of a novelist. The *Backfisch* period becomes defined as a time of investment when a girl is given the space to see her identity outside of a domestic realm and within a larger community. Simply by picking up a *Backfisch* book, the reader has opened a space for mentoring beyond what her biological mother provides. While the biological or legal mother has an *obligation* to love her daughter, the othermother/author *chooses* to love and pay attention to the protagonist/reader.

Two examples illustrate an explicit acknowledgment of the *Backfisch* novel's potential to serve a mentoring role—and the author's potential to serve as a mentor at a distance. First, from the preface to A. D. T. Whitney's *Faith Gartney's Girlhood*:

> I began this story for young girls. It has grown, as they grow, to womanhood. It makes no artistic pretension. It is a simple record of something of the thought and life that lies between fourteen and twenty.
>
> I dedicate it, as it is, to these young girls, who dream, and wish, and strive, and err; and find, perhaps, little help to interpret their own spirits to themselves.
>
> I believe and hope that there is nothing in it which shall hinder them in what is noblest and truest.
>
> May there be something that shall lift them—though by ever so little—up!

Similarly, in Clementine Helm's *Gretchen's Joys and Sorrows*, the first-person narrator writes:

> What I still remember of my experiences in Berlin I will now relate to you, my dear friends. They are, indeed, very pleasant remembrances for me; and as the race of backfischchen still thrives and blossoms, there is, no doubt, one or another among them who sometimes feels quite as unhappy as I did, and may these lines serve to comfort and entertain her. (4)

We have two similar addresses here, written fourteen years apart, one American, one German. In both cases, the address to the reader points toward a shared female experience. The othermother author also takes on one of the two roles that are further developed in each novel through characters: the wise, single adult woman or the intimate friend. Both function as othermothers. Whitney speaks to the reader directly as the author of the novel and as a mentor. She makes it clear that her audience is young girls in need of some sort of help. They are also vulnerable, and part of her task (and the task of the girls' book) is to leave out those scenes that might "hinder" the girls' growth. Whitney's mothering role is protective as well as encouraging. She defines girlhood as a time of looking forward to the future—to "dream, and wish, and strive, and err . . ."—and of looking inward "to interpret their own spirits to themselves." This is a preface addressed to readers who are in a state of being made and making themselves. The expectations are high; they are to develop what is noblest and truest in themselves. And the novel offers the potential to help in this process.

In *Gretchen's Joys and Sorrows*, the address to the reader comes directly from Gretchen, the narrator and protagonist of this first-person narration, who is representative of the peer othermother. It comes at the end of the first chapter, rather than as a preface, so readers have already gotten to know Gretchen as a teen and a character. At this point in the text we are taken out of the narrative to a point in the present, in which Gretchen is now an adult, able to look back and advise others. The affection of the address, "dear friends," implies that the reader and narrator understand each other, that they have an intimate relationship that allows Gretchen the narrator to influence and reassure the reader. As Gretchen looks back on her past, she and the reader enter an intimate world of shared unhappiness and growth.

Both of these passages serve to encourage the girl reader that things will get better, and in the meantime, here is a book "to comfort and entertain." Significantly, the American book has more of a focus on its ability to support moral growth, while the German book suggests that the reader just needs a source of pleasure. In both cases, there is something about this period from "fourteen to twenty" in which a girl needs mothering other than that which her biological mother can provide. These authors both attempt to provide some of that mothering themselves through their novels and suggest other models of mothering that the girl reader can then reach for in her own life.

Mentors as Othermothers

Most explicitly, these novels provide examples of single, adult women, either relatives or teachers, who serve as othermothers. Each of the four novels I discuss includes a plot centered on the protagonist's departure from home to live with a woman who is not her biological mother. In this, as Carroll Smith-Rosenberg describes, they mirror the situation of many mid-nineteenth-century American girls: "In the process of leaving one home and adjusting to another, the mother's friends and relatives played a key transitional role. Such older women routinely accepted the role of foster mother; they supervised the young girl's deportment, monitored her health and introduced her to their own network of female friends and kin" (18). Like the twentieth-century communities of women of color Patricia Hill Collins describes in *Black Feminist Thought*, mid-nineteenth-century German and American women relied on the support of other adult women to help raise their daughters, and this social reality is mirrored in novels of the period. What is surprising about these novels is that they focus not on the story of the girl's developing relationship with her future husband, but on the intimate relationships she develops with an older, single woman and with peers. Rather than moving directly from her father's home to that of her husband, the heroine of the *Backfisch* novel enters an intermediate space where she is free to develop intimate relationships with other women and girls. While the first of these novels is linked to the sentimental novel with a focus on the girl's relationship with God, even this role is subsumed by a female mentor as the genre develops.

In the earliest of the American *Backfisch* books, Elizabeth Prentiss's *The Flower of the Family*, we are introduced to fifteen-year-old Lucy as "'old things were passing away and all things becoming new'" (24). Lucy's mother is loving but exhausted. She lacks the time and money to nurture Lucy as it seems clear would best benefit her, and it appears that Lucy is headed toward a life of drugery and repression. Instead, Lucy's plot shifts when her mother's brother takes her away to his wife in the city to be cosseted and educated. Travel away from home relieves the heroine of the domestic grind; it also allows her to see how others live and the variety of choices there are to make. In particular, Lucy meets Miss Prigott, a spinster and childhood friend of her mother, who imagines herself as Lucy's mother, saying: "'And have I not tried to be a mother to you, ever since you came?'" (124), and who ultimately offers to adopt her. In later *Backfisch* books, single women like Miss Prigott will be positive sources of both emotional and financial support. In this novel, with its ties to an evangelical literary tradition, Miss Prigott is a trial to Lucy rather than a solace. She is constantly critical of what she sees as Lucy's self-centeredness and "insufferable pride" (123)—to the surprise of both Lucy and her reader, for Lucy seems much more a paragon of female virtue than a child in need of discipline. On Lucy's birthday, Miss Prigott dismays her by giving her several tracts and suggesting that Lucy might want to consider becoming a Christian. Since Lucy already sees herself as Christian, this gift causes a painful identity crisis, as Lucy wonders if she has failed her parents and her God in this new community: "The longer she looked at herself, the more discouraged and wretched she became" (126). In despair, she turns to God: "Amid the multitude of her thoughts within her, the idea of God alone offered repose. To Him then she turned. To Him she confessed her capricious, changeful temper; her doubts, fears, mistakes; and besought Him now and once for all to fasten her to Himself" (135). In this passage, God is given several attributes that will be applied to othermothers in later novels—God offers "repose," a confessional, the solace of forgiveness, and a solid place to stand. This sounds much like the message of the sentimental novel in that real education comes from a relationship with God and that it is better to invest in that relationship than in any human relationship. It also echoes the words Lucy's mother speaks when Lucy fears that she will be homesick away from her biological mother: "But, my dear Lucy, you will find God as truly there as He is here. And He is better than many mothers" (99). This passage suggests that not only is God better than most mothers, but God is better than multiple mothers; it points towards the girl's need for more than one mother and reinforces the sentimental idea that divine love is the only solid thing a girl can rely on. But the presence of Miss Priggott, and the fact that she instigates Lucy's embrace of God as mentor, hints at the way the classic girls' book will develop. In later *Backfisch* books, the idea of God as mentor recedes into the background as a human mentor helps solve what increasingly become social and domestic problems rather than spiritual ones.

Just as Lucy herself first sees Miss Prigott in terms of "her disagreeable qualities," she comes to "see that underneath them she has something good" (148). The girls' book as a genre makes a similar step as it moves from stereotyping spinster women as abrasive and unlovable (Aunt Fortune in *The Wide Wide World* is a prime example of this model) to imagining the spinster as a mentor who is devoted, loving, and able to contribute directly to the education of a young woman. The single woman who wants to be a mentor is only partially successful in *The Flower of the Family*, and that pattern remains one option in the genre (think of Aunt Miranda in *Rebecca of Sunnybrook Farm*), but the novels in the discussion that follows add another pattern, that of the woman whose lack of a male partner and children empowers rather than stigmatizes her.

The benefits to an adolescent girl of being mentored by a woman who is not her mother become clear in later novels for girls; what is articulated in *The Flower of the Family* is that while Miss Prigott explicitly wants to convert Lucy to Christianity, implicitly she wants to convert herself into a mother and Lucy into her daughter. Miss Prigott expresses her desire for affection from Lucy: "'From the very first hour I loved that young girl!' she said within herself; 'and my foolish old heart hoped for love in return. So it is after fifty years' experience of life; I am still childish, still hopeful, yet still disappointed'" (Prentiss 164). Though Miss Prigott never succeeds in nurturing Lucy, she does remind us that othermothering can serve not only the protagonist but also the othermother herself. Like later books such as *Rebecca of Sunnybrook Farm* and *Anne of Green Gables*, *The Flower of the Family* shows how othermothering allows spinsters or widows to express love and nurturance, to guide and educate children, without having biological children of their own. And while these early novels for girls tend to focus on the girl's own transformation, *The Flower of the Family* hints toward a key element in later novels—the protagonist's ability to effect the transformation of adults.

Ten years later, in 1863, the German *Gretchen's Joys and Sorrows* and the American *Faith Gartney's Girlhood* were published. Both continue to explore the complex ways in which adolescent girls are mothered and mother. Like Lucy, Gretchen and Faith need to establish an independent identity, something they cannot do at home. Their mothers are too tired and/or lack the knowledge their daughters need—in short, they aren't perfect. Gretchen's mother is worn down by "many children and much sickness" (Helm 3), and Faith's mother "had not been strong for years. Moreover, she had not a genius for cooking" (Whitney 120). Significantly, it is not that these mothers are absent or morally lacking, it is simply that they don't have the skills and experience that will allow them to help their daughters develop into their full potential. Rather than criticizing mothers for not being able to provide everything their daughters need, these novels suggest that mothering is a shared enterprise. Gretchen's mother is honored as having provided a solid foundation that gives Gretchen a "childish cheerfulness" and "the quiet, domestic virtues upon which the happiness of her home was founded" (Helm 3). Gretchen tells the reader:

> Her teachings formed the foundation of all that I learned in after life, and through them my heart and understanding received their early development. But my mother well knew that I could nowhere better receive the additional

instruction that I so much needed, than at the hands of Aunt Ulrike, for she herself sincerely honored her excellent, highly educated sister-in-law. (3)

Gretchen's and Faith's mothers recognize their inability to teach their daughters all they ought to know and encourage them to be mothered by another woman; they are not abandoned by their mothers through death or moral weakness. As we read in *The Flower of the Family*, "All the mother's wisdom fails to supply to her child the place of that each must acquire for herself" (Prentiss 118). As these girls move into the transformative space of adolescence, they need to be in a physical space that balances the education they have received from their biological mothers with other perspectives and skills. While Gretchen goes to the city for her education and Faith moves to the country with her family, both are taken in hand by aunts who are themselves single, independent, successful women and who are able to othermother through love and mentoring.

As *Gretchen's Joys and Sorrows* opens, Aunt Ulrike is described as "motherly" and "a motherly friend" (Helm 1, 3). We learn later that she is a widow (39) and that she still misses her husband—she is clearly a mentor who will advocate for marital bliss, though she herself seems to be quite content with her independent life, full of friends and with financial independence. The dramatic shift from Miss Prigott, whose desperate neediness sends Lucy closer to God, to Aunt Ulrike, whose calm confidence leads her to take on a godlike role in Gretchen's life, reveals the power of the single woman as mentor. Aunt Ulrike is both mentor and othermother; she combines training for life as a woman in society with emotional and physical support. Even the language Gretchen uses to describe Aunt Ulrike mirrors that which Lucy uses as she finds comfort in God. When Aunt Ulrike tells Gretchen her cousin Eugenie will be joining their household, Gretchen worries that she will be neglected in the shadow of this new member of the family. Aunt Ulrike reassures her: "'Have no fear my child,' said she softly; 'you shall suffer no loss through our new comer. I shall stand by your side to help and protect you, and my love will support you when it is necessary. Only trust to me, and be of good cheer'" (41). Gretchen's response could as easily be addressed to God and echoes key phrases from Lucy's prayers: God's ability to know her thoughts, God's role as a confessor, God as comfort and refuge from fear and embarrassment: "It was as if she had read all the fears of my poor heart; for without my speaking a word she seemed to know how weak and fearful I had been. Blushing deeply I now confessed my egotistical thoughts to her, and took good heart for all that might come, trusting full in her who had so often been my comfort and refuge" (41). Aunt Ulrike also takes a godlike role in establishing guidelines for Gretchen's behavior; she "begin[s] at once to call attention to these things which she wished me to change" (8), and Gretchen seeks to improve herself to please Aunt Ulrike rather than God.

The first thing Gretchen must learn is that her change in place also marks a change in status. Aunt Ulrike makes a clear distinction between the freedom allowed a child and the responsibilities that come with womanhood: "Children are allowed to do many things; but you are here to learn what is proper for grown persons, and to lay aside children's shoes" (8).

Writing from the perspective of many years of experience later, Gretchen tells us that Aunt Ulrike "instructed me with care and faithfulness in the quiet, domestic virtues upon which the happiness of her home was founded, and never in my life can I sufficiently thank her for it" (3). While Gretchen's education includes proper comportment for social calls and balls, the focus of the novel is on creating a system that keeps one's fingernails clean and one's guests comfortable; it is the rituals of daily life that lead to happiness and successful participation in community.

Faith Gartney's Girlhood is also the story of finding a community; it is complicated by the fact that it has not one but two protagonists. The *Backfisch* of the novel is Faith Gartney, the well-loved, white, middle-class girl whose story the novel appears to tell. But the novel also tells the story of Glory, an orphaned Irish girl whom readers discover working for her keep in a home where she is not appreciated and is certainly not mothered. Both girls end up being mothered and mentored by Aunt Faith, who is able to meet their very different needs successfully. While Glory yearns to be part of a family and to love and be loved, Faith longs for productive work and purpose. Yet both despair that there are, in Glory's words, "such lots of good times in the world, and she not in 'em!" (Whitney 139), and ultimately this novel provides multiple avenues toward being in the "good times." It is through interactions with a single woman, one who models independence, that these girls and the reader see the multitude of options laid out before them. While Faith's story becomes a fairly typical romantic story, Glory's is not (she never marries, yet othermothers four orphaned children); both end up with the feeling of being "in the good times" (139). Significantly, Aunt Faith adds a third element to the mentoring and mothering role of othermother; in her will she leaves both young women the financial means to do the work each has chosen.

The Adolescent Girl as Othermother

What quickly becomes clear in the *Backfisch* novel is that the mothering behavior these protagonists learn from their aunts and teachers is translated into their relationships with their peers as well. While the final plot resolution comes with an engagement or marriage, the emotional closure comes when readers see that the heroine has learned to mother others, that she is herself a successful othermother. That this behavior is possible before she is a biological mother further separates mothering behavior from motherhood. As Smith-Rosenberg reports of nineteenth-century American girls:

> Even more important to this process of maturation than their mother's friends were the female friends young women made at school. . . . [O]ne woman might routinely assume the nurturing role of pseudomother, the other the dependency role of daughter. The pseudomother performed for the other woman all the services which we normally associate with mothers; she went to absurd lengths to purchase items her "daughter" could have obtained from other sources, gave advice and functioned as an idealized figure in her "daughter's" imagination. (19)

All four novels provide examples of what Smith-Rosenberg calls "pseudomothering." It is through the psychological and domestic labor that allows them to care for others that these protagonists are transformed into happy, satisfied women, with or without husbands. By the end of *The Flower of the Family*, Lucy will be glorified with the title "sister-mother" (348), and we see her earning that title from the first pages of the novel: when the baby is hurt, only Lucy can comfort him; when her older sister is home late from school, Lucy takes on her domestic tasks; and when one of her brothers brings home strawberries, he splits them between his mother and Lucy with a smile. Gretchen othermothers her cousin Eugenie (helping her dress, modeling loving interactions) and is herself othermothered by her friend Marie (who eases her through the etiquette of her first ball and proper sidewalk manners). Faith's desire to do meaningful work is first recognized in her care for her brother when she takes over the work of the unsatisfactory nursery maid: "Kind, sisterly fingers helped Hendie now, in his morning robings; and sweet words and pretty stories replaced the old, taunting rhyme" (Whitney 184–85). In *An Obstinate Maid* Ilse learns to othermother first by being othermothered by schoolmates. Her roommate, Nellie, helps her put away her clothes, teaches her to wash herself properly, and loves her unconditionally. Later, Ilse's love for a younger student, Lilli, leads her to finally learn to sew so she can make clothes for Lilli's doll. What is more, she nurtures Lilli and calms her on her deathbed. When Ilse returns home, the skills she demonstrated in that relationship are replicated in her care of her newborn brother. In all of these instances, mothering is shown to be a diverse, communal project that extends beyond biological connection, and the ability to mother, rather than marriage, serves as the real marker of the adolescent girl's shift to womanhood.

The Story as Othermother

By the 1880s, the genre of the *Backfisch* novel was firmly established, and Emmy von Rhoden's *Der Trotzkopf* (1885) [*An Obstinate Maid*] elucidates the ways themes of othermothering persist. While the protagonist Ilse's birth mother is dead, and it is her stepmother who fills the role of legal mother, Ilse calls her stepmother, Frau Anne, "Mama," and nowhere does the novel suggest that her difficulties with Ilse result from a lack of biological connection. Rather, this novel helps us see the ways that legal obligation—the formal role of mother, whether biological or not—interferes with the education of a daughter. Othermothers are effective largely because they mother without obligation; they choose willingly to love, educate, and nurture their otherdaughters.

Ilse leaves home because her parents confess themselves completely unable to educate her. Something must be done with this wild tomboy, or she may some day be called "unweiblich" (unwomanly), a "furchtbar" (dreadful) thought (9). What is at stake here is not just Ilse's happiness and well-being but also her parents' pride and the integrity of the community. Ilse's parents have a responsibility to send out a well-behaved young woman into the world. If they can't do it themselves, they must find someone else who can. In this case, the chosen method is a boarding school. There Ilse finds two potential mentors: Fräulein Raimar, the director, who tries, unsuccessfully, to impose her will on Ilse; and Fräulein Güssow, a young teacher, who succeeds in mentoring Ilse through a combination of love and storytelling.

This novel and its translation also highlight ways that the German and American *Backfisch* novels diverge.[2] On several occasions, the American translator of *An Obstinate Maid* adds Christian language to the text that is not present in the original and shifts some of the power of othermothering to God and away from the girl and her mentor. Translator Mary Ireland adds this sentence to the scene in which Ilse's father is being convinced to send her to boarding school: "Fräulein Raimar, the principal, is a noble Christian woman, Ilse will be under the best of influence, and I tell you truly that nothing but the grace of God in the heart of your child will enable her to overcome the stubborn, disobedient disposition and refine her reckless manner" (16–17). In the German original, the line praises Fräulein Raimar and then moves to describing the beautiful setting of the school—the mountains and clean air—without any Christian reference (9).

Similarly, when Ilse is told that she must go to school, she storms to her bedroom to weep. Her stepmother longs for the day when Ilse will recognize her love. The Ireland translation reads, "She could only lift up a prayer to God that her step-daughter might in time learn to love her who was trying to be a true and faithful friend to her husband's only child" (22). In contrast, the original German version states that Frau Anne "stayed behind and longed for the time when Ilse's good heart would help her find the way to her motherly love" (13). The original is more typical of the *Backfisch* book, in which it is the girl's own "good heart" that is key, not God's grace. In a third example, describing Lucie's transformation, the Ireland translation reads, "She learned to cast all her care upon her Saviour, and He gave peace to her soul" (108), while the original German simply states, "She went forward quietly and earnestly and her exuberant laughter disappeared" (80). This American translation shifts the responsibility onto God and away from the girl and her othermothers.

In contrast, the original German embraces the notion of the *Backfisch* as othermother. Ilse is most successfully mothered by young women—the young teacher, Fräulein Güssow; her friend Nellie—and even by the ridicule of other less friendly schoolmates. After being corrected for improper table manners by the principal, Ilse storms to her room and insists that she will leave the school. Her roommate, Nellie, calms her down: "Fräulein Raimar is right, she means well and isn't trying to criticize you. It's the same with all of us. We are young and dumb and need to learn" (43). While Nellie's perspective does not change Ilse's view of Fräulein Raimar, it does convince her to stay at the school, where her behavior is modified by a double program of the ridicule of her peers (especially around her table manners) and the loving compassion of Fräulein Güssow. Ilse may not recognize her need for change, but the reader can see clearly that Ilse's current path will not be a pleasant one. Her "good heart" and lively ways seem likely to lead only to more tears unless she can somehow change her fundamental attitude. Ilse writes to her father, "I would so much rather have stayed at home; then I wouldn't know how stupid I am . . . I have learned only that I am very, very dumb" (58). This is perhaps significant progress and opens up the possibility that Ilse will be able to learn something of use to herself.

The opportunity to learn comes with yet another battle with the principal, this one over the quality of Ilse's sewing. On the verge of being expelled for her bad temper, Ilse is warned by the young teacher, Fräulein Güssow:

> "A child must be able to ask forgiveness! And a girl particularly. O Ilse! You must also learn this; it is not yet too late!" said Fräulein Güssow with excitement. "O Ilse, if only my words are able to arouse you from your blindness! Learn to give in, my child, learn above all else to restrain yourself! If you don't, life will take you to a hard school and prepare for you heartbreak and suffering. Believe me, defiance and obstinancy are evil weeds in a girl's heart and often obscure the best, most sacred feelings! Go downstairs, child, ask Fräulein Raimar's forgiveness. Overcome your temper today and you will have triumphed forever!" (69–70)

When Ilse still resists, Fräulein Güssow tells a story-within-the-story that lies at the center of this novel and marks a transformation point for Ilse: if she can't master her own temper, she will be expelled from any loving community.

By hearing the story of Lucie, the girl whose obstinancy costs her her fiancé and her happiness, Ilse is able to take the first steps to humbling herself, a step that leads her toward happiness and away from obstinancy. Ilse's successful transition to womanhood is marked by a maturity that is enabled by othermothering: "The early rising, the order and punctuality had been difficult, but Nellie had stood by her, and had helped her over many a hard place, often by a word or look quelling the spirit of obstinancy that was about to rise. But more than all, the story of Lucie had fallen upon good soil, and had brought forth fruit" (Ireland 111). Here the story-within-the-story provides not just a moral lesson but also a model of reading behavior. As Ilse responds to Lucie's story, so should the girl reader of *Der Trotzkopf* respond to Ilse's story. In the telling of stories, a community of othermothering is formed, and the trials of adolescent girlhood are shown to be shared.

Just as the authors of the *Backfisch* book directly address readers not as experts or authority figures, but as friends and peers, these characters help one another through stories that emphasize shared experiences and challenges. Ilse's transformation comes not from reading the Bible and deferring to God, but from the physical care of peers, the story of another girl's life, and her own opportunities to othermother. Though protective of biological mothers (they are generally good women who are loved by their daughters), these novels avoid essentialism and celebrate the individual's ability to function in a variety of roles as a loving and loved member of her community. While one plot arc for the *Backfisch* suggests that the awkward young girl must be polished so that she is a suitable wife and ready to mother her own children, these stories focus instead on mothering within a world of women, where men are largely invisible and nonessential. The world is full of children and friends who need mothering; with or without biological children, the work of womanhood is to mother and be mothered. Ultimately, the "romance" that illuminates these texts is not a heterosexual romance or a Christian romance, but a romance of othermothering, as girls learn to mother one another without the distractions of husbands or children.

Notes

I am grateful to LeeRay Costa, Lee Talley, and Lisa Radcliff for their encouragement and thoughtful readings of this essay.

1. Patricia Hill Collins takes the word "othermother" from the work of Rosalie Riegle Troester.
2. *Der Trotzkopf* was translated twice in 1898; I use the more skillful of the two translations, Mary Ireland's *An Obstinate Maid*, as well as my own translation of the German.

Works Cited

Clark, Roger, Joel McCoy, and Pamela J. Keller. "Teach Your Children Well: Reading Lessons to and about Black and White Adolescent Girls from Black and White Women Authors." *International Review of Modern Sociology* 34.2 (Autumn 2008): 211–28. Print.

Collins, Patricia Hill. *Black Feminist Thought: Knowledge, Consciousness, and the Politics of Empowerment*. New York: Routledge, 1991. Print.

———. "Shifting the Center: Race, Class, and Feminist Theorizing About Motherhood." *Mothering: Ideology, Experience, and Agency*. Ed. Evelyn Nakano Glenn, Grace Chang, and Linda Rennie Forcey. New York: Routledge, 1994. Print.

DiQuinzio, Patrice. *The Impossibility of Motherhood: Feminism, Individualism, and the Problem of Mothering*. New York: Routledge, 1999. Print.

Glenn, Evelyn Nakano. "Social Constructions of Mothering: A Thematic Overview." *Mothering: Ideology, Experience, and Agency*. Ed. Evelyn Nakano Glenn, Grace Chang, and Linda Rennie Forcey. New York: Routledge, 1994. Print.

Helm, Clementine. *Backfischens Leiden und Freuden*. Leipzig: Georg Wigand's Verlag, 1880. Print.

———. *Gretchen's Joys and Sorrows*. Trans. Helen Dunbar Slack. Boston: Williams, 1877. Print.

Prentiss, Elizabeth. *The Flower of the Family: A Book for Girls*. New York: Randolph, 1883. Print.

Rhoden, Emily. *Taming a Tomboy*. Translated from the 25th edition by Felix Oswald. New York: Allison, 1898. Print.

Smith-Rosenberg, Carroll. "The Female World of Love and Ritual: Relations between Women in Nineteenth-Century America." *Signs* 1.1 (Autumn 1975): 1–29. Print.

Troester, Rosalie Riegle. "Turbulence and Tenderness: Mothers, Daughters, and Othermothers in Paule Marshall's *Brown Girl, Brownstones*." *SAGE: A Scholarly Journal on Black Women* 1 (1984): 13–16. Print.

Von Rhoden, Emmy. *Der Trotzkopf. Eine Pensionsgeschichte für junge Mädchen*, 1885.

———. *An Obstinate Maid*. Translated by Mary E. Ireland, 1898. Print.

Whitney, Mrs. A. D. T. *Faith Gartney's Girlhood*. Boston: Houghton, Mifflin, 1892. Print.

Wiggin, Kate Douglas. *Rebecca of Sunnybrook Farm*. New York: Grosset and Dunlap, 1903. Print.

PART II

Mothering in Modernity:
Shifting Cultures and Subjectivities

Chapter 4

The Women Who Sent Their Children Away: Mothers in Kindertransport Fiction

Adrienne Kertzer

One of approximately ten thousand children and adolescents who left Germany and German-annexed territories (Austria and Czechoslovakia) on a Kindertransport (children's transport) between 1 December 1938 and 1 September 1939, Lore Groszmann arrived in England in December 1938 as a precocious ten-year-old determined to write letters and passionate "Hitler stories" (Segal, "Preface" x) in order to obtain work permits for her parents.[1] One of the Kinder,[2] Groszmann would later discover that a "tear-jerking letter full of sunsets" (Segal, "The Bough" 241) was surprisingly successful; her parents were granted a married-couple visa that permitted them to enter England in March 1939 and work as domestic servants. Although the incident confirmed her sense that she was a writer, by the time she emigrated to New York in 1951, she was less confident that she had a subject worth writing about. She changed her mind when someone at a party asked her about her childhood, and she experienced "the peculiar silence of a roomful of people listening" (245). She had discovered that she "had a story to tell" (245).

Other People's Houses, the autobiographical novel Groszmann published under her married name, Segal, is unusual in two ways: in its nuanced portrait of Segal's mother, Franzi Groszmann, and in its publication in 1964, long before many others wrote about their Kindertransport experiences. While Segal's ability to create this detailed portrait was undoubtedly enabled by her parents' arrival in England, that alone does not account for the difference between *Other People's Houses* and the patterns of maternal representation in recent Kindertransport fiction. The passage of time also plays a role in that contemporary authors and the focalizers they invent rarely share Segal's close relationship to the woman who sent her daughter away. But equally important to how mothers are represented in recent fiction is our current understanding that nearly all of these refugee children were orphaned by the Holocaust.

Phyllis Lassner has cautioned that the commonalities associated with the Kindertransport can produce a "problematically homogenized understanding" of the children's more varied experiences (20). Frances Williams agrees that "there was no typical experience for the Kindertransportees in Britain" (xxxii) and for that reason prefers the term "Kindertransportee" to the more widely known "Kinder," which she claims has "become entrenched in the popular imagination of the group identity of those who used the Kindertransport" (xxv). In juxtaposing *Other People's Houses* with recent fiction such as Mona Golabek and Lee Cohen's *The Children of Willesden Lane: Beyond the Kindertransport: A Memoir of Music, Love, and Survival* (2002), Linda Newbery's *Sisterland* (2003), and Alison Pick's *Far to Go* (2010), I support Lassner and Williams's critique and propose that the contemporary narrative, in which nearly all the mothers who sent their children away were murdered by the Nazis, results in mothers being mythologized, misrecognized, and misunderstood. In her memoir, *The Tiger in the Attic: Memories of the Kindertransport and Growing Up English*, Edith Milton admits that it took her "twenty years to recover from the disappointment" (68) of her reunion with her mother after the war. Here too, the passing of time makes a difference in that the maternal memories of orphaned children do not evolve. All of the Kindertransportees in the recent work I examine have memories that are frozen by the trauma of separation.

Publishing individual chapters initially as stories in *Commentary* in 1958 and in *The New Yorker* between 1961 and 1964, Segal was unusual in writing about her experiences in the 1960s. When Karen Gershon (another Kindertransportee) began the project that culminated in her edited collection *We Came as Children: A Collective Autobiography* (1966), she was driven by her realization that there was so little documentation by and about the Kindertransportees (Baumel-Schwartz 225). In contrast, since the first international reunion held in 1989 (the fiftieth anniversary of the rescue mission), there has been a proliferation of writing; one Kindertransportee, Olga Levy Drucker, directly attributes her decision "to write a book about [her] childhood, *for children*" to the reunion (144). As a result, historian Tony Kushner has described this group of refugee children as "the most famous and commemorated group of refugees coming to Britain, increasingly memorialized nationally and internationally" (10).

Scholars frequently note how "For a long time, the story of the Kindertransports . . . lay in the shadow of historical research on the Holocaust" (Benz, Curio, and Hammel 1). According to Rebekka Göpfert, the first Kindertransport reunions could not take place until the majority of survivors of the death camps were already dead (25) as though the refugee children were aware that their experiences were so different from those of the death camp survivors that they were not worth paying attention to. Initially regarded as transmigrants who were issued temporary travel visas because it was assumed that they would return to their home countries once "the crisis was over" ("Kindertransport, 1938–1940"), the Kindertransportees are today regarded as Holocaust survivors, a perspective reinforced by widespread reference to how 90 percent never saw their parents again (Lassner 24; Drucker 141; Travis 178n15; Segal, "Baby Terrors" 96). This dreadful percentage resembles the statistics for how many Polish Jews were murdered by the Nazis and is significantly higher than figures for many other countries, including those from which the majority of Kindertransportees departed ("36 questions"). Heading the FAQ section of the American Kindertransport Association website is the question "What is a Holocaust survivor?" When the answer defines "the Kindertransport children [. . . as] child Holocaust survivors," the figure of 90 percent makes psychological sense. They may not share "the horrific experiences of those who had survived camps and ghettos" (Baumel-Schwartz 228), but they share with other child Holocaust survivors the traumatic loss of nearly all family members. However, the results of a 2007 survey sent to 1500 former Kindertransportees indicates that "54% of *Kinder* parents were believed to have been killed," and about 60 percent of the Kindertransportees "never saw one of their parents again" (Hirschberger 250). These revised percentages are still distressing, but they are far from the picture in recent fiction, where we might well conclude that hardly any parents survived.[3]

Juxtaposing *Other People's Houses* with more recent work thus highlights four major differences. First, because the mothers do not survive, maternal representation is viewed through a traumatic childhood memory of rupture and loss. Second, romanticizing maternal representation through the lens of postmemory, second-generation authors (that is, the children of Kindertransportees) are really primarily concerned with the children who were sent away. Third, because of the temporal delay in depicting the Kindertransport, in young adult fiction granddaughters, rather than daughters, are the primary writers and focalizers. Finally, as a result of the delay, traumatized childhood memories prove harder to access, and this has major implications for the representation of the women who sent their children away, a pattern evident not only in young adult fiction but in adult fiction as well.

We learn very little about the mothers who sent their children away in *The Children of Willesden Lane* and *Sisterland*; we know even less in Alison Pick's adult novel *Far to Go*. In a novel that concludes "Soon there'll be nobody left to remember" (308), Pick stresses that the time for remembering is rapidly coming to an end. The novel gives plentiful evidence that it may be already too late, given the narrator's admission that, unable to learn much about her mother, she has invented a story about her. That she tells her story to console a dying man who has spent his adult life misrecognizing his own mother in a photograph that accompanied him on the Kindertransport is also characteristic. Postwar, photographs served as evidence of Nazi atrocities, but in recent Kindertransport fiction, photographs prove harder to decipher.

Maternal Storytelling in Lore Segal's *Other People's Houses*

Adding the subtitle *A Novel* to *Other People's Houses* in 2004, Segal had already explained in her 1994 preface that she chose to write about herself "in the manner of the novelist" (Segal, "Preface" xi) because fiction was the only way she could write about her past. The adult author admits that the cost of such role-playing was high: "Cut yourself off, at ten years old, from feelings that can't be mastered and it takes decades to become reattached" (Segal, "The Bough" 246). Nevertheless, she attributes to her protagonist, Lore, similar survival strategies. Boarding the train, Lore controls her feelings by thinking of herself as performing a role: "This is me going to England" (*Other* 29). Ten years later on a ship that would take her to the Dominican Republic, she masks her disappointment about leaving England by seeing herself as a glamorous traveler: "this is me, lying in a deck chair listening to the midnight guitar" (*Other* 186).

Just as critics have disagreed on whether *Other People's Houses* is a children's novel (Baker),[4] a memoir for young adults (Travis 73), or an adult novel ("Lore Segal"), readers may well wonder where "autobiography stopped and fiction began" ("Preface" xii), especially since Segal often treats *Other People's Houses* as autobiography. When she talks about how Mr. Cohen, the old man in her first foster home, offered her a sixpence and "winked at [her] to signify secrecy" (Harris and Oppenheimer 145), the only difference between this interview and the description in *Other People's Houses* is that in the interview, she uses his real name and not the pseudonym, Mr. Levine, that she gives him in the novel. The majority of the other details, such as how Segal ended up in an Orthodox foster home even though she had no idea what Orthodox meant, and her feeling of relief when she learned of her parents' arrival, are identical. In contrast, in the interview, Segal's mother is more open about her agony upon her daughter's departure from Vienna. As is evident in the novel, both daughter and mother do not always tell each other the truth, at least initially: Lore lies to her mother about her difficulties at the County School (Segal, *Other* 108); Franzi does not tell her daughter for years about her struggles the first few weeks of widowhood (146). The mother and daughter relationship is revealed not only in how Segal draws on her mother's memories, but also in what they do not tell each other.

That Segal dedicates *Other People's Houses* to her mother does not on its own signal the major role Franzi plays in the creation of the text, for Franzi is not only a character, but also a contributor to the story. Serving as a witness to events that Lore could not observe, she tells Lore about her husband's bout of illness so that Lore can imagine the attack "as if it were a memory out of my own life" (*Other* 135). Segal acknowledges that she could not have witnessed such details of her father's chronic illness and thereby draws attention to the complicated way our memories are formed: "He told my mother, and my mother must have told me" (135). She has so internalized her mother's voice that even though she has no memory of her mother telling her this, she is convinced that Franzi must have told her. How else could she remember what she did not witness?

Segal not only incorporates mother-daughter conversations that took place both before the Kindertransport and years after, but she also relies heavily on letters her mother wrote, such as those outlining her parents' first day as domestic servants to the Willoughby family (79). Versions of the phrase "My mother tells me" appear throughout *Other People's Houses* but are especially significant in chapter 4, "'Illford': The Married Couple." Since Kindertransportees could not live with their parents if they were working as servants, the chapters about the parents' domestic service are highly dependent on Franzi's written correspondence and later conversations.

In addition to contributing to the narrative, Franzi plays an important role in Segal's analysis of the class implications of refugee status. Torn between her sympathy for servants and her attraction to the world of "the drawing room" (*Other* 153), the child who once took "cues from [her] mother . . . in matters of taste" (148) is like a chameleon who determines as an adolescent that she wants to become English and criticizes her mother's clothing for its difference from English style (162). In contrast, Franzi never aspires to become English, and in her letters to Lore, she is highly self-conscious about her sudden demotion from being an affluent Viennese housewife who owned a Blüthner piano to a domestic who is told she can play her sponsor's piano only when everyone is out (78). Dealing with her lower status by regarding the English inability to appreciate her *apfelstrudel* as proof that they are incapable of recognizing superior baking (85), she finds subtle ways of resisting her employers' view of her as an inferior. But as Segal demonstrates through Franzi's account of how her employers took for granted that her falling down the stairs from exhaustion was really caused by her husband knocking her down, a refugee can have little impact on entrenched class attitudes.

As Lore grows increasingly delighted with the genteel English lives of her fifth foster family, Franzi challenges the memory her daughter constructs: "My mother tells me a story that I seem to have chosen to forget, for I want nothing to spoil my infatuation with that formal, gentle town" (*Other* 120). Franzi's memory of how the English humiliated her husband by treating him as no more than a two-legged animal when he worked as an assistant gardener for the Lambston family not only undercuts her daughter's memory of life in an idyllic "gentle town," but also provides insight into her father's physical collapse: "My mother says that one day Mrs. Lambston thought the donkey was looking tired and told my father to unharness the poor dear and pull the cart himself" (121). Given that the child feels only shame regarding her father's behavior and chronic illness, it is clear that the novel's complex perspective requires the insight provided by Franzi. Even as the daughter emphasizes that she had no recollection of this incident, she incorporates her mother's story. This narrative practice distinguishes *Other People's Houses* from more recent fiction on the Kindertransport.

Maternal Idealization in Mona Golabek and Lee Cohen's *The Children of Willesden Lane*

Undoubtedly, Malka Jura, the mother who sent her daughter away, plays a critical role in Mona Golabek and Lee Cohen's *The Children of Willesden Lane:*

Beyond the Kindertransport: A Memoir of Music, Love, and Survival. However, it is important to note that in contrast to *Other People's Houses*, the memoir is not authored by Jura's daughter, Lisa Jura. Instead, Lisa is a character in a postmemory work coauthored by her own daughter, Mona Golabek, and writer Lee Cohen. Although Golabek credits Cohen with researching her mother's story ("About the Author"), in the author's note that prefaces *The Children of Willesden Lane* she provides a somewhat different account when she refers to how her own research filled in the gaps in her mother's memory (x). As is evident in the acknowledgments where she thanks Cohen and in the way her name appears before his on the title page, Golabek is the driving force behind the book. Although *The Children of Willesden Lane* demonstrates how Lisa's memories of the woman whose parting words, "You must promise me . . . that you will hold on to your music" (Golabek and Cohen 28), dominate Lisa's subsequent life, it is revealing that in the epilogue, Golabek's daughters attribute these words, not to Malka, their great-grandmother, but to their grandmother Lisa (Golabek and Cohen 272). Our understanding of Malka is doubly mediated: first by her daughter and then by the granddaughter/coauthor. Golabek claims that "the spirit of the story" ("Author's Note" x) is her mother's, but given that Lisa had died by the time Golabek published her fictionalized account, we only have her word for it. If Golabek is indeed true to the spirit of her mother's story, then Lisa's sudden separation at age fourteen from her mother, Malka Jura, appears to have produced a very narrow maternal portrait.

Second-generation accounts often simultaneously mythologize and demonstrate uncertainty about key facts (Kertzer 36–37). Despite claims about the research Golabek and Cohen carried out, there are several historical inaccuracies in *The Children of Willesden Lane*, particularly about dates. Whether these demonstrate the inadequacy of the authors' research or the shape of the story Lisa passed on to her daughter is unclear. Thus while most accounts of departure from Vienna's Westbahnhof Station (including Segal's) stress that the parents were forbidden to walk the children to the trains, perhaps Lisa claimed to remember her mother doing so (Golabek and Cohen 26). Perhaps it was also Lisa who imagined the impact of Kristallnacht disrupting the sanctity of the Jewish Sabbath, even though Kristallnacht began the night of 8 November 1938, a Wednesday, not a Friday (Golabek and Cohen 13). Most first-generation memoirs give an exact date for the child's departure (for example, Segal notes that she came on the first train that left Vienna on 10 December 1938). In contrast, Golabek and Cohen write vaguely that Lisa left a week after Chanukah. But if she left the final week of December 1938, what explains her August 1939 reference to the "loneliness of the last six months" (70)? It is not just Lisa's memory that is "clouded by time" (Golabek, "Author's Note" x).

Such temporal inaccuracies have not affected Golabek's ability to carry her mother's "legacy" further. *The Children of Willesden Lane* has been remarkably successful, possibly because among all the works this essay discusses, it comes closest to Kushner's assertion that by the beginning of the twenty-first century, "The *Kinder* . . . had become a safe story, put together neatly and with a redemptive ending" (165). Search for "*Kindertransport* fiction" on Amazon.com and *The Children of Willesden Lane* consistently shows up close to the top of the list.[5] Unlike most Kindertransport fiction, *The Children of Willesden Lane* is currently in its eighth printing. In 2003 Golabek created a nonprofit organization *Hold on to Your Music Foundation* "to expand awareness and understanding of the ethical implications of world events such as the Holocaust, and the power of the arts, especially music, to embolden the human spirit in the face of adversity" (*Hold on*). In support of this goal, the foundation provides several teaching guides and videos, and according to the foundation's website, numerous projects, including a PBS documentary and an interactive website, are planned. Golabek, herself an accomplished pianist, has performed a musical adaptation called *The Pianist of Willesden Lane*, which tells "how the most beautiful music in the world saved her [mother's] life" (*Hold on*).

As is evident in the title of the website *Hold on to Your Music*, in the music that begins as soon as we click on the website's link, and in the novel's dedication to Lisa saying that "the music of your soul is eternal," Golabek conceptualizes her own mother's "legacy" solely in terms of music (Golabek, "Author's Note" xi), and this strongly affects how *The Children of Willesden Lane* depicts Malka Jura. Golabek is undoubtedly committed to telling the story of her own mother; but in the course of doing so, Golabek's grandmother, the woman who sent Lisa on the train, is both celebrated and erased.

It is also striking that Lisa said nothing about Malka in a brief memoir that she contributed to Bertha Leverton (who organized the first international reunion) and Shmuel Lowensohn's 1990 collection *I Came Alone: The Stories of the Kindertransport*. One of the entries in this collection of brief memoirs is by Lisa Golabek Roberts, the woman whose story is retold in *The Children of Willesden Lane*. Another entry is by her sister Sonja Marco (called Sonia Jura in *The Children of Willesden Lane*), who, unlike Lisa, acknowledges "the terrible feeling of never seeing my parents again"

(Leverton and Lowensohn 207). Consistent with Kushner's assertion that Leverton and Lowensohn likely edited out the "trauma of separation from [one contributor's] parents" (164), Golabek Roberts says nothing about her parents; instead, just as her daughter would twelve years later, she stresses the "lucky day" that led to her winning a scholarship to the Royal Academy of Music (Leverton and Lowensohn 123).

The sisters' entries in *I Came Alone* differ in both their facts and their emphases from what we find in *The Children of Willesden Lane*. Golabek Roberts begins her entry with the factual statement, "I left Vienna with a children's transport in 1938, aged fourteen, for London, where I stayed with relatives and looked after babies" (Leverton and Lowensohn 122). In her second paragraph she mentions living in a hostel (presumably the hostel located at 243 Willesden Lane that is the novel's setting), and in her third paragraph she focuses on her music. In her final paragraph, she briefly recounts meeting her first husband in Paris, his death in 1977, and her remarriage in 1981.

Several of the details in Golabek Roberts's account are either revised or omitted from *The Children of Willesden Lane*. In the latter, the relative (called Sid in the novel just as he is in Sonja Marco's account) proves unable to give Lisa a temporary home;[6] Lisa meets her future husband, Michel Golabek, in London, not Paris; and there is no reference to her remarriage. Instead *The Children of Willesden Lane* ends with Lisa's postwar concert, which evokes not just her personal memories of wartime loss but also the "tale of so many in war-torn London" (Golabek and Cohen 266). Concluding with Chopin's "heroic polonaise," she makes the entire audience relive "their proudest, bravest moments—their courage under the bombing, their unshakable resolve, their ultimate victory" (267). Among the London audience is Lisa's future husband. Adding to Lisa's triumph is her conviction that her mother is "watching from above" (269). Despite all the losses of the war, Lisa's "heart filled with joy as she realized she had done it. She had fulfilled the promise she had made to her mother. She had held on to her music" (269).

It might be argued that the differences between Golabek Roberts's account and the novel can be credited to how Golabek Roberts's memories were "clouded by time" (Golabek, "Author's Note" x). However, given that Golabek Roberts was only in her fifties when she wrote her account, it is more likely that the differences are deliberate narrative choices made by Golabek and Cohen. Lisa becomes more heroic after Sid is unable to give her a home and she must find a new home independently. When her future husband attends the concert, it is hard to separate his admiration of her performance from his attraction to her beauty (reinforced by the photograph of a stunning Lisa Jura that immediately follows). Taken in 1947, it is the only photograph in the novel.[7] In *The Children of Willesden Lane*, Mrs. Cohen (called "Mrs. Cohn" in Sonja Marco's account [Leverton and Lowensohn 208]) tells Lisa that her music has inspired all of the residents of 243 Willesden Lane (258). In contrast, although at least five other contributors to *I Came Alone* refer to residing temporarily at the hostel at 243 Willesden Lane, no one ever mentions Lisa or the impact of her music.[8]

While such differences may be occasioned by Golabek and Cohen's determination to tell Lisa's story in a heroic romantic mode—as well as Malka's conviction that her daughter was "special" (8)—there is another detail in *The Children of Willesden Lane* that implicitly reveals the limits of the authors' ability to portray the woman who sent her daughter on the Kindertransport. Just before Malka parts from Lisa at the train station in Vienna, she thrusts a photograph into her daughter's hand. Described as a "photograph of Malka standing straight and proud, taken on the day of Lisa's last recital at school" (29), the photo bears an inscription "*Fon diene nicht fergesene mutter*," which is translated differently in two simultaneously published editions. In one edition, the inscription is translated as "From the mother who will never forget you" (Grand Central Publishing 29); in the other, it reads, "So that you will never forget your mother" (Warner Books 29).[9] As though Malka's intention is overridden by the oft-cited general imperative to never forget, the two translations reverse the subject and object of the forgetting. On the website *Hold on to Your Music*, Golabek writes of the impact of the day she first saw the photograph and uses the translation found in the Warner Books edition:

> On the back in shaky handwriting was written the following: "So that you will never forget your mother. . . ." I was so overwhelmed by the love my grandmother showed in sending her daughter away, losing her forever to save her, that I vowed to share this story with the world.

Whatever accounts for the different translations or for the decision not to include the photo in *The Children in Willesden Lane*, the sentence is ungrammatical and incoherent, likely a sentence written by someone who "was not a German native speaker" (Strzelczyk).[10] I do not know whether Golabek and Cohen copied the inscription correctly, or whether the photo even existed. Assuming that the photo existed but is not displayed in the novel or in the Lisa Jura Photo Gallery that is part of the *Hold on to Your Music* website because it disappeared, we are left with a conundrum regarding Malka's intention. The mystery about these words highlights numerous additional questions about Malka. Was German her native language? Where did she grow up? Did she receive a formal education and for how long? These questions are impossible to answer because other than in her role as Lisa's first music teacher and a "wonderful pianist" (Golabek and Cohen 261), Malka is presented in the most generic terms. Like many mothers in Kindertransport memoirs and fiction, she bakes *apfelstrudel* that is "the best in all of Vienna" (3). Other than that, readers learn that she is an observant Jew who respects the Sabbath, compares Hitler to the biblical tyrant Haman, and disapproves of her three daughters wearing makeup. The inscription, the only writing by Malka that readers see directly, suggests that the woman who inspires Lisa's behavior and Golabek and Cohen's novel had a life whose details we can never know. *The Children of Willesden Lane* is ultimately a novel that celebrates the power of music, Mona Golabek's tribute to the mother she cannot forget. But despite Golabek's act of maternal ventriloquism, Malka Jura, the mother who saved her daughter's life, remains hidden and indecipherable. That is also the case with the mother who sent her daughter away in Linda Newbery's young adult novel, *Sisterland*.

Maternal Rejection in Linda Newbery's *Sisterland*

Although Linda Newbery's *Sisterland* differs from *The Children of Willesden Lane* in that it scarcely celebrates the mother who sent her daughter away, it resembles *The Children* to the degree that a granddaughter plays a central role. However, Newbery does not ground her novel in her own family's experience in the Kindertransport. Instead, using a contemporary setting, she relies on an adolescent narrator, Hilly Craig, to discover the truth of her grandmother's past and juxtaposes this truth with multiple examples of current racial and sexual bigotry. The truth has been hidden for decades because Hilly's grandmother denied her Jewish identity to such an extent that she abandoned her birth name, Sarah Reubens, and postwar adopted the name Heidi Schmidt. Supporting the premise found in other Kindertransport novels that repressed Holocaust memories are likely to emerge in fragmented form with the onset of dementia in old age, *Sisterland* also demonstrates how the delay in regarding the Kindertransportees as legitimate

Holocaust survivors affects character roles in young adult fiction. Contemporary novels about Kindertransportees routinely rely on grandchildren to unveil their grandparents' hidden past. While slightly more than half of the Kindertransportees were female (Hirschberger 249), this does not explain why the grandchild who discovers the grandparent's past is nearly always female. With the exception of Ransom Riggs's *Miss Peregrine's Home for Peculiar Children*, I can think of no young adult novel where the grandchild who discovers this truth is male.

Even the pseudonym Hilly's grandmother adopts contributes to the novel's representation of mothers. Taking the name Heidi after the heroine of the book she takes with her on the train, she initially links the book to her mother's voice and thinks that she will "have to imagine Mutti's voice reading" (Newbery 60). Perhaps because of the difficulty of doing so, she chooses instead to imitate Johanna Spyri's heroine by starting to read from the beginning, "because Heidi in the story was setting out just like this, to a new life" (63). Once in England, the novel proves therapeutic: when she is teased by English children, she escapes by reading about the heroine who is always grateful, loved, and most advantageous, neither German nor Jewish. Even though she sometimes hates the novel because its optimism and the heroine's cheerfulness conflict with her own moroseness, in 1945, after she watches graphic details of Bergen-Belsen on Allied newsreels, she returns to *Heidi*. The solace is short-lived. A few days later, after she destroys the novel as though it is emblematic of her need to break with a past that is now dead to her, she decides that her new name will be Heidi: "She had been jealous of Heidi, but now she. . . . would be as happy and as lucky as Heidi had been" (261).

Spyri's novel fuels Sarah's desperate determination to reconstruct her life by offering an alternate narrative for her childhood. Decades later, giving the novel to Hilly when she turns seven—the same age she was when she came to England—she tells Hilly that her parents named her Heidi "Because I was always such a happy little girl" (Newbery 236). A further advantage to adopting the heroine's identity is that the cheerfulness of Spyri's heroine is independent of a mother's support. In *Heidi*, the mothers of the principal child characters, Heidi and Clara (the crippled child Heidi befriends) are both dead. In choosing her false identity, the orphaned Kindertransportee imitates the orphan narrative of canonical children's literature.

Mothers become irrelevant in multiple ways in *Sisterland*. The first way is by having Heidi's mother—known only by the generic nickname Mutti (mommy)—die twice: once in a gas chamber, and once more symbolically when her daughter refuses to remember her. Second, Rose (Heidi's daughter and Hilly's mother) displays no interest in uncovering her mother's secret. Vaguely aware that her mother's story about coming to England postwar as a German refugee does not really make sense (why would a woman who claims she lost her parents because of Allied bombing want to immigrate to England?), Rose goes along with her mother's fictional identity. The minimal role Rose plays in her daughter Hilly's uncovering of Heidi's identity is itself a form of maternal erasure by reducing Rose's role in the narrative. A third form of erasure involves the photograph that initiates Hilly's quest. Unlike the maternal photo that governs *The Children of Willesden Lane*, the photograph Hilly accidentally finds is of Heidi's sister. Aided by her friend, whose first name, Reuben, occasions several anti-Semitic comments by Heidi, Hilly unearths the truth that her grandmother came to England on a Kindertransport and that Rachel, the name inscribed on the back of the photograph, is Heidi's older sister. Only after the revelation of Heidi's Jewish identity does Hilly realize that her grandmother's anti-Semitism was a further strategy of erasing her maternal lineage since Judaism is inherited through the mother.

Like the photograph of Rachel, the novel's title also foregrounds that the author's primary interest lies in exploring the relationship of sisters. Although the contemporary conflicts of Hilly and her sister, Zoë, are different from the earlier tensions between Heidi and Rachel, Newbery is clearly interested in examining how sisters move from misunderstanding to reconciliation. Hilly and Zoë quarrel about room boundaries and the suitability of boyfriends, but eventually reconcile. In contrast, Heidi, unable to understand why her parents are sending her away, tells Rachel (who is too old to go on a Kindertransport) that she hates her and never reconciles with her. In striking contrast to her continuing distress over her fight with Rachel, it is fairly easy for Heidi to reject her parents as impostors: "Mutti can't be my real mother, or Vati my real father, or they wouldn't send me away" (Newbery 48). During the war, she dwells on her inability to make amends with her sister and regrets that she failed to bring Rachel to England. After the war, when she learns that her parents died in gas chambers, she appears less disturbed by this news than by the fact of her sister's remarkable survival. Her parents' death ironically means that she does not have to think about how they died. What troubles her about Rachel's survival is that she fears that Rachel will resemble one of the people in the photographs taken by Allied soldiers: "the nearly-dead [sic] people who had reached out to the soldiers and begged silently" (324). The "nearly-dead" in the photographs were begging for food, but Heidi fears that Rachel will beg Heidi to confront the reality of what happened in the death camps. This is a reasonable fear given that the novel makes Rachel a survivor of three years in Auschwitz (326). Forced to participate in a postwar meeting where Rachel proves to be "not quite like the living skeleton of her dreams" (328), Heidi refuses to have anything to do with her sister. In the novel's conclusion, Hilly is flying to Israel to meet her great aunt. That reconciliation is denied Heidi, who remains in England, slipping further into dementia, suspecting confusedly that she "might have had a sister, once" (364) and not once thinking about her mother. The last time Heidi appears in the novel, she is unable to recognize herself or her sister in the photos Hilly has discovered, and she struggles to remember a word. Consistent with the representation of mothers in *Sisterland*, Heidi's memory struggles have nothing to do with the word "Mother."

Maternal Invention in Alison Pick's *Far to Go*

Alison Pick's adult novel *Far to Go* treats the absence of maternal memory as a figure for the traumatic losses of the Holocaust. Highly self-conscious about readers' expectations regarding Holocaust fiction but never questioning its premise that the Kindertransport is a story in which the majority of the parents died and the children never recovered from a loss that paradoxically they could barely remember, it begins by warning readers that this will not be a happy story. The novel's narrator, Lisa, is a retired professor who specializes in recording Kindertransport oral histories and does not reveal for most of the novel that she has a personal and traumatic relationship to this history. It is only close to the end that she confides that the mother who abandoned her at age six and then died in a DP camp in 1946 was Marta, the Czech governess of six-year-old Pepik Bauer, who was sent to England on a Kindertransport.

Connecting with Pepik when he is elderly and dying of cancer, Lisa learns that he has spent his life ignorant that he was born into a Czech Jewish family. Because of the shock of his journey to England and also because his initial foster mother misidentified his mother in a photograph that accompanied him, he has spent his life convinced that Marta is his mother. He is incredulous when Lisa tells him that his mother is the other woman in the photo, the one "holding herself slightly apart" (Pick 286). Lisa understands why the foster mother misidentified Pepik's mother; our expectations about how mothers behave frame how we recognize them in photographs.

Full of secrets, betrayals, and traumatic journeys, *Far to Go* saves its deepest secret until the end, when Lisa reveals that she is Pepik's half-sister, the result of a relationship between his father and Marta. Readers also learn that much of what they have just read is actually a "bedtime story" Lisa has invented as a way of comforting the dying Pepik (Pick 287). Admitting that despite her professional expertise she knows very little about the Bauer family's life in the months leading up to Pepik's departure, she has filled in the blanks in his story by imagining it from the perspective of her own mother. The story is intended as an act of kindness, giving Pepik "some sense of completion, some resolution—even imagined—to the tragedy that opened his life" (289). Lisa regards the story she creates as an act of maternal love to the man she imagines could have been her child. It is also her way of imagining the mother she could never know. Unable to know who her mother was, she invents a story about her.

The Women Who Sent Their Children Away

We bring our expectations about how mothers behave to more than photographs. We also bring them to our longing to reconcile the behavior of the women who sent their children away with ingrained beliefs about how mothers should behave. Just as Lisa regards her storytelling as an act of maternal love, in *Hold on to Your Music*, Mona Golabek writes of feeling "so overwhelmed by the love [her] grandmother showed in sending her daughter away . . . that [she] vowed to share this story with the world" (*Hold on*). Even in *Sisterland*, the novel least concerned with maternal behavior, Heidi comes to a realization that her mother lied about the Nazi imprisonment of her father in order to protect her.

Other People's Houses confronts the challenge the Kindertransport poses to our understanding of maternal behavior when Lore invites another lonely refugee child to play house. The rules of the game are very simple: "You be the child. You have to cry and I'll make you feel better" (56). Lore is unable to understand why the other child refuses to play. The child's refusal captures the difficulty in reconciling the actions of the Kindertransport mothers and our expectations that mothers make us feel better. It is precisely this longing for reconciliation that lies at the heart of the maternal idealization of *The Children of Willesden Lane*, the maternal erasure of *Sisterland*, and the maternal invention of *Far to Go*.

Our expectations regarding maternal behavior also contribute to the gendered nature of these narratives. Pick's narrator recognizes that in telling one story, "the other versions slip through the cracks" (307). What slips through the cracks in contemporary Kindertransport fiction are not only the stories of the women who let their children go, their motivations for doing so, and their lives, however brief, following their children's departure. The stories of the fathers also disappear. Lisa is fascinated by the photograph that Pepik shows her because it is the first time she sees her biological father. Inventing a story about her mother, she also invents a story about the man who fathered her. In the novel's final paragraph, she admits that she "*would* give anything—for a single memory of [her] father" (308). But while he is as lost to her as the mother who sent her away, Pick chooses to have her narrator tell another story. As willing as she is to interrogate the conventions of Kindertransport fiction, she respects the way that this fiction focuses upon maternal figures. Even when the decision to send the child away was initially the father's (and that fact is acknowledged in most of the works discussed here), what compels our interest in Kindertransport fiction are the stories of the women who sent their children away.

Notes

1. "[A] small group of German Jewish refugee children" (Baumel-Schwartz 109) whose families were of Polish extraction were deported from Germany in late October 1938 and then refused admission to Poland. Some of these children came to Britain as part of the Kindertransport as did a group of forty refugee children who fled the Netherlands on 14 May 1940.

2. The term "Kinder" has come to collectively identify these Jewish and "'non-Aryan' Christian children (Jewish converts to Christianity or children of mixed marriages)" (Baumel-Schwartz 1).

3. In contrast, collections of testimonies include many more reunions with one or more parents (Fox and Abraham-Podietz).

4. In 1974 part 1 was published in a series titled Books for New Adults with an introduction by children's author Naomi Lewis. Julia Baker refers to this edition (which bore the subtitle *A Refugee in England, 1938–48*) as a children's novel (Baker 199n4). Its eight stories trace Segal's life from childhood in Vienna to the moment when she reluctantly departed for the Dominican Republic.

5. It appeared as second out of twenty-seven entries 6 Apr. 2014. It appeared as fourth out of thirty entries 24 Aug. 2014.

6. Sonja Marco states that she lived with her "cousins Rose and Sid" (207) when she first came to England. In contrast, Golabek and Cohen call the female cousin Dora, and Sonia lives with a Quaker family in the north of England (98).

7. On the dust jacket of the Grand Central Publishing edition, a photo of Lisa is imposed on top of train tracks that clearly evoke Lisa as a Holocaust survivor.

8. Marga Goren-Gothelf, Martin Lewis, Dennis Schwartz, and his wife, Gina, mention 243 Willesden Lane.

9. Throughout this chapter, my citations refer to the Grand Central Publishing edition; however, the pagination in the two different editions is identical. The only difference is that page 29 in the Grand Central edition has a font size that is smaller than the rest of the volume.

10. I am indebted to my colleague Florentine Strzelczyk for responding to my questions regarding the inscription. Initially I had wondered if the words had been written by someone who spoke Yiddish, but the *"nicht"* suggests German.

Works Cited

"About the Author." *Teaching the Children of Willesden Lane: Resources to Help You Teach the Book*. Web. 21 July 2014.

Baker, Julia K. "From Other People's Houses into Shakespeare's Kitchen: The Story of Lore Segal and How She Looked for Adventures and Where She Found Them." Hammel and Lewkowicz. 185–203.

Baumel-Schwartz, Judith Tydor. *Never Look Back: The Jewish Refugee Children in Great Britain, 1938–1945*. West Lafayette, IN: Purdue UP, 2012. Print. Shofar Supplements in Jewish Studies.

Benz, Wolfgang, Claudia Curio, and Andrea Hammel. Foreword. Trans. Toby Axelrod. *Shofar: An Interdisciplinary Journal of Jewish Studies* 23.1 (Fall 2004): 1–2. Project Muse. Web. 20 Apr. 2014.

Drucker, Olga Levy. *Kindertransport*. New York: Holt, 1992. 140–46. Print.

Fox, Anne L., and Eva Abraham-Podietz. *Ten Thousand Children: True Stories Told by Children Who Escaped the Holocaust on the Kindertransport*. West Orange, NJ: Behrman House, 1999. Print.

Gershon, Karen, ed. *We Came As Children: A Collective Autobiography*. London: Gollancz, 1966. Print.

Golabek, Mona. Acknowledgments. *The Children of Willesden Lane: Beyond the Kindertransport: A Memoir of Music, Love, and Survival*. By Mona Golabek and Lee Cohen. New York: Grand Central Publishing-Hatchette, 2002. vii-viii. Print.

———. Author's Note. *The Children of Willesden Lane: Beyond the Kindertransport: A Memoir of Music, Love, and Survival.* By Mona Golabek and Lee Cohen. New York: Grand Central Publishing-Hachette, 2002. ix-xi. Print.

Golabek, Mona, and Lee Cohen. *The Children of Willesden Lane: Beyond the Kindertransport: A Memoir of Music, Love, and Survival.* New York: Grand Central Publishing-Hachette, 2002. Print.

———. *The Children of Willesden Lane: Beyond the Kindertransport: A Memoir of Music, Love, and Survival.* New York: Warner, 2002. Print.

Golabek Roberts, Lisa. Leverton and Lowensohn. 122–23.

Göpfert, Rebekka. "Kindertransport: History and Memory." Trans. Andrea Hammel. *Shofar: An Interdisciplinary Journal of Jewish Studies* 23.1 (Fall 2004): 21–27. Project Muse. Web. 20 Apr. 2014.

Harris, Mark Jonathan, and Deborah Oppenheimer. *Into the Arms of Strangers: Stories of the Kindertransport.* London: Bloomsbury, 2000. Print.

Hammel, Andrea, and Bea Lewkowicz, eds. *The Kindertransport to Britain 1938–39: New Perspectives.* New York: Rodopi, 2012. Web.

Hirschberger, Hermann. "The AJR Kindertransport Survey: Making New Lives in Britain." Hammel and Lewkowicz. 247–54.

Hold on to Your Music Foundation. Web. 6 Apr. 2014.

Kertzer, Adrienne. *My Mother's Voice: Children, Literature, and the Holocaust.* Peterborough, ON: Broadview, 2002. Print.

The Kindertransport Association. Web. 26 Nov. 2013.

"Kindertransport, 1938–1940." *Holocaust Encyclopedia.* United States Holocaust Memorial Museum. 6 Jan. 2011. Web. 29 Apr. 2012.

Kushner, Tony. *Remembering Refugees: Then and Now.* Manchester and New York: Manchester UP, 2006. Print.

Lassner, Phyllis. *Ango-Jewish Women Writing the Holocaust: Displaced Witnesses.* New York: Palgrave Macmillan, 2008. Print.

Leverton, Bertha, and Shmuel Lowensohn, eds. *I Came Alone: The Stories of the Kindertransport.* Sussex: The Book Guild, 1990. Print.

"Lore Segal." *Something About the Author.* Vol. 163. Detroit: Gale, 2006. 183–86. Web.

Marco, Sonja. Leverton and Lowensohn. 207–8.

Milton, Edith. *The Tiger in the Attic: Memories of the Kindertransport and Growing Up English.* Chicago: U of Chicago P, 2005. Print.

Newbery, Linda. *Sisterland.* 2003. London: Red Fox Definitions, 2004. Print.

Pick, Alison. *Far to Go.* Toronto: Anansi, 2010. Print.

Riggs, Ransom. *Miss Peregrine's Home for Peculiar Children.* Philadelphia: Quirk, 2011. Print.

Segal, Lore. "Baby Terrors." *Under Fire: Childhood in the Shadow of War.* Ed. Elizabeth Goodenough and Andrea Immel. Detroit: Wayne State UP, 2008. 93–96. Print. Landscapes of Childhood.

———. "The Bough Breaks." *Testimony: Contemporary Writers Make the Holocaust Personal.* Ed. David Rosenberg. New York: Times-Random House, 1989. 231–48. Print.

———. *Other People's Houses.* New York: New Press, 1994. Print.

———. *Other People's Houses: A Refugee in England, 1938–48.* Intro. Naomi Lewis. London: Bodley Head, 1974. Print.

———. Preface. *Other People's Houses.* ix-xi.

Spyri, Johanna. *Heidi.* Trans. Eileen Hall. Illus. Cecil Leslie. 1880. Harmondsworth: Penguin, 1969. Print.

Strzelczyk, Florentine. Email to the author. 2 Apr. 2014.

"36 Questions about the Holocaust." *Simon Wiesenthal Multimedia Learning Center.* Web. 14 Aug. 2014.

Travis, Madelyn J. *Jews and Jewishness in British Children's Literature.* New York: Routledge, 2013. Print. Children's Literature and Culture.

Williams, Frances. *The Forgotten Kindertransportees: The Scottish Experience.* London: Bloomsbury, 2014. Print.

Chapter 5

Minority Mama: Rejecting the Mainstream Mothering Model

Dorina K. Lazo Gilmore

The strong mother described in the following lines from Pat Mora's profound poem and picture book, *The Desert Is My Mother/El Desierto Es Mi Madre*, is a mother rarely championed in mainstream literature, especially children's literature.

I say teach me	*Le digo, enséñame.*
She blooms in the sun's glare,	*Y florece in el brillo del sol,*
the snow's silence	*en el silencio de la nieve,*
the driest sand.	*en las arenas mas secas.*
The desert is my mother.	*El desierto es mi madre.*
The desert is my strong mother.	*El desierto es mi madre poderosa.*

She does not fit in with the ideal of the "good mother" that our culture has created and continues to replicate in children's books. Psychologist Shari Thurer, in her book, *The Myths of Motherhood*, traces our society's concept of the "good mother." According to Thurer, each culture and age defines the myth of the "good mother" (xv). If we see the mother concept as a tree deeply rooted in the soil of society, each culture adds a new ring to the trunk of our ideals. Thurer describes the contemporary "good mother," who performs all the domestic duties of the home with ease—raising children, housekeeping, and providing food. Putting it into contemporary rhetoric, our "good mother" is expected to be Supermom—with superpowers to be everywhere, doing everything, for everyone. Thurer explains the guilt these expectations cause: "A sentimentalized image of the perfect mother casts a long, guilt-inducing shadow over real mothers' lives" (xi). This statement begs the question: Is there an alternative? Will mothers ever have the opportunity to show they are individual, dynamic, and independent of this unrealistic, idealized image imposed by notions of the good mother?

In recent years, the plethora of mommy bloggers have expanded the conversation about mothering work and questioned some of the popular images presented of mothers. Meanwhile, the "mommy wars" continue as women debate topics such as staying home to raise children or working outside the home, breastfeeding versus formula, sleep schedules, school choices, and the list goes on. What is surprising is that the best-selling children's books of our time continue to heap superpower expectations on mothers' shoulders. If we reach outside the mainstream model of mothers revealed in best-selling picture books, however, an alternative model already exists. Mothers from ethnic minority backgrounds depicted in children's picture books reject the mainstream "good mother" model and prove more multidimensional, serving as a different mothering example for the future.[1] These mothers are naturally emotional and resilient, creative, and in touch with their sexual identities, all the while encouraging independence, promoting education, and preparing their children for challenges such as dealing with racial oppression.

Images of the Good Mother in Best-selling Picture Books

In order to properly contrast the alternative mother with the mainstream notions of the "good mother," it is important to first examine briefly how the "good mother" is depicted in mainstream children's picture books. I will then examine several picture books that reveal the mother of color and discuss how these alternative mothers reject the mainstream model. Finally, I will explore why it might be easier for a minority mother to redefine mothering apart from the mainstream myth and what all women can learn from the minority mama[2] depicted in children's picture books.

Despite expansion of the conversation about the mother's role in the mainstream media, "traditional mothering ideology" is often propagated by best-selling children's book series and trade books. Lisa Rowe Fraustino delves into this topic in her article, "The Apple of Her Eye: The Mothering Ideology Fed by Best-selling Trade Picture Books," which notes some of the patterns promoted by this ideology. Fraustino says the "mother-child relationship is often intense, one-on-one, all consuming. There's no career for the woman, no interest in nondomestic activities" (68). Fraustino follows this "traditional mothering ideology" through one of the most popular best-selling picture books of our time, Shel Silverstein's *The Giving Tree*, originally published in 1964. By the fiftieth anniversary edition of the book in 2014, more than 10 million copies had been sold, pointing to its popularity and influence (Maughan). A popular interpretation of the book is to celebrate the sweetness of the mother-son relationship. Fraustino explains a different interpretation: "Young readers see that boys are allowed to go off and do what they want, unlike girls, who by gender affiliation are assigned the tree's rooted role, doling out apples" (60). The book idealizes an ever-sacrificing mother model. *The Giving Tree* proves to be one of those books containing images of the "good mother" that continues to sell and be attractive to a large segment of Western society.

The "smothering mother" is another popular image in mainstream picture books. She can be found, for example, in Robert Munsch's popular *Love You Forever*. Perhaps the most surprising illustration in the book depicts the mother when she grows older fixing a ladder to her car, then driving to her adult son's house and climbing in his window so she can rock him to sleep. Like *The Giving Tree*, many read Munsch's book with a nostalgic lens, viewing it as a depiction of the circle of life—a mother's love being passed through the generations. Of course, there are multiple interpretations of Munsch's book, including the backstory that he wrote it for his two stillborn babies.[3] Again, it is important to consider what this book reveals about the "good mother" as a "smothering mother," one who does not release her child to grow and become independent. She is not willing to accept that he has moved into new stages of life in which he is no longer dependent on her rocking and comforting. The mother acts out of nostalgia for the past. Clinical psychologist and psychoanalyst Donna Bassin, in her essay, "Maternal Subjectivity in the Culture of Nostalgia: Mourning and Memory," might call this a path of "incomplete mourning." Bassin suggests that a healthy way for mothers to mourn is to move beyond nostalgia and recognize that a child is moving to a new stage in life and then supporting his or her independence (168–69). This leads us to an alternative portrait of a minority mother who models and encourages independence in her children.

Images of minority mothers presented in picture books are, of course, diverse in both personality and culture. However, some patterns become evident as we compare recent picture books featuring characters outside white, middle-class culture. This chapter will examine six contemporary picture books as a representative sampling to reveal the alternatives these mothers of color can offer in contrast to mainstream "good mother" myths. These books include: *Mama, Do You Love Me?*, by Barbara M. Joosse; *Mama Does the Mambo*, by Katherine Leiner; *The Desert Is My Mother/El Desierto Es Mi Madre*, by Pat Mora; *Calling the Doves*, by Juan Felipe Herrera; *Imani's Moon*, by JaNay Brown-Wood; and *Little Melba and Her Big Trombone*, by Katheryn Russell-Brown. The mothers in these books can be characterized by maternal resilience, confidence, strength, creativity, ambition, compassion for their communities, and their ability to equip their children to survive racial oppression.

Showing Maternal Resilience

Barbara M. Joosse's *Mama, Do You Love Me?* is an exceptional book published in 1991 that, through lyrical text, tells a familiar story about mother and child in a culturally specific Arctic setting. The book opens with the Inuit daughter asking, "Mama, do you love me?" The mother answers, "Yes I do, Dear One." These lines are reminiscent of countless other mainstream picture books such as Margaret Wise Brown's *The Runaway Bunny*, Anna Pignatori's *Mama, How Long Will You Love Me?*, and Laura Leuck's *My Monster Mama Loves Me So* that talk about how much a mother loves her child. These books tend to show "good mothers" who accept their children no matter what mischief or harm they cause. For example, the baby on the cover of Munsch's *Love You Forever* is clearly destroying the bathroom. He has pulled the toilet paper from the roll and dumped an array of cosmetics on the floor. How does this mother react? She rocks her child and says she'll love him forever. She is not allowed an emotional reaction to his mischief. She accepts her man-child and coddles him no matter what. As Thurer describes, the "good mother" "exists bodily, of course, but her needs as a person become null and void" (xvii). Joosse writes a new script. Her Inuit mother shows unconditional love, but still responds humanly and emotionally to her daughter's challenges. When the daughter asks her mother, "What if I put salmon in your parka, ermine in your mittens, and lemmings in your mukluks?" the mother answers with hands on her giant hips, "Then I would be angry." The vibrant watercolor illustrations on this page show the mischievous daughter giggling as she puts fish in her mother's parka and small white weasels (ermine) in Mama's mittens, then coaxes mouse-like lemmings into Mama's boots. On the opposite page, we see the world from the child's perspective, looking up at her great mama whose facial expression and hands on her hips express her anger. These pages show a mother who has permission to express anger when her child misbehaves—an image less frequently depicted in mainstream picture books and unaccepted in American culture.

Joosse's Inuit mother displays healthy "maternal resilience" when she reacts to her child's questions. In her essay "Mothering, Hate, and Winnicott," Elsa First describes the importance of "maternal resilience" for the development of young children. In this stage of the child's development, "A mother, to stay resilient, has to recognize potentially constructive energy in the attack [in this case filling mama's clothes with fish and small animals] and to identify with it and even, for the child's sake, to enjoy it while protecting herself" (159). Joosse depicts the Inuit child asking her mother: "What if I turned into a polar bear, and I was the meanest bear you ever saw and I had sharp, shiny teeth, and I chased you into your tent and you cried?" The mother shows her resilience: "Then I would be very surprised and very scared. But still, inside the bear, you would be you, and I would love you." The mother answers truthfully, saying she would be surprised and scared, but she also recognizes the playfulness in this question and points out that the child would still be worthy of loving even as a bear. The mother expresses her unconditional love when she welcomes the child back into her arms for the final lines of the book: "I will love you, forever and for always, because you are my Dear One." Joosse's minority mama shows realistic emotions that are generally considered negative, such as fear and anger, as well as resilience in this text, while still sending that important message of unconditional love to her child.

Modeling Confidence and Sexual Identity

Mama Does the Mambo by Katherine Leiner published in 2001 shows the minority mother in a new light: she is at once a confident and "sexy mama" while still connected to her child. This is a surprising picture book because the story starts with a Cuban girl, Sofia, dealing with her father's death. The book opens: "After Papa died, Mama stopped dancing. Just like that, the dancing in our house stopped. Of course, how could it not. There was no one in our house for Mama to dance with" (1). As the story progresses, we see the child take interest in how her father's death has affected her mother, and ultimately, their family. She reminisces about when her father was alive and she would watch her parents dance. Leiner writes,

> Papa held the beat, and Mama, the rhythm. The sound of their hands when they came together was like palm leaves flapping in the wind: Mama's against Papa's. Papa's against Mama's; her crimson skirts whipping a million lights, Papa like the sparrows in the tamarind tree, the two of them their own hurricane. (8)

This confident and "sexy mama," who expresses creativity and emotion through dance, presents a different view from the picture of the asexual mother so often emphasized in the "good mother" myth. Thurer elaborates in *The Myths of Motherhood*, "Sex and motherhood have not mixed well since the demise of the goddess religions, when men began to split women into madonnas or whores in every sphere. Presumably a good mother extinguishes her libido with conception or else expels it along with her placenta in childbirth" (xx). *Mama Does the Mambo* presents the alternative to the "good mother" as Mama's character is sexy, confident in her body, creative, and not afraid to show it. This is a stark contrast to the mother figure in *The Giving Tree*, who sacrifices her own body and identity for the boy throughout.

In *Mama Does the Mambo*, the child narrator steps outside her own needs and desires and focuses on finding her mother a dance partner for the Carnival festivities. This represents her understanding of her mother's need for male companionship. She says, "Perhaps I am worried for nothing. Because people come from all over Havana. It seems everyone wants to dance with Mama. Selvagio from *el mercado*, Esdras from *la farmacia*, Pablo from *la oficina de correos*, and Miguel in his shiny red Chevrolet. They all come to the courtyard" (Leiner 15). Sofia sorts through her mother's suitors, trying to choose the best dance partner for her mama. Eduardo is the only one who spends time developing a relationship with both Sofia and her mother. He cooks them food, takes them on walks, teaches Sofia games, and plays music—but, of course, he can't dance. Sofia explains, "Eduardo trips over Mama's feet. She trips over his" (23). The book culminates with the Carnival festivities and dancing. Sofia looks on as Mama smiles at Eduardo. But then she stretches out her hand and motions for Sofia to be her partner. This is an important moment because Leiner shows the strong relationship between mother and daughter here. They survive the tragedy of the father's death by depending on each other and ultimately becoming dance partners.

This mutual love and growth echoes what Alice Walker describes in her essay "One Child of One's Own": "We are together, my child and I. Mother and child, yes, but sisters really, against whatever denies us all that we are" (392). The final image is illustrator Edel Rodriguez's painting of Mama and Sofia dancing the mambo together. Leiner writes, "Our skirts whirl around us and I am lost in the motion, lost in the wind of our dance. Mama holds the beat and I am the rhythm. And there, in front of all of Havana, I am dancing with Mama, and Mama is dancing the mambo again" (29). This is a satisfying ending that also emphasizes how Mama has taught her daughter this expression of creativity and emotion through dance. As readers, we can guess that Mama chooses Eduardo for a life partner and Sofia will grow up independent and confident like her Mama. Even in the final illustration Sofia appears more mature and confident dancing with Mama.

Revealing Strength and Creativity

Another image that is rare in mainstream children's picture books is the strong and creative mother found in Pat Mora's *The Desert Is My Mother*, which won the Skipping Stones Honor Award in 1995. The book features a poetic depiction of the desert mother as the provider of comfort, food, spirit, and life. Mora is a renowned Hispanic poet for children, and her poem is presented in both Spanish and English. In the opening of the poem, Mora sets the pattern: "I say feed me. She serves red prickly pear on spiked cactus." Across from the text, artist Daniel Lechon has painted a cactus with a close-up of a brightly colored prickly pear. This image sets the tone that our earth-mother has an alternative way of nurturing than we are accustomed to seeing in mainstream books—one that allows prickles. The poem continues, "I say tease me. She sprinkles raindrops in my face on a sunny day." Here we see the ironic side of Mother Nature. She is smart and clever, creating rain on a sunny day. We see Mother Nature's ability to express emotion when "she shouts thunder, flashes lightning." This can be contrasted to her ability to caress and nurture the narrator: "She strokes my skin with her warm breath." In her final lines, "The desert is my mother. The desert is my strong mother," Mora explicitly states that the natural image of a mother is strong. Her poem returns to an ideal of the indigenous people in Mexico and Native Americans in the United States—a profound respect for Mother Earth, but also for mothers in general. About this broad understanding of motherhood, Patricia Hill Collins writes: "A culture that sees the connectedness between the earth and human survival, and that sees motherhood as symbolic of the earth itself, holds motherhood as an institution in high regard" (72). This mother is very different from the mainstream "good mother," who seems to have no personality of her own. Mora's desert mother is truly multidimensional. She is emotional, yet nurturing. She gives physically of herself, but she also challenges her children intellectually. She is beautiful, confident, and strong. She is representative of the multidimensional mothers revealed in many other picture books depicting minority mothers.

Encouraging Dreams and Ambition

Imani's Moon by JaNay Brown-Wood is a more recent book on the scene published in 2014, depicting a mother of color who encourages her young daughter to dream big and believe in herself. The book tells the story of Little Imani of the Maasai people who, despite her size, longs to do something great—touch the moon. The book was named the Children's Book of the Year by the National Association of Elementary School Principals in 2014. Imani's mama builds confidence in her daughter through storytelling. She tells her about the goddess of the moon who triumphed over the god of the sun in a great battle. She tells her about Anansi, the small spider who captured a snake to gain a name for himself. These proverbs lead to real-life encouragement: "'A challenge is only impossible until someone accomplishes it,' Mama said. 'Imani, it is only you who must believe'" (12). Despite many discouraging voices in Imani's world telling her she cannot touch the moon and she should quit, her mama's voice comes through with strength and dignity. Mama's strength is illuminated in the illustrations by Hazel Mitchell. Mama holds her Little Imani on her lap and encourages her to look up at the stars. This posture symbolizes the way Mama encourages Imani to dream and look beyond her circumstances to the greater world. There is a progression through the book as the next spread shows Imani seated next to her mother listening to her stories and looking up at the sky. She is moving out of Mama's lap and tasting independence. She is beginning to dream on her own with a new ambition to touch the moon. The book concludes with Imani returning from her adventure to the moon, this time with a story for her mother. Imani's growth is clear. She stands proudly holding a moon rock, offering it to her mother as evidence of her realized dream. Brown-Wood writes:

Mama listened as Imani told her story.

"Where did you hear such a tale?" asked Mama.

Imani opened her hands and revealed the glowing moon rock, so small and beautiful.

"It is my story, Mama," said Imani. "I am the girl who touched the moon and was welcomed by Olapa. I am the one who believed" (29).

These words show that Imani has gained the confidence Mama instilled in her. She dreamed of touching the moon, she put in the work to get there, she defied the odds against her, and she shared the victory with her mother, who was brave enough to set her free to pursue her ambition.

Extending Her Arms to the Community

Chicano poet Juan Felipe Herrera's bilingual book *Calling the Doves*, winner of the 1997 Ezra Jack Keats Award, introduces a Latino woman who is a mother not just to her son but also to the greater migrant worker community. The book is a poetic first-person story of a boy who grew up traveling the mountains and valleys of California with his Mexican farmworker parents. The mother depicted in this book, Lucha, is multidimensional. She performs typical mothering work, but she is also a poet. Herrera writes:

> Sometimes my mother would surprise us at dinner by reciting poetry.
>
> Over a plate of *guisado* (a spicy tomato stew) and a hard flour tortilla, she would rise to her feet with her hands up as if asking for rain.
>
> Rhyming words would pour out of her mouth and for a moment the world would stop spinning. (15)

The richly colored illustrations by Elly Simmons show the mother as the central figure in this spread. The boy is looking on, but clearly Mama is the center of attention while she recites poetry with her hands lifted toward the sky. She has an organic power expressed through her poems.

Calling the Doves sets up a traditional nuclear family structure found in many mainstream children's books, yet the mother in the book also has an independent identity in the community beyond raising her child. The boy explains:

> My mother was a healer.
> When a fast sparrow would crash into our square house, Mama would pick it up gently and rub its head with alcohol and eucalyptus tea.
> Sometimes she would visit the neighborhood children who were sick. "For a fever," she would tell me, "you need *plantillas* for the feet."
> "First you mix shortening and baking soda in a bowl. Then you rub this on the legs and feet. Gently, you wrap the feet with newspapers."
> In the morning, cool and surprised, the children would jump out of bed in their squeaky paper boots. (19)

Lucha is depicted here as a *curandera* or healer in the community. The *curandera* is traditionally revered in Mexican culture much the way the work of midwives is sacred and respected in Mayan and other cultures. Lucha extends her mothering work to nurture the people around her as well as her immediate family. Collins, in her essay "Shifting the Center: Race, Class, and Feminist Theorizing about Motherhood," explains how a mother's work extends to the community for many women from ethnic minority backgrounds: "'Work for the day to come' is motherwork, whether it is on behalf of one's own biological children, children of one's racial ethnic community, or children who are yet unborn. Moreover, the space that this motherwork occupies promises to shift our thinking about motherhood itself" (59). Rather than the image of the "good mother" who is dependent on her child for her identity, Lucha is independent and models independence for her child. Her role as a *curandera* also alludes to alternative ideas about community parenting used by some groups of farmworkers. In this tight-knit community, the mothers and fathers both work in the fields, and everyone has to look out for the children of the community. We see how both father and mother influence and share in the raising of the child. This, of course, defies the "good mother" myth in mainstream books where fathers are often absent from the book, and the mother and child form an isolated pair.

The mother in *Calling the Doves* is a Mexican farmworker who works in the fields with her husband, mothers her child, and extends her branches to heal the community. Also implicit in her act of mothering is dealing with the racism and discrimination in the dominant society where her family must live and work. Although Herrera does not venture into these conflicts in his text, it is clear that the strong mother, Lucha, gives her son the tools to navigate life through the challenges of being poor and in a minority. Collins highlights this difficult mothering task: "Latino mothers face the complicated task of shepherding their children through the racism of the dominant society and the reactions to that racism framing cultural beliefs internal to Hispanic communities" (71). Lucha proves successful at this task because her son can see the memorable and positive aspects of his life.

At the close of the book, Lucha announces that it is time for the family to settle down in one place and send Juanito to school. She recognizes the importance of education. The narrator also recognizes some of what he has learned through his migratory life. Herrera writes:

> I was eight years old and I had gathered the landscapes of the Valley close to my heart:
> my father curling a tractor around the earth,
> my mother holding her head up high with song.
> Our little square loaf house swerved down the spiral of the mountains into the cities of Southern California.
> As the cities came into view, I knew
> one day I would follow my own road.
> I would let my voice fly the way my mother recited poems, the way my father called the doves. (29)

Herrera leaves us with the image of the strong poet-mother and the father with the power to call the doves. This is certainly not the stereotypical image of the poor, uneducated farmworker woman so often depicted in literature and the media. This mother understands the power of education and art, and she passes that value on to her son.

Equipping Children to Survive Racial Oppression

Perhaps one of the most unique and important tasks that minority mothers must face is equipping their children to shape their identities despite bias and racism. Dorothy E. Roberts articulates this unique experience and task in her article, "Racism and Patriarchy in the Meaning of Motherhood." She writes:

> Most white women do not know the pain of raising Black children in a racist society. It is impossible to explain the depth of sorrow felt at the moment a mother realizes she birthed her precious brown baby into a society that regards her child as just another unwanted Black charge. Black mothers must bear the

incredible task of guarding their children's identity against innumerable messages that brand them as less than human. (5)

I would argue that a similar pain extends to all mothers of children who are not part of the ethnically dominant culture. Like Herrera's Lucha, who is of Mexican descent, the African American mother in Katheryn Russell-Brown's *Little Melba and Her Big Trombone* has to help her child navigate through racism and sexism. Russell-Brown's book features the story of Melba Doretta Liston, a jazz virtuoso who was one of the first women, of any race, to become a world-class trombone player, composer, and arranger. The book was awarded the Coretta Scott King Illustrated Award Honor in 2014. Russell-Brown is a professor of law and director of the Center for the Study of Race and Race Relations at the University of Florida. Her work informs her writing.

In *Little Melba and Her Big Trombone*, we see how Melba's mother invested in her daughter early on, helping to shape her character. Momma recognizes the trombone is a big instrument for her daughter, but she grants her daughter a vote of confidence by purchasing it. "Momma Lucille bought the shiny trombone on the spot. She couldn't say no to her only child. Melba beamed from ear to ear and squeezed her new friend." Melba goes on to teach herself to play trombone with the encouragement of her mother and Grandpa John. Russell-Brown writes, "Before long, Melba and her horn were making magic. She was only eight when the local radio station invited her to play solo. Momma Lucille and Grandpa John were so proud as they watched little Melba play her big trombone." Melba's mother encourages her to be an overcomer as the two move to Los Angeles in 1937 during hard times. Melba learns to turn prejudice and hurt feelings into "soulful music," which comes into play later when "jealous boys call her bad names." Throughout her career, Melba has to deal with sexism. The book details, "Still, Melba was lonely. She was the only woman in the band. Some of the men were cruel. Others acted as if she wasn't there. Melba let the music in her head keep her company."

Even eight decades after Melba was born, our current events prove a need for books like this one. In 2014, a series of high-profile shootings of unarmed black males in places like Ferguson, Missouri, by police officers—as well as retaliatory shootings of police officers by civilians claiming to be acting on the behalf of those unarmed black victims—led to widespread protests, rioting, and much public debate about where the United States stands today in terms of historical, institutional, and personal racism. The volatile nature of this social conversation is clear evidence that mothers, particularly mothers of color, still face the task of navigating racism with their children. Russell-Brown writes about the racism Melba faced:

> Rough times came when Melba traveled down South with singer Billie Holiday and her band. Some white folks didn't show good manners toward folks with brown skin. Hotel rooms were hard to come by, and the band members often had to sleep on the bus. Restaurants didn't always want their business. In the clubs, audiences sometimes just sat and stared at the band, or didn't show up at all.

Although Melba wants to quit, her fans won't let her. Perhaps digging deep for that "overcomer" character quality modeled by her mother, Melba goes on to pursue her music career and play with some of the jazz greats, including Dizzy Gillespie, Duke Ellington, and Quincy Jones. Collins, in "Shifting the Center: Race, Class, and Feminist Theorizing about Motherhood," discusses this issue of how minority women have to negotiate relationships that are marked by racism and also teach their children how to do so. Collins writes that "women of color's motherwork requires reconciling two contradictory needs concerning identity. First, preparing children to cope with and survive within systems of racial oppression is essential," and "a second dimension of this mothering tradition involves equipping children with skills to challenge the systems of racial oppression" (68, 69). Melba's mother helps equip her to survive the racism she must endure later in life. Melba defies stereotypes and eventually becomes a pioneer in the world of jazz. The mainstream "good mother" is rarely depicted dealing with the complications of race relations because, as Collins points out, most mothers in the majority culture are not forced to reconcile this for themselves or for their children.

Multidimensional Minority Mamas

These noteworthy children's books give us a window into the lives of a more multidimensional mother. As we have identified, the minority mother often defies the patterns of traditional mothering ideology still prevalent in mainstream best-selling children's books. She is resilient and confident, strong and creative, sexual and smart. This mother encourages dreams and free choice in her children, extending her arms to the community and equipping them for survival in the sometimes difficult and even racist world around them. She is not to be viewed as the opposite of the "good mother," but she is an alternative mother from whom we all can learn.

Roberts explains, "The meaning of motherhood in America is molded on the basis of race as well as gender" (6). This is a key point as we consider why children's books depicting mothers from ethnic minority backgrounds provide a different script from the reproduction of "traditional mothering ideology" in mainstream books. Is it easier for minority mothers to redefine mothering apart from the mainstream myth? Perhaps minority mothers are better equipped to defy the myth of the "good mother" because they already sit at the fringes of mainstream culture and do not feel the pressure to fit into a middle-class, white-generated stereotype of the "good mother." Black writer Rosemarie Robothom speaks to this issue in "Making Up the Truth," the introduction to her anthology *Mending the World: Stories of Family by Contemporary Black Writers*. Robothom writes:

> Marginalized as we are in the societies of the New World, Black writers were faced with "making up" the truth, literally writing ourselves and our experiences into being. In doing so, we chose to reject the more negative images of ourselves reflected by others in favor of defining our own realities. (xx)

In a sense, minority mothers like writers of color have already been rejected, so they have a blank canvas on which to paint their own picture. Maya Angelou paints her own picture of motherhood in her essay "Great Expectations," the preface to Robothom's *Mending the World: Stories of Family by Contemporary Black Writers*. Angelou's experience deepens our understanding of how it is different for a mother of color. She describes the unique gift she gave her son:

> I didn't have a great mansion to give him, or the storied names to make people shiver in the marketplace, and I didn't have large packets of everlasting earth, and I didn't have bank accounts and cash. So I told him, "You're the best, you're the greatest, you're the finest, by gosh." And he was. And he is. And he *believed* it. (xii)

Angelou, a strong woman, an iconic writer, and an admired mother, was able to rewrite the script of the "good mother" by passing her survival skills as well as her deep sense of self-worth on to her son. She believed, so he, in turn, believed there was a different ending to the story.

Another well-known writer-mama, Alice Walker, joins Angelou in rewriting the mother story. In her poem "A Woman Is Not a Potted Plant," she gives a glimpse of a woman who is free from the confines of the myth of motherhood. Like Angelou, she moves beyond the "giving tree" image, freeing women from the roots of the "good mother" myth. The poem opens,

> A woman is not a
> potted plant
> her roots bound
> to the confines
> of her house.

These words set the tone for the poem. Walker may be providing a rebuttal to the "giving tree" image, where the mother is bound to her home and can only wait for her son to come visit or asking for something. The poem goes on to describe how women are not defined by sex or race or how they provide nourishment for their children, but rather a woman is

> a wilderness
> unbounded
> holding the future
> between each breath.

We can learn from Angelou and Walker just as we can learn from the diversity of mothers already highlighted here. They each provide a call and response to the *Giving Tree* mother image, freeing not just themselves, but other women as well, from the strangling roots of the "good mother" myth. The voices of these women are an inspiration, a call to action that all of us have the ability and opportunity to rewrite the story and share a new vision of motherhood with future generations.

Notes

1. Very little scholarly attention has been paid to mothers of color in children's books despite the recent growth of interdisciplinary interest in the topic. See the publishing list of Demeter Press, particularly Andrea O'Reilly's *Mothers, Mothering and Motherhood Across Cultural Differences: A Reader*.

2. While I am aware that the more scholarly term is "mothers of color," I have chosen to use the term "minority mothers" because not all ethnic groups under discussion

identify themselves as being "of color." Further, each ethnic group under consideration has historically experienced a level of systemic oppression as a minority population in North America.

3. On his website Munsch writes of *Love You Forever*: "I had written it as a memorial for two stillborn babies we had in 1979 and 1980." This backstory has been widely publicized.

Works Cited

Angelou, Maya. "Preface: Great Expectations." *Mending the World: Stories of Family by Contemporary Black Writers*. Ed. Rosemarie Robotham. New York: BasicCivitas, 2003. ix-xx. Print.

Bassin, Donna. "Maternal Subjectivity in the Culture of Nostalgia: Mourning and Memory." *Representations of Motherhood*. Ed. Donna Bassin, Margaret Honey, and Meryle Mahrer Kaplan. New Haven: Yale UP, 1994. 162–73. Print.

Brown-Wood, JaNay. *Imani's Moon*. Waterton: Mackinac Island, 2014. Print.

Collins, Patricia Hill. "Shifting the Center: Race, Class, and Feminist Theorizing about Motherhood." *Representations of Motherhood*. Ed. Donna Bassin, Margaret Honey, and Meryle Mahrer Kaplan. New Haven: Yale UP, 1994. 56–74. Print.

First, Elsa. "Mothering, Hate, and Winnicott." *Representations of Motherhood*. Ed. Donna Bassin, Margaret Honey, and Meryle Mahrer Kaplan. New Haven: Yale UP, 1994. 147–61. Print.

Fraustino, Lisa Rowe. "The Apple of Her Eye: The Mothering Ideology Fed by Best-selling Trade Picture Books." *Critical Approaches to Food in Children's Literature*. Ed. Kara K. Keeling and Scott T. Pollard. Children's Literature and Culture 59. New York: Routledge, 2009. 57–72. Print.

Herrera, Juan Felipe. *Calling the Doves/El Canto De Las Palomas*. San Francisco: Children's, 1995. Print.

Joosse, Barbara M. *Mama, Do You Love Me?*. San Francisco: Chronicle, 1991. Print.

Leiner, Katherine. *Mama Does the Mambo*. New York: Hyperion, 2001. Print.

Maughan, Shannon. "Celebrating Shel Silverstein: Five Book Birthdays." *Publisher's Weekly*. 21 Oct. 2014. Web.

Mora, Pat. *The Desert Is My Mother/El Desierto Es Mi Madre*. Houston: Piñata, 1994. Print.

Munsch, Robert. "All About Robert Munsch." *Robertmunch.com*. Web. 17 Jan. 2015.

———. *Love You Forever*. Richmond Hill: Firefly, 1986. Print.

O'Reilly, Andrea. Ed. *Mothers, Mothering and Motherhood Across Cultural Differences: A Reader*. Toronto: Demeter, 2014. Print.

Roback, Diane. "Hollywood Comes Calling." *Publisher's Weekly*. 252 (28 March 2005): 36–46. *Academic Search Elite*. Wyndham Robertson Library, Roanoke, VA. 27 July 2005.

Roberts, Dorothy E. "Racism and Patriarchy in the Meaning of Motherhood." *Journal of Gender and the Law* 1 (1993): American University Washington College of Law, Washington, DC. Web. 18 December 2014.

Robotham, Rosemarie. "Introduction: Making Up the Truth." *Mending the World: Stories of Family by Contemporary Black Writers*. Ed. Rosemarie Robotham. New York: BasicCivitas, 2003. xvii-xxiii. Print.

Russell-Brown, Katheryn. *Little Melba and Her Big Trombone*. New York: Lee and Low, 2014.

Thurer, Shari. *The Myths of Motherhood: How Culture Reinvents the Good Mother*. Boston: Houghton Mifflin, 1994.

Walker, Alice. "One Child of One's Own." *In Search of Our Mothers' Gardens: Womanist Prose*. San Diego: Harcourt Brace, 1983. 371–93. Print.

———. "What Can I Give My Daughters Who Are Brave?" *Anything We Love Can Be Saved: A Writer's Activism*. New York: Ballantine, 1997. 89–107. Print.

Chapter 6

Cultural-Historical Activity Theory and the Expansive Cycle of Mothering while Black

Lauren Causey and Karen Coats

Langston Hughes's poem "The Negro Mother" begins to shade an understanding of why the *context* of mothering is of equal merit with discussions about the *process* of mothering in children's and young adult literature depicting African Americans. He writes:

> Oh, my dark children, may my dreams and my prayers
> Impel you forever up the great stairs—
> For I will be with you till no white brother
> Dares keep down the children of the Negro Mother.

While white Western culture stresses individual autonomy and focuses on the nuclear family as the most significant site of mothering activity, Hughes's invocation of a mother who transcends such autonomy and specificity emphasizes the interconnectedness of the black community, bound together by a systemic oppression that conditions the experience of mothering in specific ways. Hughes's "Negro Mother" crosses generations and works within social structures that decenter her own individual experience with her children; she mothers her children in the contexts of a fraught history and a present that continues to be dangerous, as evidenced by the tolling bell of names that are burned into our public conscience: Emmett Till, Trayvon Martin, Jordan Davis, Michael Brown, Tamir Rice, Freddie Gray . . . to say nothing of the countless murdered black children whose names don't make it into the national headlines. In this chapter, we will be exploring those contexts as they appear in a set of texts that follow similar patterns of what it means to mother while black across different genres: Eloise Greenfield's three-generation memoir, *Childtimes*; Jacqueline Woodson's picture book, *Show Way*; Marilyn Nelson's heroic crown of sonnets, *A Wreath for Emmett Till*; Angela Johnson's multivoiced young adult novel, *Toning the Sweep*; and Renée Watson's young adult novel, *This Side of Home*. Our approach to these texts is through cultural historical activity theory (hereafter referred to as CHAT), a methodology that challenges the notion of individual autonomy and instead focuses on the interrelated contexts within which human activity takes place and acquires meaning and significance.

CHAT was initiated in the 1920s and 30s by a group of Russian psychologists led by Lev Vygotsky, A. N. Leontiev, and A. R. Luria as a response to their dissatisfaction with existing paradigms for how a person develops; in fact, they were commissioned by the post-1917 Soviet government to develop an approach to psychology incorporating Marxist principles that situated the individual within the larger collective.[1] Both behaviorism and certain strains of psychology and psychoanalysis position the individual as the hub of a wheel of ever-widening contexts, such as the family, society, and culture, to which he or she reacts in a pattern of stimulus and response according to inborn tendencies and capacities; these paradigms grant that a child is *influenced* by his contexts, and may even go so far as to say she is *shaped* or *constructed* by them, but they still conceive of both the individual and the contexts as static objects or entities that we approach largely through contemplation. CHAT challenges that basic assumption, emphasizing that an individual is not simply an autonomous agent reacting to outside forces. Instead, our development of a sense of self begins in activities that take place between our mothers and ourselves; a child's psyche appears interpsychologically before it appears intrapsychologically. Our use of adverbs here is intentional, as the psyche itself must be understood as an activity rather than an entity. Furthermore, the psyche as an activity is always in negotiation with wider systems of cultural rules, signs, distributed labor, communities, and tools. This is a profoundly different way of thinking about consciousness; it removes consciousness as the inborn center of human experience and does not replace it. Rather, it proposes an open structure of activity circulating among various culturally mediated elements and suggests that human consciousness is constantly emerging in and through the activities in which we partake. As Paul Prior explains,

CHAT argues that activity is situated in concrete interactions that are simultaneously improvised locally and mediated by historically-provided tools and practices, which range from machines, made-objects, semiotic means (e.g., languages, genres, iconographies), and institutions to structured environments, domesticated animals and plants, and, indeed, people themselves.

The texts that we have chosen to analyze are paradigmatic of the "historically-provided tools and practices" that condition the activity system of black mothering.

As a methodology, CHAT has not been widely taken up by literary studies. This may well be because the development of the novel, and especially the white young adult novel, has increasingly become the novel of development—that is, most novels about white young adults trace the psychological maturation of a single character whose mental changes result from reflections on his or her own experiences that take place over a limited segment of time (for instance, a school year or a summer). History and culture are, more often than not, irrelevant to the white protagonist, and mothers are usually either cautionary tales, unhelpful, or dead. But the memoirs, novels, picture book, and poetic cycle under study in this chapter do not function in this way, or, in the case of Watson's text, do not function in only this way. Instead, these works situate their characters in expansive cycles that call attention to their embeddedness in contexts of culture and history, with a strong sense of grateful indebtedness to their mothers; they each consistently conceive of their characters in nonindividualistic terms. Indeed, it is rare to find an African American children's text that does not explicitly position its characters within broader contexts of history and culture. Because of this tendency in the literature, CHAT is especially relevant as a heuristic tool with which to approach these texts, given that Engeström reflected that to navigate the theory is akin to traversing "preexisting dominant trails and boundaries made by others, often heavy with histories and power invested in them" as well as unearthing "new trails and intersections" ("Rough Draft" 313). Tracing the cycles of motherhood (old and new) within *Childtimes* mirrors the functions of the theory and allows a continually shifting focus from the granular details of the motherly lives of the authors and their ancestors to a broader focus on historical and cultural forces and back again. *A Wreath for Emmett Till* uses a poetic form that enacts the connectedness integral to its theme; *Show Way* does similar connecting work across generations of mothering using a visual form. *Toning the Sweep*, like *Childtimes*, allows multiple generations of mothers to tell their stories. And while each of these texts benefits from the understanding one may glean through a CHAT methodology, Watson's novel comes closest to its ideological imperative as a model of transformative practice (Roth et al., par. 26). The developers of CHAT were not simply interested in conceiving a new way of understanding the human psyche as an outgrowth of culture, history, and activity; as Roth and colleagues aver, "It's not just a theory for understanding. It's one that's here to assist us, perhaps, as a heuristic for going about transforming this world. . . . It's about us human beings shaping our environment and creating tools that allow us to shape it so that the world better provides for human needs" (par. 26).

A CHAT Analysis of Mothering in African American Youth Literature

The three mothers in Eloise Greenfield's[2] *Childtimes: A Three-Generation Memoir*—Eloise, Lessie, and Pattie—represent a slice of time in the litany of their ancestry. The three characters shift positions as the matriarch of *Childtimes*, a Coretta Scott King Award honor book. Eloise Greenfield, her mother, Lessie, and her grandmother, Pattie, each narrate a section of the book in a three-generation memoir that represents a dynamic interplay of the components of an activity system: tools, objects, rules, division of labor, contradictions. Their narrative bears significance as well in the context of language and theories about mothering and motherhood. The book's opening pages contain a brief section titled "Procession":

> We came, one behind the other, to our childtimes—grandmother, mother, daughter—just three marchers in a procession that stretches long and wide. Stretches across the ocean to the continent of Africa . . . all the way back to the beginning of human life on earth. Stretches outward to sisters and brothers and aunts and uncles and nephews and nieces and cousins. A long, wide, family procession with thousands of marchers. We are just three.

With these words, the women remember the historical routes that shape their own lives and that they, in turn, replicate by becoming "marchers" along the lineage that began so long ago.

In *Show Way*, Jacqueline Woodson similarly traces a lineage through eight generations of mothers in her family. The first named character is Soonie, but she is a reference point for a great-grandmother who, sold at the age of seven and reared by a storytelling caregiver called Big Mama, began the tradition in her family of making quilts with hidden messages of secret paths to freedom. Big Mama, then, is an incarnation of Hughes's "Negro Mother," dreaming, praying, but also acting to bring about the emancipation of the many children she mothered even though she didn't give birth to them. Her tools were her stories and her needle and thread as she equipped Soonie's great-grandmother with the strength to hope and perform acts of resistance with the tools available to her in the midst of her enslavement. Her legacy of activity was passed down to Soonie, who was grandmother to Georgiana, who is great-grandmother to Woodson's own daughter, Toshi Georgiana. Each generation participates in the form that the push for freedom, dignity, and civil rights takes for their time, as Soonie's great-grandma sewed "show way" quilts, Woodson's mother and aunt marched in the 1960s, and several of the women were storytellers and writers. In these two texts, we can see how the word "march" becomes a privileged signifier for the black community, linking generations through shared history and language. But we also see how mothering itself becomes a signifier for historical connectedness and transformation; each "Negro Mother" in these texts draws on her foremothers for the strength that impels her up the great stair.

Each of these sections of *Childtimes* is preceded by a brief overview of the time period entitled "Landscape." The entire book also begins with a "Landscape" section, which could in fact be read as a CHAT manifesto, given the ideology it expresses regarding the interdependence of individuals with the events of their time period:

People are a part of their time. They are affected, during the time that they live, by the things that happen in their world. Big things and small things. A war, an invention such as radio or television, a birthday party, a kiss. All of these experiences help to shape people, and they, in turn, help to shape the present and the future.

Greenfield continues, "*This is a book about family. Kinsfolk touching across the centuries, walking with one hand clasping the hands of those who have gone before, the other hand reaching back for those who will come after.*" This same sentiment is depicted through both text and pictures in Woodson's *Show Way*, and through the unusual narrative technique in Angela Johnson's *Toning the Sweep* of including first-person, contemplative stories from fourteen-year-old Emmie's mother and grandmother. While it is certainly not unusual to have a multivoiced narrative in young adult literature, the other voices are most often those of peers. Emmie and her mother, Diane, are visiting Grandmama Ola's home in the desert for a final time before moving Ola to Cleveland, where she will live with them until she dies of cancer. As Emmie videotapes scenes from Ola's beloved home and the friends she will leave behind, her mother reflects on the differences between the way she views the house and the way Emmie views it. Ola had whisked Diane away from Alabama after her husband, Diane's father, was killed by white men angry over his new car, not leaving her time to grieve her father's death. Diane left her mother as soon as she was old enough. Ola's narrative focuses on how she felt when she found out that her daughter had given birth to a daughter, and how she will need Emmie's courage to strengthen her for the days ahead. Emmie, on the other hand, has only positive memories of the desert, but she knows that both Ola and her mother need a ceremony to mark the loss of husband and father, so she calls on a tradition from the past to mark his passing, drumming on a plow to create a sound called "toning the sweep."

Each of these books thus focuses explicitly on the interconnections between culture, history, and activity as contexts for their intergenerational reflections on mothering. They each describe how mothering happened within one African American family, and the social and cultural conditions that changed what mothering meant from one generation to the next. The protagonists keep at the center of their life stories the "problem" of being black in a country that uses both institutionalized and ideological mechanisms of oppression. In James Baldwin's words, "to be born black in America is an immediate, a mortal challenge" (129), and this notion is relevant to the narratives told by each of the women. Social class, power, general and individual histories, and other sociocultural elements play key roles within activity systems. As literary works that employ multiple narrators and tell the stories of multiple generations, these texts are exemplary of the "multivoiced formation" of an activity system, a system which expands according to the "reorchestration of those voices, of the different viewpoints and approaches of the various participants" (Engeström, "Transformation" 35). Engeström further posits that CHAT is an approach "that can dialectically link the individual and the social structure" (19). Thus, the chorus of voices that appear in these texts, mingled with historical and contemporary iterations of African American mothering, is well served by a CHAT analysis.

Renée Watson's *This Side of Home* uses a different approach to reflect the "multivoiced formation" of mothering within an activity system. Her novel appears at first blush to be a relatively traditional, first-person young adult narrative. However, it soon becomes clear that Watson has developed what Bakhtin would call a polyphonic work, one which gives voice to a diversity of opinions about the gentrification of a Portland, Oregon, neighborhood. The narrator, Maya, has a twin, Nikki. They have been named after their mother's favorite poets, Maya Angelou and Nikki Giovanni, immediately establishing a connection with their cultural heritage through their mother's desire. Maya and Nikki, however, are of two minds with regard to the transformation of their neighborhood into a hipster paradise of coffee shops, health-food restaurants, and trendy boutiques; Nikki is well pleased to have a safer neighborhood with cool places to hang out, while Maya is disturbed that the businesses are all owned by white people. Most troubling, however, is that their best friend, Essence, and her mother have been priced out of their home, as their landlord evicted them and sold the place to a white family. Maya is soon in conflict not only with her sister but also within herself, as she finds herself falling for her new white neighbor. How can she be a girl who cares about race and class issues and still be attracted to a white boy? While most young adult texts would have Maya work this out as if her mother were not in the picture, Maya's mother's opinion matters to her; throughout the text, she is both role model and conscience for Maya, as Maya reflects on what her mother says and what Maya imagines she would say about Maya's actions and thoughts. Watson takes great care to individualize her characters while embedding them in communal structures: Maya and Nikki's mother is a steady, smart community activist, while Essence's mother is an abusive alcoholic. The mothers are friends, however, and Maya treats Essence's mother with care and respect, while Essence turns to Maya's mother for a place to live when her mother once again fails to stay sober.

At the heart of Watson's text is a model and context for action. Both of Maya's parents are community activists, and when her new principal implements policies that Maya sees as disempowering, she too takes on that mantle. Her mother, oddly enough, is troubled by this. She has become weary of sharing her husband with the community and wishes for more time for them as a family, reflecting, perhaps, her embeddedness in white communities of value and practice as well as more expansive black ones. She is also fearful of the violence that sometimes attends protests of racial inequality. Maya has to remind her of her own past, when she pressured the city to improve the local park for her girls, but her reluctance to see her daughter engage in activism suggests some of the complexities that underlie Engeström's model of mediated action (see figure).

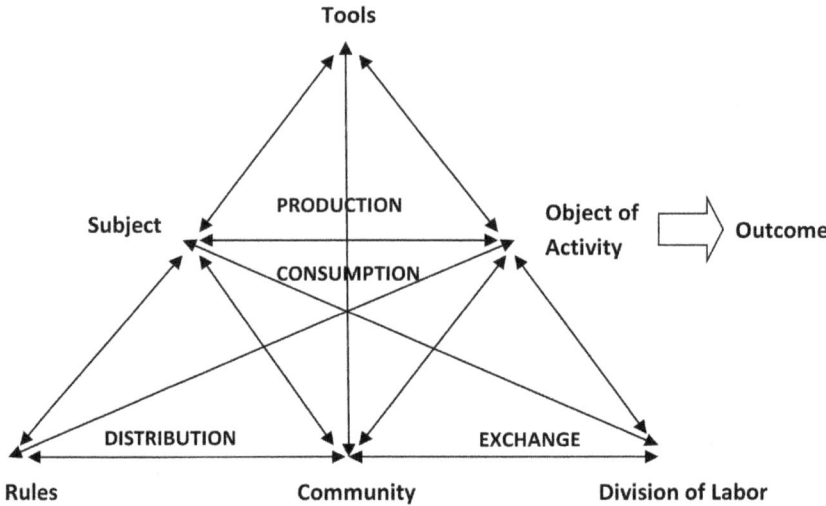

Engeström's model of mediated action

As a counter to the direct and overly simplistic stimulus/response model that dominated the psychology of his day, Vygotsky first developed the idea that human activity involves a person working toward a goal through the material and conceptual tools culture and history make available. Engeström later elaborated the model to account for at least six components (*tools, subject, object, rules, community,* and *division of labor*) that connect with and influence each other, and together they shape the *outcome* of the activity system. Additionally, other macrolevel components (*production, consumption, distribution,* and *exchange*), which some scholars overlay onto the model, are indicative of its roots in Marxist theories of material production.[3] The intention of blending so-called local factors with broader, distal-level forces is to create a system that is dynamic, rather than static, and to saturate any analysis of individual activity with reflections about sociocultural factors, and vice versa.

Engeström referred to an *object* as "a project under construction, moving from potential raw material to a meaningful shape and to a result or outcome" ("Transformation" 65). Engeström also noted that once a goal has been satisfied, a new object is then created, which is then accompanied by new actions. We conceive of *object* as the purpose of, or motivations behind, a subject's actions within an activity system. Eloise shares with her mother and grandmother the same *object* in *Childtimes*. Their stated goal for writing is to show "*black people struggling, not just to stay alive, but to live, to give of their talents, whether many or few.*" They use their book to show how, "*Through all of their pain and grief, and even their mistakes, black people have kept on going, had some good times, given a lot of love to one another, and never stopped trying to help their children get on board the freedom train.*" We can infer that Marilyn Nelson had a similar goal in mind when writing *A Wreath for Emmett Till*. She says, "I was nine years old when Emmett Till was lynched in 1955. His name and history have been a part of most of my life. When I decided to write a poem about lynching for young people, I knew I would write about Emmett Till . . . I also knew that I would write this poem as a heroic crown of sonnets." Watson's compassionate treatment of characters such as Essence's mom and her complex portrait of Maya indicate a commitment to support young people caught up in the complexities of negotiating life in a society where individual goals are overshadowed by systemic injustice and oppression.

The women, as authors and characters, are also the *subject* of the text. The term "subject" is defined by V. P. Lektorsky as the bearer of activity and can refer to an animate or inanimate individual entity or collective. Lektorsky argued that a subject has "its own aims, interests, memory, and norms"; it is "the unity of consciousness, the unity of an individual biography, and the center of making decisions" and is therefore inherently situated in cultural and social contexts (81–82). In each of the texts under consideration here, there is an explicit reference to the "aims, interests, memory, and norms" of the women in relation to these contexts. Emmie, for instance, recalls the historical tradition of "toning the sweep"; by evoking this cultural memory, she brings together the consciousness of the women in her life. Maya meets a character who is ubiquitous in African American youth literature, an older man who serves as memory keeper and tells her the history of her neighborhood, and she ends her story by bringing her friends to meet him. Woodson weaves her ancestors into the story of her own past and future. Each of these subjects demonstrates the CHAT ideology that an individual and her contexts are intertwined; in so doing, they work against the white Western model of autonomous individualism in favor of a communitarian ethic.

The *community* of *Childtimes* mostly consists of "kinsfolk" or the relatives shown in the "Family Tree" image that precedes part 1 of the book. "Procession" expresses that "we are just three" of the "sisters and brothers and aunts and uncles and nephews and nieces and cousins" who together form a procession that "stretches long and wide" (Greenfield). A *community* is defined as a grouping of participants who relate to the same object, perhaps in different ways. Jean Lave and Etienne Wenger theorize that one learns what it means to be a member of a community by apprenticing, or by participating in situated activities in which one learns by doing, rather than by observing. In *This Side of Home*, Tony, the white boy Maya is interested in, is at first reluctant to complete an assignment to learn about journalists who suffered to get out the truth about racial injustice, because he thought they were all black. Maya realizes that just as it is hard to be always portrayed as a victim, it is also hard to be always cast as an oppressor merely by virtue of your race. She points out that some of the journalists were white, and she further reflects that she has more interests in common with Tony than she does with Devin, the black boy that her mother wishes she would date. Tony's interests and commitments bring him and Maya closer to what Lave and Wenger term a "community of practice," referring to "participation in an activity system about which participants share understandings concerning what they are doing and what that means in their lives and for their communities" (98).

Within the community there exists *division of labor*, which means that each participant of the activity system enacts different roles and responsibilities toward achieving the identified goal. The three women of *Childtimes*, Pattie, Lessie, and Eloise, each take on a part of the book, and each becomes both narrator and protagonist in her own narrative. Eloise writes about chores, which her mama and grandma also have to do. She also writes about the kind of work that men in her family take up, namely, sharecropping, working on the old car, and working odd jobs at stores. Males in Eloise's section of their book are depicted as workers and family providers. Eloise's daddy goes north to "make a way for us," she writes, "looking for safety, for justice, for freedom, for work, looking for a good job" (126–27). Additionally, the storytelling work of the women in *Childtimes*, like that of Woodson in *Show Way*, is complemented by an illustrator. Nelson's work is also illustrated, and the artist, Philippe Lardy, provides a detailed note that describes his process in rendering the poetry's themes through his illustrations. But the labor of all of these works is of course completed by the readers themselves, as they coconstruct meaning from the texts.

Labor is always facilitated by *tools* and carried out according to community *norms* and *rules*. Pattie uses memory as the primary tool for reaching the book's goal. In a direct address to readers, she writes, "Yours is now, you're living your childtime right this minute, but I've to go way, way back to remember mine" (7). *Tools* (or *means*) are both immaterial and physical items, and in some cases *artifacts* (any documents, or items created by a subject) share a space with *tools* on the activity triangle. In this analysis, one of the most important tools is something we might loosely call genre—that is, even though the texts take different forms, they all share the larger designation of African American literature, which has come, over time, to possess distinctive features and thus creates contexts for its own reproduction, reception, and transformation. Nelson, for instance, adopts a form first developed in the 1300s to transform the ugly tragedy of Emmett Till's death into a legacy of sublime beauty. "The strict form," she writes, "became a kind of insulation, a way of protecting myself from the intense pain of the subject matter." For all its insulating power, however, the poetry has great affective impact on readers, sensitizing them anew to a horror that is still very much with us.

In each of the different forms of these texts, the generic conventions that we have already discussed—the explicit invocation of historical perspectives, the depiction of multiple generations, the attention to problems of systemic race-based oppression, the inclusion of multiple voices—contextualize the presentation of African American mothers. Insofar as literature itself is a mediating cultural tool, these books put forth an ideology that runs counter to white Western ideals of autonomy and the erasure of history. Considered as one element within a cultural historical activity system, African American literature thus provides a conceptual tool for understanding why the death of a single young man in Florida or Missouri or Cleveland or Baltimore can evoke such an intense and far-reaching response. The tendency of white Western thought structures is to isolate individual subjects within their immediate and specific contexts, divorced from both responsiveness and responsibility to cultural histories of oppression; while historical fiction with white protagonists is common, children's and young adult texts that represent and honor the perspectives of multiple generations within a single narrative are not. African American youth literature, by contrast, more often than not places its subjects within sociocultural activity systems so as to bear witness to the twin themes of W. E. B. DuBois's "double consciousness" and Henry Louis Gates's theory of "signifying."

DuBois posited that black people in American culture necessarily hold two different perspectives of ourselves at once: we view ourselves from our own perspective, and we also view ourselves from a perspective of how white people interpret us—that is, whether a whistle on the sidewalk might be too threatening, whether a hooded sweatshirt worn to shield one's face from a drizzly Florida night might cause one to be perceived as a suspect, and whether a turned-up radio might be enough of an annoyance to elicit gunshots. DuBois elucidated, "It is a peculiar sensation, this double-consciousness, this sense of always looking at one's self through the eyes of others, of measuring one's soul by the tape of a world that looks on in amused contempt and pity" (5). Thus, embedded within the stories that African Americans narrate is a two-pronged vantage point of interpretation, or—as in Gates's theory—a constant shifting back and forth between one's own blackness and an awareness of the significance of one's blackness in a country dominated by whites. While this shifting awareness threads through all of the texts we are considering, Watson's novel literalizes double consciousness not only through the opposite perspectives of the twins but also through Maya's frequent referrals to what her mother would think of her behavior and attitudes. Several of the sonnets of *A Wreath for Emmett Till* focus on the shifting perspectives Nelson imagines for Emmett's mother as she sought justice and remembrance for her son:

> Would you say yes, like the mother of Christ?
> Or would you say no to your destiny,
> mother of a boy martyr, if you could? (lines 12–14)

So this is the context of "The Negro Mother," who can reflect upon triumph as well as tragedy. Her sons and daughters have unique, individual lives that are rich and sufficient unto themselves, yet within their varied stories we can find familiar pathways that have been walked time and time again. These stories then become conceptual tools through which readers can experience empathy and work with greater understanding toward transformation.

Mothering for Social Change

Situated as it is within a broader Marxist framework, CHAT also takes into account the faraway forces that influence the protagonists' lives—the distal-level actions of *production, consumption, distribution,* and *exchange*. These four elements are strongly situated in Marx's philosophies put forth in his work *Grundrisse* and are therefore angled toward addressing social structures—especially the possibility of radical social change. The element of *production* is meant to yield change, and multiple thinkers have noted that activity itself results in transformation (Vygotsky; Engeström "Expanding";

Engeström "Transformation"; Roth). In fact, Roth characterized *production* as a "driver of change" (5) within the intricate activity system. By producing and publishing stories and poems that shed light on the activity system of mothering while black, these texts do a kind of mothering work in and of themselves, acting in the role of Woodson's Big Mama and Hughes's "Negro Mother," sharing stories and dreams with all children rather than only the ones to whom they physically gave birth.

Once production occurs, *distribution* is possible. Distribution can be analyzed both within the content of the texts and as the texts themselves circulate among readers. The lives of Eloise, Lessie, and Pattie can be considered to have been *distributed* according to the hand of history. The Great Migration leads Lessie to Norfolk, and Eloise to Washington, D.C., when the family lineage was begun in Bertie County, North Carolina. Economic forces are responsible for this, as the lumber mill that once made Parmele a thriving source of commerce, and which was owned by two white men, eventually closed, creating a void in the local job market. Similarly, the history told to Maya of her Portland neighborhood is one of black migration and struggle for better wages and opportunity that contextualizes and complicates her attitudes toward the gentrification that is currently taking place, where property values and quality of life are seeing gains that are good for some of her black neighbors while pushing others once again to the margins.

Such contradictions between positive and negative social and economic change also operate in *Childtimes*, either within or between activity components. Eloise participates in the Great Migration, which is a signal of both change and resistance within the text. Because her family can no longer sustain itself in Parmele, they seek a different region in which to live. Eloise's father leaves to "make a way" for the family (126), and this shows that his character displays a strong sense of agency. Rather than accepting the family's plight that there is not enough income, he moves the family north. Once in her new home of Washington, D.C., Eloise feels that she "lived in a different place, a different Washington" than the one where the White House is located (145). This feeling is created by segregation, as she further explains: "There were a lot of things we couldn't do and places we couldn't go. Washington was a city for white people. But inside that city was another city. It didn't have a name and it wasn't all in one area, but it was where black people lived" (149). The contradiction here is that although Eloise's family journeys north for better opportunities, Washington presents new challenges that the family didn't face in Parmele. Essence and her mother experience a similar sense of exclusion based on the imbrication of socioeconomic class and race when they have to leave their home for a section of the city they can afford, one that is predominately black rather than integrated like Maya's gentrified neighborhood.

As Nancy D. Tolson has written, contradictions such as these find their ways into black children's literature through the blues aesthetic, that is, the expression of the pain and suffering of past and present experience through redemptive artistic forms that comingle sadness and joy. Pattie Frances Ridley Jones, the first narrator in *Childtimes*, was born in 1884, when "White farmers were angry because they now had to pay black workers.... In many areas, black schools and homes were burned, and people were dragged from their homes and murdered.... It was hard to stay alive, hard to get jobs, hard to get an education" (Greenfield 3). She transforms these painful memories into richly evocative stories that relate not only pain but also appealing warmth and humor. Pattie's daughter, Lessie, born in 1906, writes about her mother admiringly: "Mama really knew how to tell a story. She could make it sound as if it had really happened," and "I liked being near Mama. When she cooked, I would sit in a chair right near the stove" and talk about the day's events (Greenfield 3). Nelson similarly invokes the blues aesthetic in her transformation of Emmett Till's grisly murder into a heroic crown of sonnets. In *Toning the Sweep*, Diane and Ola redeem their painful memories of tragedy and estrangement by telling their stories of mothering Emmie, and she honors their pain by toning the sweep for her grandfather as a way of helping them move into a transformed future.

These invocations of the blues aesthetic in their storytelling mark out some of the distinctive challenges of mothering while black. Eloise, Lessie, and Pattie, by writing of their daily triumph over the "mortal challenge" of being black in the United States at times of tremendous upheaval and change (Baldwin 169), reify theories of mothering that take into account DuBois's two-pronged awareness of being African American in the United States. As Dorothy Roberts notes:

> There are joys and sorrows that most mothers share.... There are also experiences mothers do not share, in part because of race. Most white mothers do not know the pain of raising Black children in a racist society.... Black mothers must bear the incredible task of guarding their children's identities against innumerable messages that brand them as less than human. (4–5)

Roberts de-essentializes scholarly conversations about mothering by discussing ways in which race and class intersect with gender, and she thereby creates new definitions of what it means to be an African American woman who is also a mother. She enhances her argument by rendering historical tracings of ways that racism and patriarchy have reshaped what motherhood means for black mothers, starting with the facts that, under slavery, many women were initiated into motherhood because of a rape by their master and that black mothers' sons and daughters were considered "property," which could be "sold" and relocated.

Besides equipping their children with strategies like the blues aesthetic, black mothers are also faced with the challenge of unequal distribution and exchange of these positive literary messages. While Woodson's text directly addresses the separation of Soonie's great-grandmother from her own mother through being sold, it is a difficult subject to broach in contemporary literature for young children, and the texts that do address it are unlikely to come into the hands of children victimized by the contemporary slave trade. Thus the imperative for production, distribution, and exchange falls into the hands of knowledgeable adults committed to becoming Hughes's "Negro Mother" by sharing these representations of mothering as a form of social activism. While Marx emphasized the interdependence of the elements of production, distribution, consumption, and exchange, the circulation of the social facts of mothering while black, in both textual representation and real life, have not yet realized his ideal. According to Marx:

> Production creates the objects that correspond to the given needs; distribution divides them up according to social laws; exchange further parcels out the already divided shares in accord with individual needs; and finally, in consumption, the product steps outside this social movement and becomes a direct object and servant of individual need, and satisfies it in being consumed. (89)

While the books under discussion certainly meet any and all definitions of good literature, the social norms and economic conditions that govern distribution and exchange still tend to marginalize these expressions of the "Negro Mother." Although Eloise did not write about having children, the stories told by Pattie, Lessie, and Eloise in *Childtimes* reflect common values of mothering among the women. These values include the passing on of family stories from one generation to the next. This is exemplified in all three women, and especially in Eloise's career choice as a professional children's book writer. The same is true for Woodson, Nelson, Johnson, and Watson, who all participate in the mothering work of sharing stories with young readers. All of these writers also exemplify the idea that being African American mothers and women necessitates daily strivings in the face of injustice.

If CHAT involves unearthing pathways "heavy with history and power invested in them," exposing those routes, and continually shifting between the here-and-now and the larger, macrolevel forces that created those well-worn pathways in the first place, then further discussion will reveal ways in which these literary mothers' burden is not unlike other women's stories today. Hughes's poem "The Negro Mother" allows us to linger on what once was (and what still remains as) a fundamental conception of motherhood among African American women—that is, protecting their children from oppressive forces (referred to by Hughes as "the white brother") and imploring and inspiring their children to ascend to their greatest potential ("the great stairs"). History provides no shortage of figures who did, indeed, ascend to soaring heights, in large part because of the effort and sacrifice of their mothers. Yet, the collective memory of storytellers in the African American tradition will also always remember the tragic cases along with the triumphant ones. The two are inextricably linked and are as important to the tenets of this chapter as the relationship between past and present ideations of mothering.

Other Mothers' Sons

The mothers of Emmett Till, Trayvon Martin, Jordan Davis, Michael Brown, Tamir Rice, and Freddie Gray—as well as others whose names have not risen to our national consciousness—have in common that they are the "mother of a boy martyr," and the "mother of sorrows, of justice denied" (Nelson, lines 14, 2). Emmett Till was lynched in 1955 in Money, Mississippi, by a gang of white men who alleged that the fourteen-year-old whistled at a white woman. The young teen was beaten, had an eye gouged out, and was strapped to an industrial fan before being thrown in a nearby river, where his body stayed for three days. Emmett Till's mother, Mamie Till-Mobley, intentionally chose an open casket to show the world what had been done to her son. Till-Mobley later reflected that the "self-confidence and a sense of life's possibilities" (Till-Mobley and Benson) that she had tried to give to her son while parenting him as a single mother in Chicago may have brought about his demise, because that disposition didn't jibe with the social codes of the Deep South at that time.

Compassion for Emmett Till's mother at the time of his death elicited worldwide attention in much the same way the spotlight shone on Sybrina Martin, the mother of Trayvon Martin, for many months after the seventeen-year-old's murder by a racist neighborhood watch volunteer in 2012 in Sanford, Florida. So too goes the story of Jordan Davis, who was also killed at age seventeen in 2012, while he sat in the back of a sports utility vehicle that was parked at a gas station and playing loud music in Jacksonville, Florida. Jordan's murder was at the hands of a different patron of the gas station, a white man who was annoyed by the music and by the presence of the African American young men who rode in the car along with Jordan. Lucia McBath, Jordan's mother, echoed nearly the same words that had been spoken decades earlier by Mamie Till-Mobley: In a 2014 interview, McBath said of her parenting style, "We always encouraged him to be strong. To speak out. We tried to teach him to speak what you feel and think diplomatically" (qtd. in Coates). Jordan Davis was a good student who had traveled internationally, and his grandfather had been the leader of the NAACP in Illinois.

Civil unrest in Ferguson, Missouri, took place following Lesley McFadden's loss of her son Michael Brown in 2014. The media zoomed in on what came to be known as simply #Ferguson, a metonym for an unarmed black teen who died because of a police officer's bullets, for the rage caused when authorities allowed his body to lie in the street (in the August sun) for four hours after the incident, and for the teen's nonexistent future. Then, #Baltimore came into existence when Freddie Gray died due to a severed spine he suffered while riding unrestrained in a police wagon in Baltimore, Maryland, in 2015. While protests at the death of Gray were swirling around Baltimore—peaceful and agitated—the actions of a black mother, Toya Graham, were captured on video, went viral, and garnered international press. Looking glamorous in a long ombré weave and false eyelashes as she attended the protest, Graham recognized her son, dressed in black, baggy sweatpants, among the crowd. She saw him pitching rocks at the riot police, and the video shows her maternal instinct to protect him from harm. Graham ran after her son, pulled at his clothes, yelled at him for taunting the police, and smacked him upside the head. Her story is interesting in that the conversations black mothers have with their sons, and, should words fail, the smacks a black mother may give her son to drill down on the idea of staying out of trouble, or just staying alive, are normally private. Graham's display of her protective love for her only son became public; it was distributed, exchanged, and consumed by millions, including the white audience who may just be becoming attuned to the historical and ongoing dangers of being black in America.

The list of black mothers' sons who have died violent deaths is too long. Nelson's elegy for the murdered Emmett Till thus speaks for all of these mothers in the expansive cycle of mothering while black:

> Surely you didn't know you would devote
> the rest of your changed life to dignified
> public remembrance of how Emmett died,
> innocence slaughtered by the hands of hate. (lines 5–8)

Our exploration of mothering in these few texts guided by CHAT is important in that it weaves together the past with the present and the tragic with the daily triumphs, told in the forms of a three-generation memoir, an autobiographical picture book, an illustrated crown of sonnets, and the multivoiced and polyphonic novel. The historically racist roots of the United States cannot be relegated to the past because they continually, and often silently, influence much of what goes on in the present day. With its dynamic heuristic making available the various components that comprise culture, history, and activity, CHAT enables us to see more clearly how the ideological gyres are reproduced and reified through a cycle of repetition and expansion over time.

The men who lynched Till in 1955 served no jail time, despite confessing to the crime. The murderer of Martin in 2012 also walked free immediately after the killing, and after a trial he was found "not guilty" and served no sentence. Davis's killer ordered a pizza after the incident and was initially not convicted of first-degree murder but is now serving jail time. At the time of this writing, six Baltimore police officers have been charged in the death of Freddie Gray, but the outcome of those charges has not yet been determined. Despite how devastating these truths are, what can provide hope is that there simultaneously exist well-trodden pathways through which African American mothers have impelled and will continue to impel their children toward light and progress, even in the face of arbitrary hatred. The activity of writing black lives, or reading them, is one such pathway.

Notes

1. In addition to its articulation in primary texts by Vygotsky, Leontiev, and later, Engeström, CHAT is most widely known through its application in educational psychology and composition pedagogy and theory, where resources abound. This, too, will be an applied discussion, so the theory will be explained only insofar as it is relevant to the current analysis. For a concise overview of the history and core principles of CHAT, we refer readers to chapter 2, "Understanding Cultural Historical Activity Theory," of Lisa C. Yamagata-Lynch, *Activity Systems Analysis Methods for Understanding Complex Learning Environments*, and Wolff-Michael Roth, "Activity Theory and Education: An Introduction."

2. An epilogue to *Childtimes* points out that Pattie Ridley Jones, Greenfield's grandmother, was deceased at the time of publication, but she had written a manuscript of life stories. Thus, only Greenfield and her mother (Little) are listed as coauthors on the book's cover in the three-generation memoir.

3. The idea of mapping onto the heuristic of the activity triangle the four Marxist principles of production, consumption, distribution, and exchange has been preconceived by scholars such as Wolff-Michael Roth. See Roth, "The Politics and Rhetoric of Conversation and Discourse Analysis: A Reflexive, Phenomenological Hermeneutic Analysis."

Works Cited

Baldwin, James. *Notes of a Native Son*. Boston: Beacon, 1990. Print.

Coates, Ta-Nehesi. "'I am still called by the God I serve to walk this out': A Conversation with Lucia McBath, Mother of Jordan Davis." *The Atlantic* 25 Feb. 2014. Print.

DuBois, W. E. B. *The Souls of Black Folk*. 1903. New York: Modern Library Edition, 2003. Print.

Engeström, Yrjö. "Activity Theory and Transformation." *Perspectives on Activity Theory*. Ed. Yrjö Engeström, Reijo Miettinen, and Raija-Leena Punamäki. Cambridge: Cambridge UP, 1999. Print.

———. "The Future of Activity Theory: A Rough Draft." *Learning and Expanding with Activity Theory*. Ed. Annalisa Sannino, Harry Daniels, and Kris Gutiérrez. New York: Cambridge UP, 2009. 303–28. Print.

———. *Learning by Expanding: An Activity-Theoretical Approach to Developmental Research*. Helsinki: Orienta-Konsultit, 1987. Print.

Gates, Henry L. *The Signifying Monkey: A Theory of African American Literary Criticism*. Oxford: Oxford UP, 1988. Print.

Greenfield, Eloise. *Childtimes: A Three-Generation Memoir*. Illus. Jerry Pinkney. New York: HarperCollins, 1979. Print.

Hughes, Langston. "The Negro Mother." *The Collected Poems of Langston Hughes*. 1931. Ed. Arnold Rampersad. New York: Vintage, 1995. Print.

Johnson, Angela. *Toning the Sweep*. New York: Orchard, 1993.

Lave, Jean, and Etienne Wenger. *Situated Learning: Legitimate Peripheral Participation*. New York: Cambridge University Press, 1991. Print.

Lektorsky, V. P. *Activity: Theories, Methodology, and Problems*. 1990. Orlando: Deutsch, 2009. Print.

Marx, Karl. *Grundrisse: Foundations of the Critique of Political Economy*. 1858. Trans. Martin Nicolaus. New York: Vintage, 1973. Print.

Nelson, Marilyn. *A Wreath for Emmett Till*. New York: Houghton Mifflin, 2005. Print.

Prior, Paul, et al. "Re-situating and Re-mediating the Canons: A Cultural-Historical Remapping of Rhetorical Activity." *Kairos* 11.3 (2007). Web. 7 February 2015.

Roberts, Dorothy. "Racism and Patriarchy in the Meaning of Motherhood." *Journal of Gender and the Law* 1 (1993): 1–38. Print.

Roth, Wolff-Michael. "Activity Theory and Education: An Introduction." *Mind, Culture, and Activity* 11.1 (2004): 1–8. Print.

———. "The Politics and Rhetoric of Conversation and Discourse Analysis: A Reflexive, Phenomenological Hermeneutic Analysis." *Forum: Qualitative Social Research* 2.2 (2001). Web. 7 February 2105.

Roth, Wolff-Michael, Luis Radford, and Lionel LaCroix. "Working with Cultural-Historical Activity Theory." *Forum: Qualitative Social Research* 13.2, Art. 23 (2012). Web. 7 February 2015.

Till-Mobley, Mamie, and Christopher Benson. *Death of Innocence: The Story of the Hate Crime that Changed America*. New York: Ballantine, 2004. Print.

Tolson, Nancy D. *Black Children's Literature Got De Blues: The Creativity of Black Writers and Illustrators*. New York: Lang, 2014. Print.

Vygotsky, Lev S. *Mind in Society: The Development of Higher Psychological Processes*. Ed. Michael Cole, Vera John-Steiner, Sylvia Scribner, and Ellen Souberman. Cambridge, MA: Harvard UP, 1978. Print.

Watson, Renée. *This Side of Home*. New York: Bloomsbury, 2015. Print.

Woodson, Jacqueline. *Show Way*. Illus. by Hudson Talbott. New York: Putnam, 2005.

Yamagata-Lynch, Lisa C. *Activity Systems Analysis Methods for Understanding Complex Learning Environments*. New York: Springer, 2010. Print.

Chapter 7

"The hills were in her bones": Living in the Blend of Mothers and Environments

Anna Katrina Gutierrez

The terms "Mother Earth" and "Mother Nature" are introduced to us from childhood to ascribe the symbiotic relationship between mother and child to our relationship with nature and the planet. Even though "Mother" and "Earth/Nature" belong to distinct categories—one a woman, the other the natural or physical world—our minds easily combine them into a unique and comprehensible mental image. We are able to make sense of the integrated ideas Mother Earth and Mother Nature by identifying similarities in the vocabulary associated with schemas of motherhood and nature/Earth, such as "nurture," "nourish," "fertile," and "fecund," and in vital relations, such as "source of food, water and shelter" and "treat with love and respect"; in other words, similarities in embodied cognitive acts that are structured in physical and cultural contexts and form the basis of scripts. Scripts describe a set of remembered actions, or "experiential repertoires," through which we filter our expectations and organize emergent information (Herman 89).[1]

Gilles Fauconnier and Mark Turner suggest that this kind of interactive meaning making comes naturally to us and, furthermore, that it is the key to human imagination. They state that the cross-linking of elements and vital relations between seemingly unrelated conceptual domains unfolds in a new emergent space rather than exists as a listing of comparisons and that this unique mental space is the product of *conceptual blending*, an automatic cognitive process in which a "third space" is formed from the inputs of two or more domains. This blended space then becomes the source of new meanings (42–44). For example, the scripts "picking fruit from a tree to eat" and "suckling from a mother's breasts" powerfully link motherhood and nature/Earth through the word "nourishment" and the recognition that food grown from the earth and milk produced in a woman's body create a similar and continuous experience of being provided and cared for. The nurturance and growth scripts contained within motherhood and nature/Earth and that link these concepts to one another undergird the coming-of-age script that lies at the heart of adolescent texts. Roberta Seelinger Trites argues that adolescence is represented in language as embodied metaphors, that is, journeying, imprisoning, awakening (66–67). In comprehending nurturing mother scripts, living Earth scripts, and adolescent coming-of-age scripts in relation to one another, Mother Earth arises as a third space that contains new and blended ideas of motherhood, childhood, and environment. From within this context, the parameters of the child-mother and child-Other relationships are transformed. Within the Mother Earth blend, all living beings are considered children of the Earth; hence, Other simultaneously means "different from me" and "a child (of Earth) like me." These new dimensions ultimately affect the development of subjectivity and agency of those who live in the blend.

The same cognitive process is activated when mothers are integrated with other types of environments. Similar transformations in child-mother and child-Other relationships occur as interactions between key concepts produce new meanings. Networks created in these mother-environment blends determine the child's perceptions and actions toward the domains he or she occupies and toward Others on the journey to adulthood. The mother's ability to provide a space of love, security, and comfort, as well as her attitudes toward social and environmental structures, are factors that shape the mother-environment blend, as are the mother's absence and the influence of other mother figures. Any of these situations affects the child's negotiations with this third space created by her own conceptual blend of mother and environment.

Although conceptual blending is an automatic operation, the meaning making that happens within the blend is a conscious process of interpretation, as described by Mary-Anne Shonoda (87). Mother-environment blends are created through the language, perception, memory, and imagination of the focalizing protagonists, who make specific statements that foreground the relationship between mother figures and the environmental space. These statements signal which facets of mother and environment are significant to the adolescent's growth and which may be passed over. Trites states, "The narratological study of adolescent literature, then, might well analyse the intersection between standard scripts (such as 'love triangles') and how the embodied adolescent characters involved will influence the adolescent reader's cognitive experience of that script" (*Growth* 69). I suggest that the intersection between scripts of nurturance, coming-of-age, and the environment's embodiment in mother figures (and vice versa) enhances the intersubjective development of the adolescent protagonist and encourages readers to think of the intersections between self, Others, and place in new ways.

In the following discussion, I offer a close examination of the child's interactive journey through mother-environment blends that either stand in opposition to or collaborate with one another. In the case of the former, the child's maturation comes from navigating the tensions between representations of motherhood wherein one negates the other. The latter shows how the combined influence of different types of mother environments reinforces the protagonist's growth into a mature and agentic subject. I explicate the cognitive processing that takes place when readers cross map mothers and environmental spaces, and the impact this blending has on emergent identities in Banana Yoshimoto's *Kitchen* (1988, trans. 1993), Gennifer Choldenko's *Al Capone Does My Shirts* (2004), and Terry Pratchett's *The Wee Free Men* (2003). The mother figures in *Kitchen*[2] are each blended with different aspects of nature and the modern Japanese home. Mikage's negotiations with these blends help her to piece herself together after a tragic loss. In *Al Capone Does My Shirts*, Moose superimposes the imagery and purpose of Alcatraz onto his relationship with his mother and autistic sister and their relationship with one another, and in doing so he finds autonomy as he finds his place on the prison island. In *The Wee Free Men*, Tiffany comes of age through her negotiations with mother-environment blends that represent conflicting views of motherhood, growth, and subjectivity. Granny Aching signifies a convergence of domestic and natural spaces, whereas the Faerie Queen represents a dangerous fusion of mother and wild magic. I have carefully chosen three popular novels that are very different from one another to show a variety of intersubjective relationships between young focalizers and mother environments. In bringing these texts together, I aim to show the usefulness of the blending framework across genres and regardless of the protagonist's gender and cultural background.

Collaborative Mother Environments in *Kitchen*

Kitchen makes ample use of the fluidity of magic realism in embodying the matrix of sociocultural relationships as domestic space. The cross-mapping of people and home spaces is made more significant when the reader engages with these concepts from within a Japanese context of social connectivity, and with the understanding that the cultural ideology of Japan subsumes the individual within family and community.

Yoshimoto's lyrical writing style and her masterful handling of traditional Japanese and modern imagery create a sense of being neither here nor there that contributes to the cross-mapping of environments and mothers and to local and international ideas of *shōjō* and adolescence.[3] Although often translated as "young women," the term *shōjo* is gender neutral and more accurately refers to a liminal period devoted to self-discovery, without the pressure of marriage and career (Treat 282–83). If Western adolescent culture yearns toward an embodied maturity, the *shōjō*'s power resides in a state of fluidity. In spite of cultural differences, the scripts and schemas of the Japanese *shōjō* and Western adolescence describe periods wherein agency develops from a heightened awareness of the self within the context of the community.

For Mikage, whose life is marked by death and loss, kitchens symbolize both the warmth and affection of familial relationships and the emptiness each person feels at the knowledge that, in spite of these loving connections, we are ultimately alone. The space of the kitchen conjures images of warmth, nourishment, and family gatherings, evoking the traditional notions of "hearth and home" and "keep the home fires burning." Because mothers are often thought of in similar terms, such as "the light of the home," and since several scripts of motherhood are performed in the kitchen, home kitchens are considered women-centered domains that reflect the emotional and psychological state of the family.

Before Mikage's grandmother dies she is only able to sleep when she brings her mattress into the kitchen, a space in which scripts for both physical and emotional nourishment are enacted. The loneliness Mikage feels at the loss of her last blood relative is heightened when viewed from the perspective of a society that considers the family name as a person's initial identifier. The kitchen is a container for global scripts of motherhood, hearth, and home, and Mikage is ultimately comforted when she imagines her own death—"breathing her last"—in the kitchen, a space associated with social nourishment (Yoshimoto 4). In envisioning her death there, she links her solitary life to an imagined community.

Mikage's memories of her grandmother and the activities that describe their bond are grafted onto the rooms of their apartment, demonstrating the emergence of the concept "home" through the integration of personal experiences of "family" scripts within a shared domestic environment. She remembers how they watched TV and told one another stories in her grandmother's room, "which hadn't changed since I was little" (20), and how her grandmother made sure the kitchen always had fresh flowers (7–8). The juxtaposition of these images with one of Mikage sleeping in a kitchen containing a vase of wilted flowers deepens the reader's empathy for her loneliness yet also highlights the comfort she receives from the mother-environment blend.

Her grandmother's flowers signify life in another way. They lead her to Yuichi, the boy from whom her grandmother bought flowers, and Eriko, his transsexual mother. They invite Mikage to live with them until she feels ready to let go of the home she shared with her grandmother and find a place of her own. Mikage consents because she "trusted their kitchen" (14) as evidence of a nurturing environment. The kitchen items are practical, of good quality, and well worn, allowing her to imagine that they have been used with ease and enjoyment. Her description of Yuichi and Eriko's terrace as a "jungle of plants" and her observation that the house was "filled with flowers" (9) draws sharp contrast to her empty apartment, made barren by the absence of a mother figure. The mother as a life-giving presence is emphasized once more through her repeated use of images of light in her representations of Eriko. Eriko "gave off a marvelous light that seemed to vibrate with life force" (11), and being in her presence left "a warm light, like her afterimage, softly glowing in my heart" (12). When Mikage watches Eriko perform activities she had associated with her grandmother, such as when she "feels an immense nostalgia . . . watching her [Eriko] pull a cushion onto the floor in that dusty living room and curl up to watch TV" (17), a fusion of mother figures occurs.

Eriko matches with the schema of the nurturing mother, yet it seems that what makes her a "powerful mother" (42) is her deviance from the norm. Readers associate Eriko's light with a mysterious glow upon learning that she owns a Tokyo nightclub and spends her nights working there and that she is in fact Yuichi's father transformed into a woman. Soon after the death of Yuichi's birth mother, a devastated Eriko came to the realization that "the world did not exist for my benefit . . . it became clear that the best thing to do was to adopt a sort of muddled cheerfulness. So I became a woman, and here I am" (81). While her resignation to "muddled cheerfulness" and her subsequent transformation expose her grief, the ambivalence of her choice foregrounds and critiques society's reliance on gender roles. But the cautious optimism that she ascribes to her metamorphosis emphasizes the tensile strength of those who are adaptable.[4] Eriko fully becomes the nurturing mother to Mikage and Yuichi, the fluidity of her form a testament to her acceptance of a world that is ever changing and her understanding that death can lead to new life.

Mikage is reborn while living in the blend of mother and environment that is Eriko's domestic jungle. She sleeps "like a baby" (22) and later finds that she has grown enough to take on the role of "housewife" (21). She finds happiness in being able to perform social and cultural scripts of nurturance. She teaches herself to cook soon after Eriko advises her that the key to independence is to care for another living being. The nourishment she receives in Eriko's unconventional home propels her into a career as a professional cook and continues to give her sustenance even after Eriko meets a tragic and violent death.

One might argue that Mikage has fallen into stereotypes that have given her a false sense of agency, but her enactment of such gender-typical roles instead plays out the tensions between cultural expectations and the personal ambitions that, as Nancy Rosenberger argues, were developing for young Japanese women in the 1990s (127). While Mikage's cooking pays homage to stereotypical women's roles, such as the housewife and the mother, it also modernizes the woman's place in the kitchen by making it a potential career. It gives her access to connect fully to the matrix of relationships symbolized by kitchens traditional and radical, which she uses to gain a deeper self-knowledge. It is through cooking that she comes of age—she would "make carrot cakes that included a bit of my soul" (Yoshimoto 59)—and from the collaboration of two distinct blends of mothers and environments emerges as an agentic subject who is herself a blend: a modern woman who is nurturing in the traditional and progressive ways of her mother figures. The kitchen is no longer only a womblike space with Mikage as the recipient of care and nourishment; rather, she steps into the role of caregiver and claims it as "a room of her own" (Kellerman 62). This agency is fully expressed when, near the end of the novella, Mikage impulsively hails a taxi and brings an order of the best *katsudon* she had ever tasted to Yuichi, who is staying at an inn more than an hour away, to comfort him after Eriko's death. "This is my profession" (Yoshimoto 92), she states of her ability as a professional cook to recognize the quality of the *katsudon*, yet it also refers to her identity as a nurturer.

The novella's inconclusive ending shows that Mikage is still in the process of change. A passage that bridges the two parts of the novella reflects that she has accepted this:

> Dream kitchens.
> I will have countless ones, in my heart or in reality. Or in my travels. Alone, with a crowd of people, with one other person—in all the many places I will live. I know that there will be so many more. (43)

The above passage expresses how Mikage and the kitchen are blended as a network of experiences (professional and personal), image schemas (of the kitchen as a place, of women and mothers in kitchens), and cultural scripts. Her "dream kitchens" simultaneously delineate and break physical boundaries. They signify the relationships yet to come and the possibilities available for her current relationships. The image captures the moment between adolescence and adulthood, when one understands that power lies in the continued ability to share the self in the face of constant change.

Imprisoning Nurturance/Imprisoned Mothers in *Al Capone Does My Shirts*

In contrast, *Al Capone Does My Shirts* challenges ideas of motherhood and home by blending this same matrix of relationships with Alcatraz, the prison island. Moose and his family move to Alcatraz when his father is given a job as guard and electrician, but he knows that the real reason for the move is that his mother wants to send his autistic sister, Natalie, to a school for special needs children located in San Francisco. Moose's mother despairs that Natalie's autism is more dangerous than Alcatraz, which echoes Choldenko's description of autism as "a prison without a key" (*Shoes* 270). Alcatraz represents a literal and figurative fusion of home and prison for Moose and his family. This blend sheds a different light on scripts and schemas of motherhood and home, in particular those of the "nurturing mother." It questions whether the "nurturing mother" fosters or smothers adolescent coming of age through Moose's experiences with his mother and, to a lesser extent, his focalized encounter with the mother of star prisoner Al Capone. Moose's focalization subtly parallels the prison island, as a space of imprisonment and rehabilitation, with the dynamics of his family, specifically the relationships between himself, Natalie, and his mother.

The cross-linking of motherhood and prison scripts represents the ambivalence between mothers and their children when the latter strain against this codependent relationship. The embodied metaphors Moose uses to describe his mother humorously foreground that resistance is futile: "My mother would be a much better jailer than my father" (*Shirts* 30) and "My mom is like a one-woman commando unit" (85). Her fierce nurturing is targeted at finding a cure for Natalie but manages instead to entrap them in a dynamic characterized by an anxiety-ridden love that emotionally distances Moose. Moose is close to his father and is comfortable around Natalie yet is angry with his mother even when he is proud of her resolve because she "never tries to imagine how I feel" (197).

Natalie is older than Moose, but as the years slip by and no cure is found, her mother attempts to mask Natalie's physical growth:

> Every year my mom has a party for her and she turns ten again. My mom started counting Nat's age this screwy way ages ago. It was just easier to have her younger than me. Then my mother could be happy for each new thing I did, without it being another thing Natalie couldn't do. (*Shirts* 11–12)

His mother infantilizes Natalie in part because she fears that society will be less likely to offer kindness and help as Natalie gets older, and in part because she assumes that Natalie herself lacks agency. In acting as Natalie's mother-jailer, she stunts her growth even as she tries to nurture her, and she suffers under an imprisoning image schema herself. Mothers are judged by their children's performance of the growth that they nurture. By keeping Natalie at ten, she attempts to protect herself from her failure as a mother, especially since autism was understood in the 1950s and 60s as a result of "refrigerator mothers," a term denoting a lack of maternal warmth (Kanner 424–26). Moose focalizes how his mother mimics Natalie's repetitive and destructive behavior when she feels a loss of control. "Things fall apart at my house," he says, when his mother learns that a prestigious UCLA program cannot diagnose Natalie's case:

> Ants in the sink. Flies on the garbage. . . . No clean dishes. Natalie in the same dirty dress . . . It was months before my mother left the house again . . . I don't remember when my mom decided Natalie was going to stay ten. But I think it might have been then. (*Shirts* 65)

The reflection of his mother's emotional state on the home adversely affects Moose's agency. When Moose babysits Natalie, acting as a "guard," the image schema that imprisons his mother extends over him as well. He is discomfited by her expectations— keeping his teenage sister clothed in little girl dresses, watching her every move—yet says nothing because he has grown into the good son: "I always do what I'm supposed to do" (28). At the same time, he is attuned to Natalie's need to widen the protective circle their mother keeps around them.

It is only when Moose encounters Al Capone's mother that he begins to imagine the difficulties of motherhood, providing a contrast to the frustration he feels toward his mother for almost the entire narrative. In the boat on the way to Alcatraz, Moose focalizes Mrs. Capone's transformation from old-fashioned and uncomfortable Italian immigrant to doting mother when she helps comfort a squalling baby. Her identity is inextricably intertwined with her son's, such that when the metal on her corset sets off an alarm she is immediately suspected of concealing weapons and is strip-searched. Humiliated, she leaves without visiting Capone and never returns, yet Moose notes that, in a way, she is also imprisoned in Alcatraz. He is deeply affected by this: "I'll bet his mama . . . held his hand when they crossed the street, packed his lunch for school and sewed his name in his jacket—A. CAPONE so everyone would know it was his. I'll bet she wishes she could do it all over again too . . . if only Al were little and she could" (134). The nurturing mother-child script that Moose bases his fantasy on juxtaposes the Capones' relationship with the reality of his relationship with his mother and its influence on Natalie. This juxtaposition encourages readers to cross-map the two representations of the script and interpret Moose's growth within the mother-prison blend according to comparisons made between himself, Natalie, and his fantasy of Al Capone the child and Al Capone the criminal.

Moose opens the door to his mother's prison of denial when he confronts her with Natalie's true age. He speaks in a whisper, but it is enough to make the family face the fact that Natalie is no longer a child. When his father asks Natalie on her birthday how old she thinks she is, she answers "sixteen" (194). In breaking the pattern of denial, Moose makes it possible for Natalie to find her own voice and for his parents to recover theirs. Their father becomes free to acknowledge them as grown-ups: "I am so very proud of my children. What wonderful people you've grown up to be" (194). His mother acknowledges him in turn when she recognizes that he acted to help rather than hinder his sister, and she acknowledges him as an agentic subject for the first time when she says, "I can't imagine how I could ask for anything more from you" (197). Her recognition of his agency allows him to see her as well so that he empathizes with her fully when Natalie is rejected from the special needs school. Readers link his family to the "godfather" script represented by Capone when he says, "I wonder if this is how my mother has always felt. . . . When you love someone, you have to try things even if they don't make sense to anyone else" (201). This blend is foregrounded when, in a secret letter to Capone imploring that he use his connections to convince the school to accept Natalie, he invokes "The Mom Rule." He name-drops Mrs. Capone because reminding someone that he has a mother "makes him act better" (210). The interplay between nurturing mother, imprisoning mother, and imprisoned mother scripts with schemas and scripts of mafia and model families in *Al Capone Does My Shirts*, along with the fusion of autism and prison, exemplifies the complex negotiations between prototypical scripts and their permutations that are essential to maturation.

Between Two Worlds: Mother-Environment Blends in *The Wee Free Men*

The Wee Free Men takes place in two distinct and contradictory landscapes represented by Granny Aching and the Faerie Queen. Both women exemplify how words and images associated with natural phenomena are used to perpetuate particular images of womanhood, and vice versa. Through her negotiations with these mother-nature blends, Tiffany Aching develops a unique relationship with the network of connections—social, cultural, ecological, and magical—that form the land called the Chalk, and becomes a powerful figure in her own right. At nine years old, she is implicitly aware of the way narrative scripts and schemas shape reality and inspire action. Her character reflects Pratchett's own cognizance of scripts and schemas, which he calls "narrative causality" and defines as "the idea that there are 'story shapes' into which human history, both large scale and at the personal level, attempts to fit" ("Imaginary Worlds" 166).

Tiffany is especially critical of and resistant to story shapes wherein power relations are based on stereotypes of gender and class: Granny Aching lives alone in a strange cottage, so she must be a witch; the Faerie Queen is benevolent because she is royal and beautiful; and brown-haired girls like Tiffany can never be heroes. She overturns such gender assumptions when she emphasizes that people are, in reality, a blend of schemas and gender concepts. Her characterization of Granny Aching, for instance, is anchored on the similarities between witches and shepherds. The description of Granny's shepherding hut as "a strange house *that moved about*" activates both wicked-witch and solitary-shepherd schemas. Her insistence that Granny could "do sheep magic and she talked to animals but there was nothing wicked about her" (29–30) infuses shepherding with witchery and at the same time makes witchcraft benign. She then declares, "That *proved* you couldn't believe the stories" (30) to underscore the purpose of the blend, which is to negate the wickedness of the witch and empower the shepherd schema. "Sheep magic" further recasts the witch schema in light of the wise and omnipresent shepherd schema, whereby the power a witch has over others is blended with the responsibility a shepherd feels for his flock, and positions Granny as guardian of the Chalk. Guardianship merges with motherhood when she observes, "lambs would find their way to it [Granny's home] when they'd lost their mothers. This was a magic place" (100). The image upholds the blend of Granny and Chalk, witch and shepherd, from which Granny emerges as an unconventional Mother Earth figure that challenges fairy-tale stereotypes.

Granny's authority over the land is such that it endures even after her death, which Tiffany demonstrates through blended images of Granny and nature: "*what Granny Aching was, was there . . .watching . . . And she was the silence of the hills*" (31). Powerful figures from political and natural spheres, such as the Baron and the Nac Mac Feegles (warrior pictsies of the Chalk), recognize her command. Her response to the Baron's demand that she exempt his dog from death, the punishment for killing sheep, underlines her influence:

> "*Those laws are on these hills and these hills are in my bones. What is a baron, that the law be brake for him?*"
> *She went back to staring at the sheep.*
> "*The Baron owns this country,*" *said the servant.* "*It is his law.*"
> *The look Granny Aching gave him turned the man's hair white. That was the story, anyway. But all stories of Granny Aching had a bit of fairy tale about them.* (88)

In describing herself as a fusion of bones, hills, and laws, Granny foregrounds that her authority spans natural and civilized worlds and overturns fairy-tale hierarchies. The blend also portrays Granny as a bastion of order, unbending and eternal. The power struggle is nuanced by Granny's use of "a baron" as opposed to the servant's "The Baron." A witch script undercuts the servant's insistence that the Baron owns the land—she turns his hair white, the color of chalk—which shows that the Baron's claim of ownership literally pales in comparison to her authority as the embodied Chalk. The scene unfolds as she watches over the flock, an act of guardianship that offsets the (rumored) display of witchcraft and, moreover, reinvents the witch schema into a protector of law and land rather than an anarchic force.

Tiffany further dismantles and reconceptualizes fairy-tale hierarchies when she states that she wants to be "the witch and *know* things, just like Granny Aching" rather than like the "stupid smirking princesses, who didn't have the sense of a beetle" (30). This inversion of power supports Tiffany's agency as she goes on a quest to rescue her brother from the Faerie Queen and to stop the Queen's world from invading the Chalk. Granny Aching passes on guardianship to Tiffany when she tells her, *"the hills is in yer bones"* (142), hence, describing Tiffany in the same fusion of concepts she had used to define herself. The kelda, mother of the Nac Mac Feegles, reinforces Tiffany's identification with Granny when she tells her she is the new witch and reveals that the meaning of "Tiffany" is "Land Under Wave" (131). The phrase describes the creation of the Chalk from the shells and bones of small "helpless" sea creatures (46); but, the kelda points out, inside the softness of the chalk can be found flints, "harder than steel" (98). The image of steel inside chalk merges with that of hills and bones and underpins the continuity between Tiffany and Granny.

The kelda's last act before she dies is to appoint Tiffany as the temporary kelda, making her the new mother of the Nac Mac Feegles. This renders Tiffany herself a mother-environment blend. Like her grandmother, she is a mother figure to and embodiment of the natural and magical planes of the Chalk.[5] And like her grandmother, she challenges the conventions of the schemas she represents. A precocious nine-year-old witch, hero, and mother figure, Tiffany personifies the unexpected strength, or the flint, of the Chalk. Her command over nature and magic is grounded on symbols of domestic nurturance, represented by the tools she takes on her quest to the Faerie Queen's world: a frying pan, her Granny's special sheep liniment, and a book on curing sick sheep.

In contrast, the Faerie Queen draws from mother schemas that strive to uphold fairy-tale hierarchies, which Tiffany insists are empty fantasies. Her world is "a land where dreams come true" (106), formed from the juxtaposition of two kinds of dream schemas: on the surface are those that refer to hopes and aspirations, yet lurking underneath are monsters and nightmares (106, 176–77). The Faerie Queen embodies her land's dual nature. The Fairyland and queen/king schemas form intertextual links (whether deliberate or inadvertent) with narratives that bolster the fantasies she projects, such as Tam Lin, Childe Rowland and Burd Ellen, Thomas the Rhymer, and the film *Labyrinth*, among others. The intertexts reveal the illusory nature of the mother-environment blend that is the Faerie Queen and underscore that she is a barren mother figure whose world cannot provide physical or emotional sustenance. For instance, she lures Tiffany's brother into her land with the promise of sweets (Pratchett 133), as happens with Edmund in *The Lion, the Witch and the Wardrobe*, and entices Roland, the Baron's young son, with her beauty and gaiety (218), as the Elf-Queen does to Thomas the Rhymer. She kidnaps them to complete a Fairyland fantasy wherein children "skip and play" (218), but once the lack of nourishment hinders their performance of this script, she loses interest and abandons them.

The Nac Mac Feegles warn Tiffany not to eat anything in the Faerie Queen's land (182), an interdiction common in all the aforementioned intertexts. She feeds people candies and dream food, which arrests their growth but fuels their ability to dream, for the vision of a green and magical Fairyland can only thrive through the fantasies of others. Like the wicked witch in the Hansel and Gretel tale, she baits people with sweets and sweet dreams only to consume them. Tiffany subverts the Queen's power over her when she uncovers the wicked-witch schema masked by the performance of a benevolent-queen mother schema and the illusion of a lush Fairyland. Yet the emptiness of the Queen's beauty and the hollowness of her land threaten to overcome Tiffany when the Queen, speaking as a "friendly, understanding" mother figure, juxtaposes the "Brave Girl Rescuing Little Brother" script with a series of scripts that recast Tiffany as a willful, egotistical "product of bad parenting" (Pratchett 268). The Queen draws on the full significance of queen, mother, and witch schemas and surrounds Tiffany with frost—the true form of Fairyland. Tiffany loses her self-confidence and experiences an existential crisis. She views herself in fragments and sensations, which she then realizes are representative of the Chalk and Granny Aching:

> *This land is in my bones.*
> *Land under wave.*
> [. . .] *I remember . . .*

> This is the million-year rain under the sea, this is the new land being born under the ocean. It's not a dream. It's . . . a memory. The land under wave. Millions and millions of tiny shells . . .
>
> This land was *alive*.
>
> All the time there was the warm, comforting smell of the shepherding hut, and the feeling of being held by invisible hands.
>
> [. . .] Now I'm inside the chalk, like a flint, like a calkin. . . . (273)

Granny's shepherding hut and the watery origin of the Chalk meld into a womb-like space, within which Tiffany is reborn into the Chalk's flint—the land under wave. The natural and domestic elements of the Granny-Chalk blend ground her in reality and empower her to strip away the story shapes the Queen relies upon and menaces her with. She defeats the Queen in a manner that alludes to Janet's own triumph over the Faerie Queen in the ballad of Tam Lin. Tiffany picks the Queen up and finds that she "was light as a baby and changed shape madly in her arms—into monsters and mixed-up beasts" (283). In shattering the Queen's illusions, Tiffany matures into the mother figure in the relationship and completely upsets hierarchies of power.

The theoretical model I have discussed extends to many other characters in children's and young adult fiction. For example, in Neil Gaiman's *Coraline*, Coraline's independence grows from her experiences with mother-home blends represented by her real mother, what Alexandra Kotanko describes as the "good-enough" mother (chapter 9), and the othermother fantasy, wherein a version of her mother focuses her entire existence on Coraline's happiness. Coraline realizes that in keeping her from hardship, the othermother is also denying her from achieving any kind of psychological agency (Kotanko). The framing of subjective agency within mother-environment blends also enables a more nuanced understanding of characters that negotiate similar dynamics in multivoiced narratives. In the *Divergent* series, for instance, Tris and Four map essential attributes of their mothers onto the factions each mother represents. Their discovery that their mothers are, respectively, divergent and factionless has a profound impact on the way they understand their own choices. In describing the coming-of-age process as the protagonist's navigation of a narrative landscape comprised of mother-environment domains, some collaborative and others in opposition with one another (or with the protagonist), I attempt to shed light on the meaning-making effect of conceptual blending, as the activation of connections between the primary text with narrative scripts, schemas, and intertexts.

Notes

1. My argument draws on John Stephens, "Schemas and Scripts" and Roberta Seelinger Trites, "Growth in Adolescent Literature." Stephens demonstrates that scripts are composed of a network of schemas: "Whereas a schema is a static element within our experiential repertoire, a script is a dynamic element, which expresses how a sequence of events or actions are expected to unfold" (14). Trites builds on Stephens's work to create a cognitive approach of growth in young adult literature, which she further develops in *Literary Conceptualizations of Growth: Metaphors and Cognition in Adolescent Literature*. For more on cognitive studies and children's literature, see Karen Coats, "The Meaning of Children's Poetry: A Cognitive Approach"; John Stephens and Sylvie Geerts, "Mishmash, Conceptual Blending and Adaptation in Contemporary Children's Literature Written in Dutch and English"; Anna Katrina Gutierrez, "Metamorphosis: The Emergence of Glocal Subjectivities in the Blend of Global, Local, East and West"; and Sung-ae Lee, "Fairy Tale Scripts and Intercultural Conceptual Blending in Modern Korean Film and Television Drama."

2. The novel *Kitchen* is comprised of two novellas (*Kitchen* and *Moonlight Shadow*) but I will only discuss the novella *Kitchen*.

3. Even though Yoshimoto is credited with bringing *shōjō* culture to global consciousness, experts criticize the tendency of her works to "end with sentimentally optimistic conclusions" (Saitō 169) as lacking the radicalness that is central to *shōjō* narratives.

4. See Lori Girshick, *Transgender Voices: Beyond Men and Women*. She makes a case for the recognition of gender identity, defined as the "extent to which a person feels masculine or feminine, a bit of both or neither," on the grounds that gender binary is a cultural concept rather than a biological one and that gender variance is rich, complex, and natural.

5. In *I Shall Wear Midnight*, the fourth book in the series, it is hinted that the Chalk may sometimes speak through Tiffany, as it seems to have done when she prophesies to Roland that she will marry him. She does, when she performs an ancient marriage ritual for him and his fiancée (Pratchett 464, 566).

Works Cited

Coats, Karen. "The Meaning of Children's Poetry: A Cognitive Approach". *International Research in Children's Literature* 6.2 (2013): 127–42. Print.

Choldenko, Gennifer. *Al Capone Does My Shirts*. New York: Puffin, 2004. Print.

———. *Al Capone Shines My Shoes*. New York: Puffin, 2009. Print.

Fauconnier, Gilles, and Mark Turner. *The Way We Think: Conceptual Blending and the Mind's Hidden Complexities*. New York: Basic, 2002. Print.

Gaiman, Neil. *Coraline*. New York: Harper Collins, 2002. Print.

Girshick, Lori. *Transgender Voices: Beyond Women and Men*. Hanover, NH: UPNE, 2008. Print.

Gutierrez, Anna Katrina. "Metamorphosis: The Emergence of Glocal Subjectivities in the Blend of Global, Local, East, and West." *Subjectivity in Asian Children's Literature and Film: Global Theories and Implications*. Ed. John Stephens. New York and London: Routledge, 2012. 19–42. Print.

Herman, David. *Story Logic: Problems and Possibilities of Narrative*. Lincoln: U of Nebraska P, 2002. Print.

Kanner, Leo. "Problems of Nosology and Psychodynamics in Early Childhood Autism". *American Journal of Orthopsychiatry* 19.3 (1949): 416–26. Print.

Kellerman, Robert. "A Room of Her Own in Banana Yoshimoto's *Kitchen*." *Pacific Asia Inquiry* 1.1 (2010): 54–63. Print.

Lee, Sung-ae. "Fairy Tale Scripts and Intercultural Conceptual Blending in Modern Korean Film and Television Drama." In *Grimms' Tales around the Globe: The Dynamics of Their International Reception*. Ed. Vanessa Joosen and Gillian Lathey. Detroit: Wayne State UP, 2014. 275–93. Print.

Pratchett, Terry. "Imaginary Worlds, Real Stories." *Folklore* 111 (2000): 159–68. Print.

———. *I Shall Wear Midnight*. London: Doubleday, 2010. iBooks file.

———. *The Wee Free Men*. 2003. London: Corgi, 2010. Print.

Rosenberger, Nancy. *Gambling with Virtue: Japanese Women and the Search for Self in a Changing Nation*. Honolulu: U of Hawai'i P, 2001. Print.

Roth, Veronica. *Allegiant*. London: Tegen, 2013. Kindle file.

———. *Divergent*. London: Tegen, 2011. Kindle file.

———. *Insurgent*. London: Tegen, 2012. Kindle file.

Saitō, Minako. "Yoshimoto Banana and Girl Culture." *Woman Critiqued: Translated Essays on Japanese Writing*. Ed. Rebecca L. Copeland. Trans. Eiji Sekine. Honolulu: U of Hawai'i P, 2006. 167–85. Print.

Shonoda, Mary-Anne. "Metaphor and Intertextuality: A Cognitive Approach to Intertextual Meaning-Making in Children's Literature and Fantasy Novels." *International Research in Children's Literature* 5.1 (2012): 81–96. Print.

Stephens, John. "Schemas and Scripts: Cognitive Instruments and the Representation of Cultural Diversity in Children's Literature." *Contemporary Children's Literature and Film: Engaging with Theory*. Ed. Kerry Mallan and Clare Bradford. Basingstoke, UK: Palgrave, 2011. 12–35. Print.

Stephens, John, and Sylvie Geerts. "Mishmash, Conceptual Blending and Adaptation in Contemporary Children's Literature Written in Dutch and English." *Never-ending Stories: Adaptation, Canonisation and Ideology in Children's Literature*. Ed. Sara Van den Bossche and Sylvia Geerts. Ghent: Academia, 2014. 193–214.

Treat, John Whittier. "Yoshimoto Banana Writes Home." *Contemporary Japan and Popular Culture*. Ed. John Whittier Treat. Honolulu: U of Hawai'i P, 1996. 275–308. Print.

Trites, Roberta Seelinger. "Growth in Adolescent Literature: Metaphors, Scripts, and Cognitive Narratology." *International Research in Children's Literature* 5.1 (2012): 64–80. Print.

———. *Literary Conceptualizations of Growth: Metaphors and Cognition in Adolescent Literature*. Amsterdam: Benjamins, 2014. Print.

Yoshimoto, Banana. *Kitchen*. 1988. Trans. Megan Backus. New York: Grove, 1993. Print.

PART III

The Mother-Child Bond:
Fantasy and Desire for the Real

Chapter 8

Animal Mothers and Animal Babies in Picture Books

Robin Calland

The disparities between the stories children's books give of animal conception, birth, and infant rearing and those that biologists tell are striking. Chia Martin, the author of *We Like to Nurse*, tells the reader, "Momma and baby panda cuddle and nurse under the bamboo" (11). The reader would never know from the text that the happy dyad portrayed there might have once been a triad and that the mother panda might have abandoned one of the twins and selected only her more robust child to live. On the page featuring an illustration of a joey with its snout buried in its mother's abdomen and no other young kangaroos in sight, the narrator of Michael Elsohn Ross's *Mama's Milk* tells readers, "She'll be there for you whenever you roam" (10). However, the biological account of kangaroo motherhood is more complex than Ashley Wolff's illustration and Ross's narrator permit it to be. The illustration of the mother kangaroo bending over the single joey with a kindly look on her face and the language on the page that promises the mother will be there waiting "whenever" the young kangaroo wants to return after wandering away suggests a mother that is endlessly devoted to this one offspring. However, the truth is that mother kangaroos have commitments that extend beyond one infant. From a biological perspective, the marsupial mothers must reproduce as many young as they can. The mother's pursuit of reproductive success probably means sustained nurturing for a joey. However, it might also mean sacrificing individual joeys. According to sociobiologist Sarah Hrdy, kangaroo mothers are "ovarian assembly line[s]" (128). They facilitate the survival of their genes in an inhospitable environment by, among other things, juggling multiple joeys at different stages of growth. As Hrdy observes, kangaroo reproduction is wired for "high turnover" (128). What's missing from Wolff's illustration is a "tiny joey latched on in her pouch" nursing at the same time as the older joey that has returned for a drink (Hrdy 128). Furthermore, a biologically accurate illustration would depict a mother who, if pursued by a predator, "can jettison, or just allow to topple out, the joey in her pouch" and quickly signal a fertilized egg-in-waiting to begin developing (128–29).

In my journey through nineteen children's books purporting to give a biological account of animal mothers, I discovered writers abandoning fact and yielding to the fantasy of mothers naturally wired to throw every last bit of themselves into caring for and protecting—successfully, of course—individual young. Indeed, this fantasy, which has become a reigning mythology, is everywhere.[1] It displaces the stories of diverse and complicated reptilian, amphibian, bird, and mammal tacticians that children's books about animal mothers could and should offer to children. The biological truths current books largely fail to tell children are that (1) animal mothers vary—within and between groups of animals; (2) animal mothers are intent on having as many viable offspring as possible over the course of their lives and, thus, juggle the needs of one generation of young with the necessity of producing new generations; and (3) inasmuch as animal mothers' strategies and environmental conditions vary, they do not universally succeed at protecting each of their young.

The omission of important aspects of reproduction appears to be guided by the assumption that human children must be reassured of the unfailing commitment and competence of mothers throughout the animal kingdom. Apparently, children require that assurance more than exposure to the variegated and challenging nature of motherhood across species. The other message such books convey is that when faced with a choice between representing animal mothers as biologists find them and propagating ideologies about human motherhood, authors and publishers should sacrifice scientific accuracy to ideology. These concessions to cultural prescriptions for motherhood are disappointing. However, it is not surprising that ideologies should suppress the multifariousness of animal motherhood in children's books presenting information about nature. As Patricia A. Larkin-Lieffers observes, although children's information books "appear relatively neutral ... [they] can be politically and socially charged" (81). I want to suggest that authors and publishers do harm when they confuse, to use Nora Timmerman and Julia Ostertag's phrase, "more-than-human others" with wishes and social expectations for human mothers (63). This practice fails to provide children with accurate and clear scientific information. Moreover, it renders animals as distortions rather than the fascinating and intricately distinct others that they are, and it denies children the possibility of seeing their own mothers as particular subjects.

Methodology

In pursuing this research, I looked for patterns in a sampling of recent children's books about animal babies and mothers. In the 1970s biologists began to recognize that the decisions mothers make play an enormous part in the survival of young.[2] Seeking to determine whether this transformation in thinking about mothers had infiltrated recent books about animal mothers, I collected nineteen of the approximately 852 books about mother animals and/or babies published between 1993 and 2013.[3] Some of these books were nonfiction and encyclopedic in nature. Other nonfiction books accounted for only one species or genus of mothers and babies. In fact, seven of my nineteen books address the maternal behavior of giant pandas. These seven books, selected from among approximately 144 children's books about pandas published between 1993 and 2013, provide the focus made possible by a smaller subset of books. Thus, with this group of books, I am able to offer a glimpse of how publishers frame the maternal behavior of one species. I did not exclude fictional accounts of mothers. When it came to fictional representations of mothers and babies, I included one book about pandas that exemplified the anthropomorphic sentimentality that often surrounds animal mothers. Otherwise, I limited myself to narratives that represented themselves as depicting with some form of scientific realism the actual behavior of mother and baby animals. The accompanying chart includes the full list of books that I chose for analysis.

Taking to heart Timmerman and Ostertag's assertion that "children under four undergo some of the steepest socio-cultural and ecological learning of their lives" (65), I looked for books targeted at children as young as two. I set the upper age limit at twelve. I was guided in my analysis of the content of all nineteen books by the following questions: (1) "Does this book acknowledge or represent in any way the variation between the mothers within a species or genus?"; (2) "Does this book represent the maternal trajectory as defined by the animal mother's focus on anything beyond one individual or one generation of young?"; and (3) "Does this book acknowledge the very likely possibility of maternal failure?" The findings garnered by those questions follow.

Title	Author	Genre	Genus
101 Animal Babies	Melvin Berger and Gilda Berger	Nonfiction	Encyclopedic
A Baby Panda Is Born	Kristin Ostby	Nonfiction	Pandas
A Mother's Journey	Sandra Markle	Nonfiction Narrative	Penguins
Animal Families	Lorrie Mack	Nonfiction	Encyclopedic
Babies in the Bayou	Jim Arnosky	Fiction	Turtles, Raccoons, Alligators
Bear Cub: At Home in the Forest	Sarah Toast	Nonfiction Narrative	Bears
I Am A Little Panda	François Crozat	Nonfiction	Pandas
If My Mom Were a Platypus: Mammal Babies and Their Mothers	Dia Michels	Nonfiction	Encyclopedic
Mama's Milk	Michael Elsohn Ross	Nonfiction	Encyclopedic
Manatee Winter	Kathleen Weidner Zoehfeld	Nonfiction Narrative	Manatees
Panda Baby: At Home in the Bamboo Grove	Sarah Toast	Nonfiction Narrative	Pandas
Panda Bear Cub	Jacqueline Moody-Luther	Fiction	Pandas
Panda Kindergarten	Joanne Ryder	Nonfiction	Pandas
Puma Range	Michael C. Armour	Nonfiction Narrative	Pumas
Pi-shu, the Little Panda	John Butler	Fiction	Pandas
Raccoon on His Own	Jim Arnosky	Fiction	Raccoons
Sisters & Brothers	Steve Jenkins and Robin Page	Nonfiction	Encyclopedic
Thank You, God, for Mommy	Amy Parker	Fiction	Pandas
We Like to Nurse	Chia Martin	Nonfiction	Encyclopedic

Picture books in study

Myth 1: The Mothers within a Species Are All the Same

Despite biologists' growing recognition since the 1970s of differences between mothers within a species or genus, all but two of the books I studied fail to dramatize the possibility of different life trajectories arising from different kinds of conception, gestation, and mothering. Instead, the books present only one mother of each genus or species and thereby give the impression that all mothers of a species or genus are interchangeable—that in essence, there is only one representative mother in a species, what I call the reduction of the many mothers within a species into The Mother. Michael C. Armour's *Puma Range*, Kathleen Weidner Zoehfeld's *Manatee Winter*, Jim Arnosky's *Raccoon on His Own*, Sarah Toast's *Bear Cub: At Home in the Forest*, and five of the seven books about pandas only show readers the intimacies and adventures of a single mother-offspring dyad or a mother and one season's litter. In Sandra Markle's *A Mother's Journey*, the reader sees the one emperor penguin protagonist amidst a group of penguins making the fifty-mile journey to the sea to fill their bodies with food for their chicks. The reader is treated to image after image of the book's designated penguin mother moving with a large number of female penguins, but the story never contrasts her strategies or fortunes with those of any of the other mothers.

The six encyclopedic books, among which I am including the books about nursing I discussed above, opt to use the small amount of space they have for each animal to present prototypical mothers. Difference in the encyclopedic books vibrates between species, not between members of a species. Lorrie Mack's *Animal Families* maintains the myth of The Mother. Pictures and text capture multiple "young hippos . . . being looked after by two moms," as well as a herd of nine large giraffes, two of which look like young giraffes, and at least five of which must be females (7). However, the text never mentions differences between the multiple mothers it presents in visual form. There's only one picture of a mother sea lion with a pup (9), and nowhere in the text or illustrations does the book reflect the research that shows that some sea lions raise their young alone, whereas other mothers in the species raise their young much more successfully in the middle of a harem (Bowen 110).

In *101 Animal Babies*, Melvin and Gilda Berger sometimes qualify the entries on animals with adverbs such as "usually" ("Pig Piglets") and "sometimes" ("Lemming Babies") and the auxiliaries "may" ("Owl Owlets") and "can" ("Lemming Babies"). However, the Bergers don't go any further and describe actual intraspecies differences. Moreover, they confidently explain that in the case of baboons, "Young baboons sit upright on their mothers' backs until they're too big at five or six months of age" (7). However, Jeanne Altman, one of the first evolutionary biologists to acknowledge the variability between mothers, documents that baboon mothers do not universally carry their babies on their backs (140). Altman records that in one study, out of fifteen baboons she observed, eleven traveled on their mothers' backs, but four did not. Altman also noted that baboon mothers vary in other ways. She identified some mothers as "restrictive mothers" who held onto their babies at all times and others as "laissez-faire" mothers who were more relaxed about releasing their young from their grip and their gaze (130–35).

Contrary to the version of animal mothers disseminated by children's pseudobiology books, there is much intraspecies variation between maternal resources and behaviors. Environments are different. Genes that give each individual in a species a range of potential ways to respond to the fluctuations in a particular environment vary. In order for natural selection to perpetuate the survival of the genes of the mothers whose strategies are suited for their environment, mothers must be different. However, according to Hrdy, the influential biologist and sociologist Herbert Spencer "reasoned (wrongly) that there was too little variation among females for proper selection to occur" (14). For years afterward, evolutionary biologists believed mothers were passive and static entities upon which natural selection did not work. That misconception began to change, however, in the 1940s with David Lack's study of birds. In the 1970s, biologists and sociobiologists began to recognize that raising young in the midst of food shortages, predators, and intraspecies infanticide required females to be as wily and resourceful as the males that compete to mate with females. Thus, biologists began to seek and find evidence that differences in animal mothers had always given natural selection much to reject and much to preserve (Hrdy 28–29).

Researchers are now recognizing that mothers also influence the trajectories of their young through mechanisms other than genes. For instance, mothers may impact their young through the nutrients they allocate to the eggs they lay or the responses to predators they teach their young. Female frogs may lay different numbers of eggs and eggs of different sizes (Warne, Kardon, and Crespi 9), and they lay their eggs in different spots (Bernardo 85). A dung beetle that lives in an area thickly populated with other dung beetles will produce male beetles with longer horns than the males produced by a relatively isolated mother dung beetle (Buzatto, Tomkins, and Simmons 118). Mouse or rat mothers in laboratories lick their young to greater and lesser degrees and thus make them more or less vulnerable to the ravages of stress (Champagne and Curley 182–87). The lives of young born to a high-ranking hyena mother or baboon will be very different from the lives of young born to low-ranking mothers (Maestripieri 259–60; Holekamp and Dloniak 240–45).

Only two of the nineteen children's texts I studied challenge the myth of the singular species mother. Joanne Ryder's *Panda Kindergarten*, a book about humans restructuring the natural habits of pandas, invites readers to recognize the potential for variability between mothers. Ryder explains that the human caretakers at the Wolong Nature Reserve in China are working to prevent panda extinction. One of the things scientists do to increase the number of living panda young is to support the mothers so they can tend to both of their young instead of abandoning one of them. Another of the scientists' strategies is to take cubs from their mothers at a fairly early age and raise them with their peers in the hopes that pandas might become less territorial. Presumably, if they become less aggressive toward strangers, this species that needs large isolated areas in which to rear young might be able to live and reproduce in smaller, more densely populated areas. Thus, Ryder's account of this intervention in panda mothering reveals that panda maternal behavior is not fixed but correlated with the conditions of mother pandas' environments.

Jim Arnosky's clever *Babies in the Bayou* gives a subtle but important nod toward intraspecies maternal differences. The book presents the bayou as home to a dangerous food chain in which savvy mothers defend their young from other mothers who want to feed the young to their babies. At first glance, the important distinctions in the book appear to be between the genera of alligator, raccoon, and merganser mothers in the bayou, not among them. But a second glance at the mother raccoon helping her young to find and eat "tasty turtle eggs" points readers to at least two different mothers of the same genera or species. On the next page, while the raccoons devour one clutch of turtle eggs, baby turtles hatch from another clutch of eggs. Thus, Arnosky makes visible a difference between turtle mothers. Site selection is one of the ways that turtle mothers distinguish themselves from other turtle mothers. The observant reader understands that while some turtle mothers lay their eggs where raccoons can find them, other mothers are luckier or more successful in finding spots that elude the raccoons. Importantly, through representations of maternal differences, children are given the opportunity to recognize that mothers are not fixed, passive vessels through which conception, gestation, and nurturing inexorably roll. Rather, children are invited to recognize mothers as responding with different strategies to environmental conditions and as playing an active role in the survival—or not—of their young.

Myth 2: The Concerns of Animal Mothers Extend No Further Than the Comfort, Security, and Survival of One Season's Young

Many, but not all, of the works I examined hide the fact that mothers are driven by agendas larger than the health and safety of one litter of young. Sixteen of the nineteen books fail to frame mothers within the larger architecture of their lives—as tacticians employing various strategies to produce, over the course of their lives, as many young as possible. The majority of the books I studied encourage children to understand mothers within the context of a sustained commitment to one generation of young. Thus, they deny readers the opportunity to develop a more challenging awareness of the maternal preoccupations that transcend the concern for one crop of young. Speaking of animal fantasy in terms that unfortunately also apply to pseudoscientific books about baby animals and their mothers, Lisa Rowe Fraustino writes, "Judging from animal fantasy, one would never know that a rabbit mother in the wild may produce seven or eight litters per season" and within "three weeks, the young are weaned, and [they] . . . leave the nest within a few days" (152). Indeed, in my research Armour's *Puma Range*, Zoehfeld's *Manatee Winter*, Arnosky's *Raccoon on His Own*, Toast's *Bear Cub: At Home in the Forest*, Markle's *A Mother's Journey*, and five of the seven books about pandas confine their coverage to the intimacies and adventures of a single season's mother-offspring dyad or litter.

Acknowledging the biological reality of animal mothers' lives would mean inviting children to step back and see mothers in terms other than devout fidelity to individual young. Such a presentation would give children a glimpse of animal mothers as, to use Hrdy's word, "flexible" strategists who assess their surroundings, calculate their odds, and pursue actions that best promote their interests (31). However, the price of gaining a more comprehensive vision of mothers is the consciousness that calculating and compromising to advance lifetime agendas might mean maternal decisions that "do not result in nurturing behavior" (Hrdy 29). It might mean a mother deciding how much energy she can invest in one season's young and how much to hold back for herself, so she will be in shape to reproduce the next season. Sometimes, preserving themselves for further reproduction means mothers take for themselves something that would make an offspring's chances more secure. For instance, Kay E. Holekamp and Stephanie M. Dloniak note that when mother cheetahs are hungry, they kill and consume prey directly and are less likely to let their young do the killing. Young who do not get adequate practice subduing prey are less prepared to survive (237).

The seven panda books I studied exemplify my findings that children's authors and publishers are often not willing to let biologists' findings dislodge stories of mothers' devotion to particular young. There's a great disparity between the realities of panda reproduction and the portraits of panda mothers and their young in the seven books. In the wild, besides abandoning one of their twins, panda bear mothers do not hesitate to initiate weaning. As biologists at the San Diego Zoo explain to a public anxious about panda weaning, conflict between mothers and cubs inevitably occurs. Cubs are unlikely to initiate separation from the comfort and constant food supply represented by their mothers. Mothers ultimately must stop pouring resources into their cubs, though, so the mothers can replenish themselves and reproduce again. Suzanne Hall, a senior research technician at the San Diego Zoo, says that when weaning time comes the zoo's panda mother, Bai Yun, "will refuse nursing or terminate bouts of nursing more frequently. She may become more aggressive about guarding her bamboo stash or become rougher during play with her cub" (Hall).

In spite of the realities of panda rearing, six of the seven children's books about panda young that I examined fail to discuss the mother's initiation of separation and in fact, end with cubs blissfully united with their mothers. Five of the six panda books end with pictures of the cubs nestled securely in their mothers' arms. François Crozat's *I Am a Little Panda* ends with the baby snuggling in his mother's arms and declaring his desire "to live here in these beautiful mountains with my mom" (20). The third-person narrator of John Butler's *Pi-shu the Little Panda* tells readers that Pi-shu, who is surrounded in the illustration by the fortress of his mother's body, would eventually "want to . . . find a place of his own to live, but right now he didn't want to change a thing" (26–27). All seven of the panda books are told from the point of view of the panda cub. In fact, all nineteen of the books for this study are told from the young's perspective—a fact that echoes Kertzer's findings that mothers' voices and realities are effaced from books that transmit widespread fantasies of perfect mothers (159–60). Nor do those six books disclose in the book proper that the ecstatic dyad is sometimes achieved by abandoning an extra baby. Only one of those six, Butler's *Pi-shu the Little Panda*, refers to the abandonment, but he does so at the end of the book in the "Panda Facts" section, explaining, "Often only the stronger of the two cubs survives." His wording suggests that the one cub's death is a matter of the cub failing to survive rather than the mother's abandonment, which makes survival impossible.

Notably, several of these books gesture to the cub's reproductive future beyond the union with the panda mother, but they all nevertheless end with the cub suspended in dependent security, not with weaning, separation, and the mother's next pregnancy. The reproductive future they point to is the baby's, not the mother's. From the children's literature on pandas, one would never know that panda mothers initiate separation in order to conceive and gestate more cubs. Readers would assume that panda babies instigate departure if and when they are ready. The panda books are not outliers. Nine more of the nineteen books limit themselves to a narrow view of mothers as faithful and cozy anchors for one season's young. However, not all of the books shy away from representing the maternal pressures that part mothers and their young. Three encyclopedic books, though they do not acknowledge that mothers within a species differ, do countenance the reality that mothers' lives transcend the birth and rearing of one offspring. In *101 Animal Babies*, the Bergers do not spare children the knowledge that mothers depart abruptly to mate and reproduce other litters. "Hare leverets," they cheerfully announce, "can live without their parents by only three weeks of age" (42). They even disclose that an opossum mother's pouch "has about 13 teats, or nipples, but only 10 or so babies attach themselves and nurse. The other joeys die" (62). Nor does *Sisters and Brothers*, the book about animal siblings by Steve Jenkins and Robin Page, presume that children need to be insulated from hard truths. It describes same-sex sibling hyenas that fight to the death, an event with which, to some degree, the mother who does not intervene is complicit.

Dia Michels's *If My Mom Were a Platypus* is also relaxed about the fact that mothers' biological schedules quickly displace and replace young. The baby koala declares, "By my first birthday my mom will be expecting a new joey. When he pokes his head out of her pouch, I will have to leave my mom. There won't be enough good leaves in her patch of trees to support all of us, so I'll have to go out and find a tree of my very own" (16). Remarkably, Michels's book suggests that children can absorb—intact—the fact of mothers' leaving young to follow their imperative to reproduce. These encyclopedic books offer children the opportunity to encounter and learn about a natural world in which young live according to different rhythms than those of humans.

Myth 3: Heroic Animal Mothers Always Succeed at Providing for and Protecting Young

Although the dance of variation, organism, and environment means that some mothers will fail, and inevitably, some young will die and others will flourish, maternal failure does not appear to be an option in the seven books that present heroic mothers who either successfully defend their young against deadly threats or provide for their young against great odds. In Armour's *Puma Range*, a female mountain lion successfully defends her kittens against a male mountain lion that seeks to kill them. The book does not explain that males commonly kill the cubs of other males in order to push females into heat and convert them into vehicles for the reproduction of their own young and genes. In Armour's book, the mother mountain lion attacks the male, and he leaves, injured and "defeated" (14). In casting the mother cougar as a fearless and victorious fighter on behalf of her young, Armour depicts a possible scenario that puts her in the most invincible and self-sacrificing light. If it is true, as Kenneth A. Logan and Linda L. Sweanor maintain, that "the greatest cause of mortality in cougar cubs appears to be male-induced infanticide" and that males sometimes kill protective mothers, then Armour evades a mother's very plausible failure (111). In *Manatee Winter*, Zoehfeld also preserves the image of mothers as committed, savvy, and indomitable where the safety of their young is concerned. Although many senior manatee mothers die in collisions with boats, and many young manatees die when they are separated from their mothers "while dodging boat traffic" (United States Fish and Wildlife 4–35), Zoehfeld tells a story of a mother manatee who skillfully shepherds her calf through the perils posed by boats. Besides a brief mention of a potentially deadly seal, Markle never admits into her story the mother penguins who do not make it back with food for their newly hatched babies. Against bookmakers' odds, every single one of the seven narratives of babies in danger showcases heroic mothers that menace or track or provide so effectively that not even a hair is harmed on their babies' bodies.

The Harms of Unenlightened Anthropomorphism

In many cases, the pressure to convey that all mothers are effective and wedded to each of their young appears to make it difficult for children's authors and illustrators to depict the complexity of actual animal mothers. Faced with a choice between representing mothers from the perspective of children's apparent needs or the perspective of mothers' goals and strategies, authors most often choose to cultivate the mother human society demands and children appear to require. One of the most obvious assumptions behind the sugarcoated content of these books appears to be that children need images that affirm their mother's care for them. Apparently, their senses of self are so fragile that they need to be shielded from the details of animal reproduction that might threaten their security. The concerted avoidance of unsettling maternal strategies and failures in the books suggests that children require the replacement of actual animals' lives with animals dressed in human maternal ideals. This dressing of animal mothers and babies in human desires and values (Timmerman and Ostertag 69) participates in the anthropomorphism, or the "attribution of human traits to nonhuman beings" (Zohar 679). As Fraustino acknowledges, humans cloaked as animals pervade children's literature and disseminate misunderstandings about animals. "Children's literature," says Fraustino, "shares in the responsibility for saturating children's culture with wrong ideas about nature" (150). Furthermore, in prioritizing animals' utility as vehicles for depicting human values, the anthropomorphism in children's books about animal mothers is anthropocentric in its framing of "experience or understanding . . . exclusively from a human perspective" (Byrne, Grace, and Hanley 37). In other words, these anthropomorphic texts put humans at the center of the universe in dispatching animals as vehicles for the human values we attach to giving birth to and raising young.

Admittedly, anthropomorphism has a role to play in pseudoscientific books helping children to learn and care about the lives of "more-than-human others" (Timmerman and Ostertag 63). Suzanne Thulin and Niklas Pramling, among many others, acknowledge how useful it can be for teaching scientific concepts to children from four to six years old. Students employ a familiar set of experiences to translate and thereby understand new scientific ideas. The researchers advise, "At times, speaking anthropomorphically. . . . can fill a 'bridging function' between the child's experience and language and the knowledge domain of science" (148). Other scholars maintain that anthropomorphism can catalyze the desire to learn about other organisms. David F. Treagust and Allan G. Harrison affirm that anthropomorphism can "motivate [older] students by maximizing their interest and cognitive understanding" (1165).

It might be possible to say that the writers of many of the books about pandas and manatees have well-founded pedagogical reasons for blurring the boundaries between human analogs and animal targets except for one important fact: the writers fail explicitly to explain their deployment of anthropomorphism and to delineate the shared and unshared attributes of the analogs and targets. While the scholars I cited in the previous paragraph endorse the pedagogical value of anthropomorphism in a teaching setting, all of them also insist that those who employ it must help students understand its role in delivering information. Treagust, Harrison, and Grady J. Venville warn teachers, "every analogy breaks down somewhere" (86). Thulin and Pramling admonish, "However, when learning science, it is important to learn to be clear and make clear to others that [anthropomorphism] is a way of speaking and making sense, not a literal description of a phenomenon" (148). None of the books that I examine in this chapter prompts children to be aware of anthropomorphism as a technique rather than truth. This failure leads me to suspect that unexamined assumptions about children and human mothers, not pedagogical strategies, lie behind intrepid manatee mothers and accommodating panda mothers.

Writers and publishers should question whether anthropomorphism that distorts the reality of animal mothers is necessary or whether it might actually do more harm than good. Thulin and Pramling suggest that anthropomorphism in biology instruction may have its roots in adult assumptions about children's limits and not in the children's cognitive needs. In a study of preschool classrooms to discover who used anthropocentrism in biology lessons and the role it played in learning, researchers garnered telling data: of the 128 anthropomorphizing statements that teachers and students made, "24 were made by the children, and 104 were made by the teachers" (147). As the numbers suggest, teachers initiated anthropomorphism much more commonly than did children. Often when children did engage in anthropomorphic talk, it was in response to the teacher's anthropomorphizing questions or statements. According to Thulin and Pramling, "The claim that children mistakenly think anthropomorphically does not appear to be confirmed in the light of the present findings. Instead, children appear communicatively . . . responsive to teacher talk" (147). The researchers' point is that adult teachers' beliefs that children need anthropomorphism to understand biology were exposed as erroneous assumptions. Thulin and Pramling pose a pointed question that pertains to the discussion here of the harm done in children's instructional books when they insulate children from biological realities: "What happens if children constantly meet teachers that maintain the notion that science is too difficult or unsuitable for children of a certain age?" (148).

Here, I want to leave the obstacles posed to learning by unenlightened anthropomorphism and turn to another of its harms. Transforming animal mothers into comforting human mirrors robs children of opportunities to recognize others beyond themselves. Reducing problem-solving animal mothers to affirmations of security blocks children's access to the otherness both of animals and of their own mothers. If we transform animal mothers into instruments of security and instruction, we deny children the experience of animal lives external to the child's subjective life—lives that may overlap in some ways with those of children but that also exceed children's experiences.

Moreover, if Ulrich Gebhard, Patricia Nevers, and Elfiede Bilman-Maheca are correct in their proposal that children simultaneously interpret "nonhuman nature" though their own experiences and their humanity through "nonhuman nature," then animal mothers present an opportunity for human children to grasp the independent existence of their own mothers. Children's books that muffle the stories of agents with obligations beyond a particular child's needs deny children the experience of their mothers as subjects, not objects. Psychoanalyst Jessica Benjamin argues that children cannot come into being as subjects if their mothers are not also acknowledged by the child to be full subjects (12–50). In order for a mother to grant the meaningful recognition that makes it possible for a child to experience himself or herself as a subject, the child must know that his or her mother is not a product of the child's own fantasies. The child must know that his or her mother exists outside his or her own interiority. Children who are given the opportunity to interpret their own mothers through varying, resourceful, and potentially flawed animal mothers may not be damaged by the experience. On the contrary, they might be stronger for knowing that their own mothers are varying, resourceful, and potentially flawed beings with commitments and roles beyond their position as a source of comfort and security.

Notes

1. Lamenting that "the selflessness of mothers giving of themselves to offspring has always seemed too vital to the well-being of too many for anyone—scientists included—to be able to examine their behavior dispassionately (xvii), Hrdy traces misguided assumptions about maternal devotion back as far as the eighteenth century. She pays particular attention to the beliefs about women's biological destiny that prevented scientists from Linnaeus to 1960s biologists and psychologists from recognizing the dynamic tactical thinking of mothers (3–29). For discussion of the framing of mothers as nurturers in children's literature, see Kertzer; Anderson; and Adams, Walker, and O' Connell.

2. See Hrdy's discussion of, among others, biologists Lack, Hrdy, Williams and Trivers, Petrie, Thornhill, Altman, and Ralls (Hrdy 29–54).

3. The Library of Congress lists 852 books that were published about animal mothers and/or babies in English between 1993 and 2013. They are under the subject headings of "Parental Behavior in Animals—Juvenile" or "Animals Infancy—Juvenile."

Works Cited

Adams, Matthew, Carl Walker, and Paul O'Connell. "Invisible or Involved Fathers: A Content Analysis of Representations of Parenting in Young Children's Picturebooks in the UK." *Sex Roles* 65.3–4 (2011): 259–70. Print.

Altman, Jeanne. *Baboon Mothers and Infants.* Cambridge: Harvard UP, 1980. Print.

Anderson, David A. "Gender Role Stereotyping of Parents in Children's Picture Books: The Invisible Father." *Sex Roles* 52.3–4 (2005): 145–51. Print.

Armour, Michael C. *Puma Range.* Illus. Simon Galkin. Norwalk, CT: Trudy Corporation and the Smithsonian Institute, 1994. Print.

Arnosky, Jim. *Babies in the Bayou.* New York: Putnam, 2007. Print.

———. *Raccoon on His Own.* New York: Puffin, 2001. Print.

Benjamin, Jessica. *The Bonds of Love: Psychoanalysis, Feminism, and the Problem of Domination.* New York: Pantheon, 1988. Print.

Berger, Melvin, and Gilda Berger. *101 Animal Babies.* New York: Scholastic, 2013. Print.

Bernardo, Joseph. "Maternal Effects in Animal Ecology." *American Zoologist* 36.2 (1996): 83–105. Print.

Bowen, Don W. "Maternal Effects on Offspring Size and Development in Pinnipeds." *Maternal Effects in Mammals.* Ed. Dario Maestripieri and Jill Mateo. Chicago: U of Chicago P, 256–91. Print.

Butler, John. *Pi-shu, the Little Panda.* Atlanta: Peachtree, 2001. Print.

Buzatto, Bruno A., Joseph Tomkins, and Leigh Simmons. "Maternal Effects on Male Weaponry: Female Dung Beetles Produce Major Sons with Longer Horns When They Perceive Higher Population Density." *BMC Evolutionary Biology* 12.1 (2012): 118. *BioMed Central.* 2012. Web. 1 May 2014.

Byrne, Jenny, Marcus Grace, and Pam Hanley. "Children's Anthropomorphic and Anthropocentric Ideas about Micro-Organisms." *Journal of Biological Education* 44.1 (2009): 37–43. Print.

Champagne, Frances A., and James P. Curley. "The Trans-Generational Influence of Maternal Care on Offspring Gene Expression and Behavior in Rodents." *Maternal Effects in Mammals.* Ed. Dario Maestripieri and Jill Mateo. Chicago: U of Chicago P, 256–91. Print.

Crozat, François. *I Am a Little Panda.* Hauppauge, NY: Barron's, 1993. Print.

Fraustino, Lisa Rowe. "The Rights and Wrongs of Anthropomorphism in Picture Books." *Ethics and Children's Literature.* Ed. Claudia Mills. Surrey, UK: Ashgate, 2014. Print.

Gebhard, Ulrich, Patricia Nevers, and Elfriede Billmann-Mahecha. "Moralizing Trees: Anthropomorphism and Identity in Children's Relationship to Nature." *Identity and the Natural Environment.* Cambridge, MA: MIT, 2003, Print.

Hall, Suzanne. "Weaning Panda Cubs." *San Diego Zoo.* San Diego Zoo, 30 Sept. 2010. Web. 15 Mar. 2014.

Holekamp, Kay E., and Stephanie M. Dloniak. "Maternal Effects in Fissiped Carnivores." *Maternal Effects in Mammals.* Ed. Dario Maestripieri and Jill M. Mateo. Chicago: U of Chicago P, 227–55. Print.

Hrdy, Sarah Blaffer. *Mother Nature: A History of Mothers, Infants, and Natural Selection.* New York: Pantheon, 1999. Print.

Jenkins, Steve, and Robin Page. *Sisters and Brothers.* Boston: Houghton Mifflin, 2008. Print.

Kertzer, Adrienne. "'This Quiet Lady: Maternal Voices and the Picture Book." *Children's Literature Association Quarterly* 18.4 (1993): 159–64. *Project Muse.* Web. 1 Mar. 2014.

Larkin-Lieffers, Patricia A. "Images of Childhood and the Implied Reader in Young Children's Information Books." *Literacy* 44.2 (2010): 76–82. Print.

Logan, Kenneth A., and Linda L. Sweanor. "Behavior and Solitary Organization of a Solitary Carnivore." *Cougar: Ecology and Conservation.* Ed. Maurice Hornocker and Sharon Jegri. Chicago: U of Chicago P, 2009. 105–14. Print.

Mack, Lorrie. *Animal Families.* New York: DK, 2008. Print.

Maestripieri, Dario. "Maternal Effects on Offspring Growth, Reproduction, and Behavior in Primates." *Maternal Effects in Mammals.* Ed. Dario Maestripieri and Jill Mateo. Chicago: U of Chicago P, 256–91. Print.

Markle, Sandra. *A Mother's Journey.* Illust. Alan Marks. Watertown, MA: Charlesbridge, 2006. Print.

Martin, Chia. *We Like to Nurse.* Illus. Shukyo Lin Rainey. Prescott, Arizona: Hohm, 1995. Print.

Michels, Dia. *If My Mother Were a Platypus: Mammal Babies and Their Mothers.* Illus. Andrew Barthelmes. Washington DC: Platypus Media, 2005. Print.

Moody-Luther, Jacqueline. *Panda Bear Cub.* Norwalk, CT: Soundprints, 2006. Print.

Ostby, Kristin. *A Baby Panda Is Born.* New York: Penguin, 2008. Print.

Parker, Amy. *Thank You, God, for Mommy.* Illus. Frank Endersby. Nashville: Nelson, 2011. Print.

Ross, Michael Elsohn. *Mama's Milk.* Illus. Ashley Wolff. Berkeley: Tricycle, 2007. Print.

Ryder, Joanne. *Panda Kindergarten.* Illus. Katherine Feng. New York: Harper Collins, 2009. Print.

Thulin, Suzanne, and Niklas Pramling. "Anthropomorphically Speaking: On Communication between Teachers and Children in Early Childhood Biology." *International Journal of Early Years Education* 17.2 (2009): 137–50. Print.

Timmerman, Nora, and Julia Ostertag. "Too Many Monkeys Jumping in Their Heads: Animal Lessons within Young Children's Media." *Canadian Journal of Environmental Education* 16 (2011): 59–75. Print.

Toast, Sarah. *Bear Cub: At Home in the Forest.* Illus. Krista Brauckmann-Towns. Lincolnwood, IL: Publications International, 1995. Print.

———. *Panda Baby: At Home in the Bamboo Grove.* Illus. Debbie Pinkney. Lincolnwood, IL: Publications International, 1995. Print.

Treagust, David F., and Allan G. Harrison. "In Search of Explanatory Frameworks: An Analysis of Richard Feynman's Lecture 'Atoms in Motion.'" *International Journal of Science Education* 22.11 (2000): 1157–70. Print.

Treagust, David F., Allan G. Harrison, and Grady J. Venville. "Teaching Science Analogies Effectively : An Approach for Preservice and Inservice Teacher Education." *Journal of Science Teacher Education* 9.2 (1998): 85–101. Print.
United States Fish and Wildlife Service. *West Indian Manatee: Multi-Species Recovery Plan for South Florida*. US Fish and Wildlife Service. US Fish and Wildlife Service, 1999. Web. 1 May 2014.
Warne, Robin W., Adam Kardon, and Erica J. Crespi. "Physiological, Behavioral, and Maternal Factors that Contribute to Size Variation in Larval Amphibian Populations." *PLOS One* 8.10 (2013): 1–9. *Academic Search Premiere*. Web. 4 Mar. 2014.
Zoehfeld, Kathleen Weidner. *Manatee Winter*. Illus. Steven James Petruccio. Norwalk, CT: Trudy Corporation and the Smithsonian Institute, 1994. Print.
Zohar, Anat, and Shlomit Ginossar. "Lifting the Taboo Regarding Teleology and Anthropomorphism in Biology Education—Heretical Suggestions." *Science Education* 82.6 (1998): 679–97. Print.

Chapter 9

A Daughter's Sacrifice: Saving the "Good-Enough Mother" from the Good Mother Fantasy

Alexandra Kotanko

A good mother, as she is often portrayed in Western culture at large, is the embodiment of sacrifice. She navigates—and perhaps struggles—within the idea that she must sacrifice her own individuality, sexuality, personal ambitions, and childhood in order to nurture these same qualities in her child. One of the first reports on this "predicament" came in 1957 and is recounted in a paper titled "Parenthood as Crisis." In this study, forty-six middle-class married couples, with at least one young child, were interviewed to determine the effects of making the transition to parenthood. Of the forty-six couples, thirty-eight "reported 'extensive' or 'severe' crisis in adjusting to the first child" (LeMasters 353). Rather than experiencing the romanticized view of motherhood that they admitted to previously holding, the mothers' actual experience included "loss of sleep . . . chronic 'tiredness' or exhaustion; extensive confinement to the home . . . curtailment of their social contracts; giving up the satisfactions and the income of outside employment . . . guilt at not being a 'better' mother; the long hours and seven day (and night) week necessary" (LeMasters 352–54). Consider the impact that this message of self-sacrifice might have on a young girl, whose future also holds the sacrifice that her mother made for her.

    J. M. Barrie's novel *Peter and Wendy* and Neil Gaiman's novel *Coraline* are two works that continue to be interpreted and reinterpreted over the decades in the forms of movies, plays, and even video games. Both stories hold solid places within Western pop culture because of the emotional truths they represent, and a central truth exposed by both stories, despite the nearly one hundred years between them, is a girl's struggle with the dialectical conflict between self-sacrifice and motherhood. *Peter and Wendy* portrays the fantasy of remaining a child forever without the limits that an adult mother would instill upon that world. In this fantasy, anything is possible, and adventures run rampant. Perhaps part of the timeless appeal of *Peter and Wendy* is the attraction children have to the fantasy of life without limits. *Coraline* also presents an appealing fantasy for children, though it is the complete opposite of that seen in *Peter and Wendy*. In *Coraline*, Coraline fantasizes about the ideal mother, who prepares her favorite meals, buys her interesting toys, and is available to Coraline all of the time.

Despite the distance between these two books in time and subject matter, this chapter examines how the female protagonists in the two stories come to the same conclusion: psychoanalyst Donald Winnicott's "good-enough mother" is the ideal mother to have and become. Winnicott coined the term in 1953, only four years before "Parenthood as Crisis" was released. The good-enough mother is able to recognize her ambivalence toward her children and is aware of both the love and the hatred that she feels toward her role as a mother. A good-enough mother does not look exactly like the mothers Hallmark refers to in their cards. Unlike a "good" mother, a good-enough mother may be reluctant to happily sacrifice herself entirely to her child's every need. According to Winnicott, this is not a bad thing. In fact, he claims that "there is no possibility whatever for an infant to proceed from the pleasure principle to the reality principle ... unless there is a good-enough mother (*Playing and Reality* 13). He goes on to describe the good-enough mother as "one who makes active adaptations to the infant's needs, an active adaptation that gradually lessens, according to the infant's growing ability to account for failure of adaptation and to tolerate the results of frustration" (13–14). As a result of the child's frustration at not having a "good," all-sacrificing mother, the child will begin to see objects as "real ... since exact adaptation resembles magic and the object that behaves perfectly [the good mother who behaves precisely the way that society has led her to believe is good] becomes nothing more than a hallucination" (13–14).

In *Peter and Wendy*, Mrs. Darling appears to represent the same ideal Victorian woman that Lynn Abrams describes in her article "Ideals of Womanhood in Victorian Britain": a "virtuous woman whose life revolve[s] around the domestic sphere of the home and family. She [is] pious, respectable and busy" (2). *Peter and Wendy* opens with a description of Mrs. Darling, who keeps "the books perfectly, almost gleefully" (Barrie 6). Mr. Darling tells Wendy that Mrs. Darling "not only love[s] him, but respect[s] him" (5–6), showing the reader that regardless of her actual feelings, Mrs. Darling is able to show the requisite Victorian "devotion to her husband" (Abrams 2). After a while, however, her housework becomes tedious, as she is only able to think about her inevitable role as a mother: "there were pictures of babies without faces. She drew them when she should have been totting up" (Barrie 6). For Mrs. Darling, the Victorian ideology is clear: "motherhood [is] woman's highest achievement" (Abrams 5). Mrs. Darling becomes a dutiful mother, who only occasionally leaves the house—but not without her daughter's bracelet, symbolic of the shackles that remain even when she is not physically in her house—and goes so far as to rearrange the thoughts within her children's minds each night, so that the pleasant ones are always on top (8).

Coraline's mother, however, appears to be the polar opposite of Mrs. Darling. At the beginning of the story, Coraline seems an annoyance to her mother, as she repeatedly comes to her in an effort to escape her boredom. Her mother suggests she go bother the neighbors instead, and at one point tells her, "I don't really mind what you do . . . as long as you don't make a mess" (Gaiman 4). In other words, don't make me do any extra work on your behalf—a typical response of a good-enough mother. Additionally, Coraline finds "only a crust in the bread bin" and has to remind her mother to get her new clothes for school (23). Unlike Mrs. Darling, Coraline's mother does not strive toward the achievement of being an ideal mother as Coraline might want her to.

In both *Peter and Wendy* and *Coraline*, there is a struggle around the maternal role. In *Peter and Wendy*, woven throughout its portrait of the ideal Mrs. Darling are hints of the ambivalence she feels toward this role. Most notably, there is a kiss—simultaneously a representation of adult sexuality and of maternal love—"perfectly conspicuous in the right-hand corner" of Mrs. Darling's mouth (Barrie 5). "Wendy could never get" this kiss, nor could Mr. Darling (5). This feeling of ambivalence is not unique to Mrs. Darling. Adrienne Rich, in her book *Of Woman Born*, boldly reflects the sentiment that many mothers likely share but would be ashamed to admit: "My children cause me the most exquisite suffering of which I have any experience. It is the suffering of ambivalence: the murderous alteration between bitter resentment and raw-edged nerves, and blissful gratification and tenderness" (21). Like Rich, and the many women who can relate to her crisis, Mrs. Darling struggles with the complete surrender of herself to the mother role. Nonetheless, it is clear that this complete surrender is not only what her family desires, but what she strives to give.

Similarly, Coraline struggles to see beyond her mother's identity as mother alone, as she longs for her to give up her own work and focus solely on Coraline. We see this through Coraline's constant interruptions of her mother's work. In her boredom, Coraline flips through her mother's book (something that she presumably reads for pleasure). The book is about native people who "take pieces of white silk and draw on them in wax, then dip the silks in dye . . . then finally, throw the now-beautiful cloths on a fire and burn them to ashes" (Gaiman 23). This description presents the "good-enough mother" in two ways. For one, it shows that Coraline's mother is able to indulge in "selfish" pleasures, away from her duties as a mother. Also, the subject of the book itself resembles "good-enough" mothering, in that the native people put work into these cloths to make them beautiful, just as a mother puts work into her child; then they burn the cloths, just as a "good-enough mother" lets her child go or at least provides room for her child to develop independently. Significantly, Coraline finds the native people's behavior in this scene "particularly pointless" (23). When Coraline's mother reads, she is simultaneously providing room for Coraline to develop an individualistic self and modeling what this self might look like. Coraline, for her part, both takes this lesson to heart (by escaping from her real mother) and rebels against it by finding what she initially believes to be an ideal mother.

That Coraline leaves her real mother can be viewed, in light of Winnicott's idea of recognizing the other, as an effort to destroy her mother. Psychoanalyst Jessica Benjamin describes Winnicott's idea: "In the course of development we do a rather paradoxical thing: we try to destroy the other person in order to discover that they survive" (135). Benjamin explains that "what [Winnicott] meant was to absolutely assert our right to have it our way and to make the other person subject to our fantasy" (136). Coraline certainly does this when she leaves her real mother and compares her to the othermother fantasy. Other Mother prepares "the best chicken that Coraline had ever eaten" and provides her with more interesting toys than she has at home, is more affectionate, and is attentive to her every need (Gaiman 27). Other Mother tells her, "We're ready to love you and play with you and feed you and make your life interesting" (58). "This is more like it," Coraline thinks to herself (28).

Like Coraline, the children in *Peter and Wendy* also need an escape. Rather than escaping to reject their mother for not fitting an ideal, they escape to find subjectivity apart from their mother, who controls them right down to the thoughts in their heads. Nonetheless, this escape can be seen as their effort to destroy the mother. Wendy, however, is unsure whether she should leave, not because she would miss her mother's dedicated care, but because she worries how her mother would continue without her children. She responds to Peter's asking her to come along, "Oh dear, I can't. Think of mummy!" (Barrie 31). To children, their self-sacrificing mothers do not exist without them, which is a mother's fear as well. Contrast this with the scene Other Mother presents to Coraline of her parents returning from a vacation: Coraline's real mother says, "Now we can do all the things we always wanted to do, like go abroad, but were prevented from doing by having a little daughter" (Gaiman 60). Thus, in both novels, the "good" mother ideal causes tension in the parent-child relationship, whether it is the mother's need to consume her children in self-sacrificial love or the child's belief that she should be the recipient of that love. This tension causes metaphorical destruction of the mother within the children's minds and an immersion into fantasy.

Unfortunately, for the children in *Peter and Wendy* and *Coraline*, the fantasy lands in which they find themselves are nothing short of horrific. Upon reaching Neverland, the Darling children realize that it is "real now, and there were no night-lights, and it was getting darker every moment" (Barrie 41). Likewise, after the initial joy upon realizing the Other World, something creepy immediately sets in: "There was something hungry in the old man's button eyes that made Coraline feel uncomfortable . . . Coraline could hear the rats whispering to each other. . . . Her other parents stood in the kitchen doorway as she walked down the corridor, smiling identical smiles, and waving slowly" (Gaiman 40–41). Coraline leaves Other World immediately, realizing the horror in the omnipotent, objectifying mother. What she originally imagined as perfection now appears unreal and even magical, like Winnicott's description in his account of the good, sacrificial mother. The children in both stories realize that something scary happens when the lines between fantasy and reality crumble, which leads them to understand the inadequacy of the mother fantasy.

Upon returning to her real house, Coraline symbolically sees her real parents stuck inside the mirror, indicating that her parents are stuck within Other Mother's fantasy world. Their appearance in a mirror that she is looking into has a couple of implications. First, it is a clue that Coraline has trapped them within her own expectations. Second, if we look at this experience through Winnicott's mirroring theory, we get a much deeper picture. Winnicott explains that "in individual emotional development the precursor of the mirror is the mother's face" (*Playing and Reality* 1). The infant wants and needs to see itself mirrored in its mother's face. In order for this to happen, the mother has to be able to reflect back what she sees and feels emotionally from the infant. This helps create a sense of self for the infant: "When I look I am seen, so I exist" (3). Therefore, a completely self-absorbed mother, one who has not matured beyond the narcissistic stage of development, would be unable to achieve this because she would only be able to display her own moods, which the infant cannot internalize. If this is the case, the infant must learn to defend himself against his mother's moods and adjust his own behavior accordingly. Thus, the mother who cannot mirror "brings a threat of chaos, and the baby will organize withdrawal, or will not look except to perceive as a defense. A baby so treated will grow up puzzled about mirrors and what the mirror has to offer" (2). If the infant is consistently limited to the "static, isolated realm of perception," then apperception, "the process of understanding something with reference to oneself," cannot be properly developed, so the infant's ability to develop an independent self will be hindered (Squier 275).

If the mother's face is the precursor to the mirror, then this first experience with the mother reflects what the child will later see of him- or herself in the mirror. Winnicott explains that when the "average girl studies her face in the mirror she is reassuring herself that the mother image is there and that the mother can see her and that the mother is en rapport with her" (*Playing and Reality* 2). We see this act of mirroring in Neverland, as well. Peter convinces Wendy to go there by telling her that she will be able to play mother to the Lost Boys. Wendy accepts and is very dutiful in her role. Soon after Wendy's arrival in Neverland, she realizes that her brothers are beginning to forget the life they came from. Much like her mother's tidying of her children's thoughts, Wendy "tried to fix the old life in [her brothers'] minds by setting them examination papers on it" (Barrie 70). She can also be found surrounded by her "children" dancing, just as Mrs. Darling brought joy to her children by coming up with and encouraging "lovely dances" (8). It does not take long, however, to see that this mothering is nothing more than an act of mirroring the roles set up by society and shown to her through her own mother, as Wendy is actually unable to provide real care for children. This is clear through the description of food: in Neverland "they had to make-believe that they had had their dinners" (61). Wendy is unable to produce real food for her "children," despite the fact that she goes through all of the motions of preparing the meals; nor is she able to keep them safe, despite her strict adherence to learned safety rules. When the Pirates come to attack Marooners' Rock, Wendy does not move because "you simply must stick to your rule about half an hour after the mid-day meal" (75). Here, Barrie subtly compares Wendy to Peter—a child unable to think beyond the rules that she may have heard from her own mother in order to actually save the Lost Boys and her siblings from the pirates. Because all Wendy has ever seen of her mother is mothering, all Wendy knows to do is to mother; however, this is mothering without thought. Psychoanalyst and sociologist Nancy Chodorow, in *The Reproduction of Mothering*, suggests that "parenting is not simply a set of behaviors, but participation in an interpersonal, diffuse, affective relationship" (33). Only through the "heightened sensitivity" that Winnicott describes—sensitivity that allows a mother to mirror her infant—can a mother know how to respond to her child's needs.

Coraline, however, has a more explicit experience of Winnicott's claims. When Coraline looks in the mirror, it is significant that she sees herself *and* her parents, though they are not physically in the room. From this, we can conclude that because Coraline's mother is a "good-enough mother"—a mother who has a strong subjective self and who has mastered the narcissistic stage, and therefore has not completely lost her entire self to the mother role—she was able to successfully mirror Coraline during infancy, which has allowed Coraline to see her mother in the mirror through her own reflection. It is also significant that this is a major turning point in the novel. This is when Coraline decides to help her parents and rescue them from the ideal mother fantasy.

A little later, Coraline again looks in the mirror at Other Mother's house: "She looked at the girl in the mirror and the girl in the mirror looked back at her. *I will be* brave, thought Coraline. *No, I am brave*" (Gaiman 59). Here we see that Coraline is able to perceive herself—she sees her physical self in the mirror and realizes that this is an independent person looking back at her. More importantly, though, she apperceives herself; she can see introspectively when she recognizes her bravery through her reflection. Interestingly, Coraline discovers that Other Mother's reflection does not show up in the mirror, unlike Coraline herself and her real parents, hinting not only that Other Mother and the world she has created are fantasy but also that her development of a true self that she can apperceive and perceive through a mirror has been hindered. In fact, when Coraline realizes that Other Mother is not in the mirror, Other Mother says, "Mirrors . . . are never to be trusted" (75). As discussed earlier, this puzzled attitude toward the mirror is exactly the consequence Winnicott describes as a result of an overly self-absorbed mother unable to mirror her infant.

Later, Coraline also becomes locked inside the mirror in Other Mother's effort to teach her how to be a loving daughter. This is symbolically a place for Coraline to reflect and discover her individual self, and it also signifies that she, like her parents, is trapped by her fantasy of the ideal mother. Here we see that not only does the mother become an object for her children's use, but the children become objects for the mother's use as well. Inside of the mirror, Coraline communicates with three ghosts of children who had also been left inside the mirror. These children, contrasted with Coraline, will never be able to look within a mirror because they are behind the glass and also because they are insubstantial beings. Despite Other Mother's ability to see physically, the fact that she does not have real, human eyes is symbolic of her inability to really see herself and those around her. If eyes are the windows to the soul, and it is clear that Other Mother can see physical objects, then perhaps the lack of eyes is symbolic of an inability to see the "soul"—the true self. As a result, the ghost children are left without any sense of self: The ghosts say, "She stole our hearts, and she stole our souls, and she took our lives away" (82). Furthermore, because Other Mother was never able to develop a sense of self, she was unable to let go of the image of the perfect child. Only through her ideal children could she acknowledge herself as an ideal mother, so she hid the children that misbehaved. Therefore, the children behind the mirror are left to die a metaphorical death, and their hope of reaching a mature adulthood has perished.

In her psychoanalytic study of fantasy and reality, Benjamin describes the idea of the need for the mother to separate from her child in order to allow the child to mature. There emerges a conflict between mother and child when they begin to separate into individualistic beings. The mother "may experience the child's demands now as threatening, as tyrannical, willful. The child is different from her fantasy of the perfect child, who would want what she wants" (Benjamin 135). This is the deeper reason Other Mother locks Coraline into the mirror. The mother "has to be willing to relinquish her fantasy that she can be perfect and provide a perfect world for her child. . . . . [This] is a step on the road to recognition" of her and her child's subjective self (Benjamin 135). The other mother, however, is unable to realize this, so without the ideal child for the mother to happily sacrifice herself to, the "good" mother cannot exist.

In *Peter and Wendy*, when the Darling children finally decide to leave Neverland, Peter recounts the story in which he tried to fly home: the window to his room was shut, and his mother was holding a new child. Chodorow might describe this as symbolic of the time in a child's life when he experiences rejection by the mother, which requires the child to face the fact that "its mother is unique and irreplaceable, whereas it is replaceable—by another infant, by other people, and by other activities" (69). Chodorow describes this as the point at which a child learns the difference between the fantasy of the mother and the reality of her. Significantly, this is the point in Peter's life at which he realizes he will never grow up, though not necessarily by choice. Assuming that "his mother would never weary of waiting for him" (Barrie 198), Peter puts off returning home to his mother in order to secure himself a little extra time to be free on his own. Once he decides to return home, he finds he is very wrong in his assumptions, as there are metal bars on the window. After calling to his mother, who does not hear him, "he had to fly back, sobbing, to the Gardens" (198–99). Chodorow goes on to suggest that a child might retaliate against this rejection by "turning the naïve egoism to hatred" (69), which is exactly what Peter does. Here we also see Winnicott's idea of destroying the other in order to see that they survive. Peter Pan has "destroyed" his mother by leaving her. Winnicott defines survival as the other's (the mother's) continuing "to be an effective, responsive, and nonthreatening presence" (Benjamin 136). When the child "feels that he has destroyed everyone and everything around him . . . he notices that everyone is just as before—still loving and still there" (Benjamin 136). This is survival. So, if the other survives, the baby or child is able "to distinguish between what he imagines and what is real" (Benjamin 136). In Peter's story, his mother does not survive according to this definition. She is no longer available, and as a result, Peter is unable to distinguish between fantasy and reality. Benjamin explains that "the flip side of Winnicott's analysis would be that when aggression is not worked through in this way . . . the whole experience shifts . . . from a feeling we can own to a projection onto the object" (136), and in this case, Peter eventually projects onto his mother a feeling of hatred of even the idea of mother. Similarly, we see Other Mother's hatred toward her own mother, possibly indicating a long line of unsuccessful rejection. Other Mother put her mother in her grave, "and when I found her trying to crawl out, I put her back" (Gaiman 91). Thus, we see that Other Mother's mother did not survive, leaving Other Mother in a permanent state of fantasy and projection. This is further indication that Other Mother was unable to develop her true self and would thus be unable to encourage this growth in a child.

Unlike Peter and Other Mother, the Darling children begin to realize that though their mother survives their attempted destruction, she may not always be there waiting to completely sacrifice herself. When the

Darling children return home, they find an open window. It appears that their attempted destruction—the escape from their mother—"damages neither the parent nor the self" (Benjamin 136). As a result, "external reality comes into view as a sharp, distinct contrast to the inner fantasy world" (Benjamin 136). Though the window is open, their mother is no longer in their room as they hoped she would be. Michael says, "It is very careless of mother . . . not to be here when we come back" (Barrie 140). The children then hear their mother playing piano in another room, signifying that though she is present, she has also been doing things for herself. Her subjectivity now has no consequence, as it did when she tried to enjoy herself at a party. Now her children do not need to escape her because she is able to allow them the space they need to play and discover their inner selves. In other words, at this point she begins to resemble a "good-enough mother." Mrs. Darling, rather than rejecting the world her children imagine—a world they use to escape her all-encompassing love—now realizes the importance of this subjective space, especially for Wendy. She offers "to let Wendy go to [Peter] for a week every year" (145). Through the Darling children's escape to Neverland, Mrs. Darling is able to recognize her children's subjectivity as well as her own. Likewise, Wendy learns to give her future daughter, Jane, this same freedom.

When Peter returns once Wendy has grown up, Wendy feels guilty being so grown-up in front of him. We see Wendy's struggle to let go of the child—both Peter as a perpetual child and her own nostalgia for her child self, with all of its immature perceptions and fantasies, who cries "Woman, woman, let go of me" (149). This comes just at the time she struggles to allow her daughter, Jane, to visit Neverland. In order to transform and grow, however, Wendy must both accept the loss of the child within and allow her daughter the space to discover her true self, as Wendy discovered hers. It appears that through this process, the adult Wendy experiences nostalgia, as Donna Bassin describes it in "Maternal Subjectivity, Culture of Nostalgia." Bassin suggests that nostalgia is "an attempt to reenact reunion with the lost object" (168). In Wendy's case, the lost objects are the childhood fantasy of Neverland and the instilled idea of being the ideal, self-sacrificing, good mother to Jane and the Lost Boys. The state of nostalgia is a result of "incomplete mourning" of loss (Bassin 168). Bassin explains that "although the nostalgic fantasy seeks metamorphosis and transformation, it is devoid of a sense of internal agency and thus remains trapped in a process of endless seeking" (168). We see this clearly in Peter and the Lost Boys' consistent longing for and seeking of a mother—"A lady to take care of us at last," they proclaim upon Wendy's arrival in Neverland (Barrie 57). Luckily, Wendy is not devoid of a sense of internal agency. This is something she gained through her going to and returning from Neverland. Thus, she realizes that it would be untrue to Jane to continue to hold onto this nostalgia. She lets go and tells Peter with confidence that she has grown up. After this, we see Wendy's mourning as complete: "She was not a little girl heart-broken about him; she was a grown woman smiling about it all" (151). Her growth then allows Jane to travel to Neverland one week each year, and Jane allows her own daughter, Margaret, the same. Here we see a new idea of good mother emerge, one that allows the mother and her children their own individualistic freedom along with recognition of fantasy as fantasy.

Likewise, at the end of *Coraline*, the fantasy of the self-sacrificial mother unravels. Chodorow explains that if the mother is unable to relinquish control of her maturing child, the child "has two options. Either it must remain permanently regressed and merged with its mother, or it must totally reject its mother, even though this mother has, until now, been a 'good mother'" (84). Therefore, Coraline must save not only her real parents from the expectations she has instilled upon them, but also herself. As Coraline succeeds in rescuing her parents, the ghost children, and herself from Other Mother's world, the world itself begins fade. Upon reaching her real house, Coraline sees her real parents, and they "never seemed to remember anything about their time in the snow globe" (Gaiman 147). It appears that her parents, like Mrs. Darling, have survived. Thus Coraline successfully separates her fantasy from reality. Just when she does so, however, Other Mother's hand creeps back to get the key to the door separating the fantasy world from the real one. In the end, the hand is defeated: Coraline uses her dolls, which her real mother points out she has grown too old for, as "protective coloration," camouflaging herself as a child to lure Other Mother, symbolized by her hand, to her death. Thus, unlike Wendy, Other Mother is defeated by nostalgia.

Wendy and Coraline are successful because they are able to separate fantasy from reality, despite the differences in time period and type of fantasy. Benjamin explains that "in the best of circumstances, we do not get rid of dangerous fantasies; rather the fantasies exist in tension with reality" (132). She goes on to explain that "it is the breakdown of the tension between these two modes, and not the existence of fantasy per se, that is detrimental to the recognition of other subjects" (132). By drawing the line between fantasy and reality, while holding both simultaneously within themselves, Wendy and Coraline are able to develop individualistic selves and mourn the loss of the ideal childhood or ideal mother. Wendy and Coraline display hope of holding on to this true self once they become mothers, thereby giving hope to the girls who read their stories.

Works Cited

Abrams, Lynn. "Ideals of Womanhood in Victorian Britain." *BBC*. BBC, 9 Aug. 2001. Web. 25 July 2013.
Barrie, J. M. *Peter Pan: Peter and Wendy and Peter Pan in Kensington Gardens*. New York: Penguin, 2004. Print.
Bassin, Donna. "Maternal Subjectivity in the Culture of Nostalgia: Mourning and Memory." *Representations of Motherhood*. Ed. Donna Bassin, Margaret Honey, and Meryle Mahrer. New Haven: Yale UP, 1994. 162–73. Print.
Benjamin, Jessica. "The Omnipotent Mother: A Psychoanalytic Study of Fantasy and Reality." *Representations of Motherhood*. Ed. Donna Bassin, Margaret Honey, and Meryle Mahrer. New Haven: Yale UP, 1994. 129–46. Print.
Chodorow, Nancy. *The Reproduction of Mothering*. Berkeley: U of California P, 1999. Print.
Gaiman, Neil. *Coraline*. New York: Harper, 2008. Print.
LeMasters, E. E. "Parenthood as Crisis." *Marriage and Family Living* 19.4 (1957): 352–55. Web. 4 October 2014.
Rich, Adrienne. *Of Woman Born*. New York: Norton, 1976. Web. 4 October 2014.
Squier, Susan. "Mirroring and Mothering: Reflections on the Mirror Encounter Metaphor in Virginia Woolf's Works." *Twentieth Century Literature* 27.3 (1981): 272–88. Web. 25 July 2013.
Winnicott, D. W. *Playing and Reality*. New York: Routledge, 2005. Web. 25 July 2013.
———. *The Child, the Family, and the Outside World*. Middlesex: Perseus, 1992.

Chapter 10

"The Mother Was the Mother, Even When She Wasn't": Maternal Care Ethics and Children's Fantasy

Mary Jeanette Moran

In the introduction to *Feminist Moral Philosophy*, Samantha Brennan makes broad claims about what constitutes feminist ethical scholarship; she includes reconsideration of "mainstream historical figures or theories, . . . [applying] feminist thought . . . to mainstream . . . problems" and even work by scholars who identify politically as feminists but "whose feminism hasn't changed the theoretical commitments guiding their approach to moral theorizing" (viii-ix). While these approaches all enrich the feminist import of philosophical study, I would argue that the development of care ethics constitutes feminist philosophy's most distinctive and significant contribution to the field. Scholars such as Carol Gilligan, Nel Noddings, Sara Ruddick, Virginia Held, and Fiona Robinson argue that relationships of care should serve as the basis for ethical decisions in the public as well as the private sphere. Our relationships with others constitute our identities and also create the responsibility to respond to others in an ethical fashion.

Care ethics has the potential to revolutionize both community structures and individual interactions, but it has also created a significant amount of controversy, in no small part because scholars such as Noddings and Ruddick identify the maternal relationship as the exemplar of ethical care. Simply founding an ethical paradigm on the association between women and caring raises concerns that the paradigm will replicate the damage that women have suffered as nurturers under patriarchy, a system that depends on care yet also views that care as a threat to autonomy. Focusing on maternal care introduces yet more questions. For example, does using a nonbiological definition of motherhood marginalize women's bodily experiences? Can we rely on a biological definition without falling into essentialism? How can the dynamic of the mother-child relationship, with its inherent power imbalance, serve as a model for relationships between adults or communities in which some level of parity is a desired goal, if not a present reality?

Children's fantasy, with its imaginative reinterpretations of subjectivity and interpersonal relationships, offers new ways to consider a maternal basis for care ethics.[1] In Philip Pullman's *His Dark Materials*, Marisa Coulter's vexed maternity illuminates the complex ethical negotiations that can occur even within one mother-child dyad. Coulter's sudden conversion into a devoted mother makes more sense when considered as part of, rather than separate from, the drive to power that has characterized her throughout the text; because the political environment affects this mothering relationship so significantly, the novel emphasizes how important it is for practitioners of care ethics to consider the particular circumstances of the maternal images that underlie this ethical system. Robin McKinley's *Spindle's End* attempts to rewrite the Sleeping Beauty tale's representations of femininity; with a host of characters who conspire to nurture and protect the young princess, McKinley's text complicates images of motherhood as well as the goals of what Ruddick calls maternal thinking, in which anyone can take up the tasks of mothering. Madeleine L'Engle's *A Swiftly Tilting Planet* presents what seems to be the most conventional image of motherhood among these texts, in that Meg Murry's pregnancy has nothing supernatural about it, and it limits her range of movement to the domestic sphere. However, as Meg's brother, Charles Wallace, travels through time by inhabiting the bodies of others, he is the one to experience the loss of self and agency that can be the negative result of motherhood in a patriarchy, while Meg maintains the ability to act for them both. With their variations on maternal relationships, these texts enable us to participate in the ongoing effort to think critically about how ideas of motherhood contribute to feminist ethics of care.

Maternal Images in Ethics of Care

Carol Gilligan's *In a Different Voice: Psychological Theory and Women's Development* is perhaps the most well-known example of feminist ethics (1982).[2] In this groundbreaking work, Gilligan points out that dominant psychological theories, based as they are on men's experiences and the worldviews resulting from those experiences, validate separation from others as the most significant marker of maturity. Not surprisingly, this kind of patriarchal system also uses various manifestations of separation to determine the rightness of ethical decisions; in order to act ethically, a person must take an objective and rational stance, make universalizable decisions, and aim at the ultimate goal of impartial justice. All of these criteria require the person to separate himself or herself from emotion and from the particular details of the situation in question. As a result, people who value connection, whether as the basis for their ethical decisions or in other parts of their lives, seem to be immature and insufficiently ethical (8–9). Gilligan found that women often fall into this category, in large part because patriarchal societies encourage women to build and maintain connections between people; as she puts it, "the very traits that traditionally have defined the 'goodness' of women, their care for and sensitivity to the needs of others, are those that mark them as deficient in moral development" (18). Rather than seeing the "masculine" or "feminine" side of the equation—separation or connection—as the sole indication of success, Gilligan argues, we need to realize that a combination of both qualities is necessary for each individual to live a fulfilling life and to make ethically sound decisions that balance concern for the self and for others. While it is certainly possible to strike this kind of balance using traditional systems of ethics, the key difference between these systems and feminist ethics is in the worldview that contextualizes and characterizes the ethical decisions. According to Gilligan, those who follow an ethics of care will see people "arrayed not as opponents in a contest of rights but as members of a network of relationships on whose continuation they all depend" (30). Once we have moved away from a paradigm that values separation above all else, care emerges as a legitimate goal of ethical decisions in addition to, or perhaps even instead of, justice. Within an ethics of care, moral decisions not only *can* take existing relationships into consideration, but they *should* aim to maintain these relationships and create new caring connections.

Other scholars have taken up the idea of care-based ethics, developing the theory and investigating how an ethics based on care could be extended from the private to the public realm. Nel Noddings and Sara Ruddick were among the first to claim that maternal care should be the model on which care ethics depends. This line of thought extends the goals of feminist ethics by challenging the idea that mothering is an instinctive and therefore almost animalistic behavior. For Noddings, the mother-child relationship exemplifies how care ethics should work because for the mother, responding to her child is an ethical imperative, a feeling that "I must" act to address another person's needs (*Maternal* 13). This interaction demonstrates what Noddings calls "natural caring," which she delineates as distinct from rule-based ethical decisions: "*Natural caring* is not a conceptual contrivance. It is a state we see in everyday life—a practical, empathetic mode of responding to one another. It is a social way of interacting with others, and we treasure it" (*Maternal* 17). According to Noddings, natural caring leads to and serves as a model for an ethics of care that goes beyond our already established emotional connections so that the "purpose of *formal morality* from the perspective of care theory . . . is to sustain and expand the community of natural caring" (18). Like Noddings, Ruddick attempts to present a new image of maternal care as the basis for an ethical paradigm that applies to the public sphere as well as the private. She argues that what she calls "maternal thinking" has particular elements that would benefit our consideration of moral issues other than that of raising children. According to Ruddick, our understanding of motherhood "demands" that mothers meet at least three goals; they must ensure the "preservation, growth, and social acceptability" of their children (17). In turn, these demands require that mothers engage in "preservative love, nurturance, and training" (17). Noddings and Ruddick, as well as later proponents of maternal care ethics such as Virginia Held, stress the amount of conscious, deliberative thought necessary for mothers to care for their children effectively. By emphasizing biological maternity in the content and language of their analysis, Noddings and Ruddick suggest that there is something special about the mother-child bond, something that makes this particular caring relationship the best model on which to found a prescriptive moral theory.

The proponents of maternal care ethics must walk a fine line as they attempt to forge an integral connection between mothering and philosophy; while these two fields both concern themselves with the well-being of others, they had previously been seen as separate and distinct modes, with mothering based in bodily practices that seemed antithetical to the realm of intellectual abstractions. Maternal care ethics thus faces a dual challenge: radically redefining existing notions of motherhood, which evoke strong (though varied) feelings in almost everyone, while also relying on and revaluing those notions as building blocks for a new ethical paradigm. In their choice to use the terminology of mothering, rather than parenting, Noddings and Ruddick do not wish to suggest that only women can function within an ethic of care. In fact, each writer takes pains to stress that men can enact caring ethics; Ruddick even asserts that according to her definition of mothering, men can be mothers too (40), while Noddings provides this disclaimer: "Readers should understand that I am not claiming that the path from maternal instinct is the only path to full moral life, but it is one primary path that has been neglected" (*Maternal* 6). However, Noddings contends that women have a biological propensity toward empathy that is enhanced by cultural standards like the ones Gilligan describes (13–16), while both Noddings and Ruddick use feminine pronouns when they speak of mothers. There are good reasons for these linguistic choices, of course; Ruddick should not need to remind us, "Throughout history and still today women assume disproportionately the responsibilities of caring for children" (xxvii). Moreover, even as *mothers* garner a certain kind of reverence (at least in certain cultural contexts and provided they conform to societal norms), *mothering* receives a lower level of respect than many jobs, the intellectual work of mothering gets little recognition, and systemic injustices that hinder good mothering go unaddressed. Add to these problems the fact that not only mothering, but childcare of all sorts, gets caught in a misogynist feedback loop—undervalued because it is associated with women, assigned to women because it is undervalued—and we can see why Noddings and Ruddick would choose to emphasize the feminine side of parenting, even if one of the ideal results of their work would be to encourage men as well as women to take on the work that mothering entails. This political statement is necessary and valuable, but the perhaps inevitable consequence is that by using mothering instead of parenting or childcare as the basis of their ethics, these authors risk idealizing mothers, reinforcing limiting stereotypes about them, and excluding those who cannot be or choose not to be biological or adoptive mothers.

    Ruddick herself addresses the difficulties facing maternal care ethics at some length (28–57). I find her arguments persuasive but not conclusive, a response that she seems to anticipate when she says, "In reflecting on these . . . resistances to my project, I do not mean to anticipate objections or to still dissent, but rather to make open discussion more likely" (29). Both Gilligan and Ruddick use literary references to identify pervasive cultural images of femininity, maternity, and care, so as part of this open discussion, it seems natural to consider how literature can contribute to or comment on the ethics of care that they have developed. If, as Ruddick claims, our images of motherhood are powerfully influenced by the perspectives of daughters, then literature for young people should provide especially productive material for this kind of study ("Maternal" 346; *Maternal* 36, 38–39). Maria Nikolajeva argues that fantasy literature, especially when compared to fairy tales, has responded to our post-quantum-physics world by moving "From a limited, positivistic view of the world . . . to a wider, more open view of life" that allows it to depict "the postmodern human being's split and ambivalent picture of the universe" (140). Building on all these ideas, I turn to examine how mothering practices connect to an ethics of care in young adult fantasy.[3] While the topic warrants extended attention, here I will discuss one novel at length and provide brief overviews of two others as a way of indicating how much has yet to be said on the issue.

Conflicted Motherhood in *His Dark Materials*

Marisa Coulter, the mother of protagonist Lyra in Philip Pullman's three-volume novel *His Dark Materials*, is a complex mother figure to say the least. When we first meet her, she is luring children away from their homes to an isolated research station. There they undergo medical experiments that culminate in intercision, the violent separation of the children and their daemons (the concrete embodiment of a soul that exists in their world). She abandoned her own infant daughter, conceived during an extramarital affair, and Lyra grows up believing her mother is dead. Mrs. Coulter uses physical violence to control Lyra at several points in the book, but she saves her from intercision and seems horrified that Lyra nearly had to undergo the process. When she discovers that Lyra has been prophesied to undermine the church to which Coulter has devoted her life and on which much of her power depends, she initially seems to abandon Lyra to the mercies of church officials and then experiences a drastic and unexpected change of heart that leads her to protect Lyra at all costs. This protection first takes the form of absolute control when she drugs Lyra to keep her from acting against the church even unwittingly. After Lyra escapes, however, Coulter continues to watch over her from afar, risking and eventually giving her life so that Lyra may grow to adulthood in freedom and happiness.

Coulter's sudden conversion into a doting mother has intrigued and frustrated critics, and their comments reveal some of the cultural approaches to motherhood with which maternal care ethics must contend. Nikolajeva holds that Coulter's "ultimate reformation, ostensibly driven by her sudden maternal instincts, is psychologically implausible" but then suggests that it is nevertheless believable, since "human nature is enigmatic and inconsistent, and the character of Mrs. Coulter is a good illustration" (148). Mary Harris Russell finds Coulter's transformation more credible, especially when compared with that of Lyra's father, Lord Asriel; she claims that after Lyra escapes her mother's imprisonment, Coulter "is apparently speaking the truth about her conversion to motherhood" and that "Perhaps because Pullman has spent so much time with Marisa Coulter . . . her conversion to totally support Lyra's cause comes as less of a surprise than Asriel's does" (216, 221). Nikolajeva's comments imply that maternal attachment cannot develop quickly and/or that this maternal attachment is inconsistent with Coulter's previous behavior, including being "keen to see [the children] pulled apart" in an earlier and crueler form of intercision than the guillotine that Lyra encounters (Pullman 202). Russell, on the other hand, sees Coulter's transformation as gradual, locating the beginning at the moment when she physically reacts to Lyra's impending intercision: "Lyra saw her totter and clutch at a bench; her face, so beautiful and composed, grew in a moment haggard and horror-struck" (Pullman 205). Russell suggests that when viewed as a slow development, Coulter's growing attachment to Lyra is plausible despite how she has acted toward others and that her change represents a move away from "the quest for knowledge" and toward "the quest for maternal identity" which motivates her ultimately to sacrifice herself for her child (216).

Both of these interpretations indicate how the character of Mrs. Coulter presents problems from the perspective of maternal care ethics, and potentially *for* that perspective as well. If, as Nikolajeva appears to think, it is impossible to activate maternal instinct through a brief though traumatic interaction with one's biological child, then Coulter's transformation is implausible. However, if this kind of spontaneous bond is possible and leads Coulter to value her child's well-being above her own, as Russell's argument implies, then we seem to be left with an image of motherhood that reinforces the antifeminist stereotypes that critics of maternal care ethics fear. For example, Coulter's conversion, if authentic, supports the assumptions that motherly care is a biological, instinctive drive to which all mothers are subject and from which nonmothers are excluded, and that the essence of motherly care is the sacrifice—mind, body, and soul—of the mother for her children. After all, as Russell points out, the narrator's last mention of Coulter is not by name but as "Lyra's mother." As she plunges to her death in order to destroy the being who poses a great threat to Lyra, both action and language reinforce the idea that her maternal role has consumed her entirely (Russell 216–17; Pullman 847). Like Nikolajeva, Amelia Rutledge expresses skepticism about Coulter and Asriel's new parental priorities—"Viewed in terms of narrative sequence, her parents' pro-Lyra stance seems sudden and undermotivated" (129–30)—but she also parallels Russell when she argues that Coulter's intent and eventually her motivation become clearer and at least somewhat credible as the novel progresses.

I would argue that we can see Coulter's transformation as a turn from a patriarchal system of ethics, focused on objectivity and abstraction, to an ethics of care. When viewed in this way, Coulter's change in priorities becomes more plausible, but her conflicted, inconsistent brand of motherhood reminds us of the need to consider the maternal images at the base of care ethics with as much specificity as the moral decisions that draw on that ethics. Rutledge contends that "until Coulter *acts* on her resolve to aid Lyra—departing to seduce Metatron [an angel who intends to destroy Lyra]—her motivations remain ambiguous, which is part of the power of Pullman's characterization" (123). Care ethics would agree with Rutledge here, due to the precept that care cannot simply be an attitude; it must be enacted with respect for the specific details of each situation in order to have any moral power. Noddings identifies as dangerous the moments when "caring, which is essentially nonrational in that it requires a constitutive engrossment and displacement of motivation, may gradually or abruptly be transformed into abstract problem solving" (*Caring* 25). For example, when Coulter learns that her daughter is destined to be "Eve, again!"—to be tempted, fall, and become "mother" to a new reality in which the church loses much of its power—she initially responds according to objective logic rather than considering Lyra's particular needs, as care ethics would require. Although the revelation of Lyra's destiny occurs long after Coulter saves Lyra's life by rescuing her from intercision, in this later scene Coulter demonstrates the kind of abrupt transformation that Noddings describes; she immediately says, "Why, I shall have to destroy her [. . .] to prevent another Fall. . . . Why didn't I see this before? It was too large to see." Then "she clapped her hands together softly, like a child, wide-eyed" (Pullman 528). Coulter's "Why" sets up the following comment as an obvious consequence of her new information; she has lived her life according to the doctrine of her church, conforming to its ideas of good and evil in order to achieve what power she can in her patriarchal society, and if she is to continue within this paradigm, a hierarchical structure in which believers must follow ethical and behavioral rules without question, then she has no choice: she will "have to destroy" Lyra. This is exactly the kind of "abstract problem solving" that Noddings criticizes. Coulter does not take into account the fact that she is Lyra's mother, but she simply applies her existing rules to the situation and deduces the logical outcome. Her approach to the problem opposes the emphasis that an ethics of care places on maintaining relationships; this distancing method is so alienated from the particular identities and relationships of the people involved, in fact, that it is almost "too large to see," and it tramples over Coulter's will as well as Lyra's, reducing her to a powerless child who can simply look "wide-eyed" in wonder as the sequence of ideas unfolds.

By contrast, when Coulter comes upon Lyra in the grip of the intercisor during the earlier scene, it is clear that she is reacting to the particular elements of that ethical dilemma: while she could watch other children undergoing the process without compunction and even with relish, she springs into action upon seeing *this* child about to be irreparably harmed. If this is an example of Noddings's maternal "I must," then it might seem that biological motherhood holds some mystical power to reform even a child molester and murderer. Another possibility, of course, is that she has not been reformed at all and that she only values Lyra because of the girl's relation to herself. Caring ethics sheds a slightly different light on this relational reading, since an ethics of care depends on the idea that relationships with others *constitute* each person's identity. In Susan Sherwin's words, "relational theory requires us to supplant the familiar ideal of the independent, rational, self-interested deliberator of liberal individualism with a relational subject who is (at least partially) constituted by social interactions" (288). This approach neither exalts nor erases the self but values the relationship between self and other. As Robinson says, "the relational ontology of care ethics claims that relations of interdependence and dependence are a fundamental feature of our existence" (4). Rather than being struck by Lyra's value as an object, Coulter may be reacting to the realization that the relationship between them is significant. Indeed, Pullman's phrasing emphasizes this relationship, for in the same quote that Russell references from this scene, we read not simply of Coulter's reaction but also of Lyra's perception of that reaction: "Lyra saw her totter and clutch at a bench; her face, so beautiful and composed, grew in a moment haggard and horror-struck" (Pullman 205). Lyra is as aware of her mother as Marisa Coulter is of her, and their relationship helps define each of them whether they like it or not.

Even if maternal care ethics helps to make Coulter more sympathetic and her behavior toward Lyra more understandable, we are still left with the problem posed by the kind of mother Coulter becomes. A self-abnegating mother would seem to contradict feminist aims; a mother who uses her maternal identity to manipulate others would seem to undermine the ideal at the heart of maternal care ethics—and Coulter appears to be both. She sacrifices her privileged position in society, her ambitions, and finally her life in order to protect Lyra. (True, her idea of protecting Lyra includes holding her captive, but the sacrifice is there nevertheless.) However, Coulter's renewed partnership with her previously estranged lover, Asriel, undertaken in the last moments of their lives as they work together to bring down the oppressive power structure threatening Lyra, indicates that she may be developing an awareness of relational or mutual autonomy, a feminist ethical concept that rejects the isolated, individualist definition of autonomy that patriarchy supports. Virginia Held comments,

> There can be more, or less, self-direction within the interdependencies that surround us, and caring relations often contribute to such autonomy. But more self-sufficiency is not always better. Cooperative activity involves mutual dependence. The critique of domination basic to the ethics of care can contribute to fostering appropriate kinds of autonomy. (Held 55)

Rutledge suggests something similar when she says that after Coulter and Asriel "realize that working for Lyra is not a 'zero-sum' gesture that jeopardizes their autonomy, they can reverse the separation" between them (130). And another character comments of Asriel and Coulter's destruction of Metatron, "They could not have done it alone, but together they did it" (Pullman 900). In other words, while Coulter's maternal relationship motivates her to abandon many of her old priorities, it also gives her the potential to build other relationships and to take an active role in reshaping the power dynamics of her world. She sacrifices much for her child but maintains and even strengthens her relational autonomy; she does not need to obliterate her identity in order to enact a maternal ethics of care.

Although Coulter's efforts to protect Lyra do lead to Coulter's death, it is the political context of her mothering, not the maternal relationship itself, that necessitates this ultimate sacrifice. This destructive dynamic highlights the importance of considering maternal care ethics within a political context. As Robinson puts it, "relations of care and intimacy are of great political significance in that their form and nature are determined by relations of power that play out in a variety of different contexts—from the household to the global political economy" (5). While these relations of power eventually lead to Coulter's demise, her awareness of them also allows her to manipulate her maternal identity to her advantage. After being captured by Asriel's rebel forces, Coulter speaks passionately about her growing love for Lyra in order to convince one of Asriel's commanders, King Ogunwe, to trust her. She uses the language of instinctive attachment in order to project a maternal ethos, claiming that "something stirred in [her] heart" when Lyra faced danger (Pullman 699). Coulter's emotions seem to overwhelm her as she continues in broken phrases, "Oh, I felt such a love, such a tenderness . . . I lay beside her at night, I cradled her in my arms, I wept into her hair, I kissed her sleeping eyes, my little one" (700). The narrator does not give us a clear indication of whether Coulter's words are sincere; Asriel thinks that she is speaking "barefaced lies," although he is not necessarily a reliable judge of his former lover's character (700). However, another of the commanders, who has no history with Coulter, parallels Asriel's skepticism about her statements; he "sensed in her a nature as close to that of a scorpion as he had ever encountered, and he was well aware of the power in the sting he could detect under her gentle tone" (700). Coulter may very well have Lyra's interests at heart when she successfully manipulates King Ogunwe into trusting her, but the associated images of deception, volatility, and danger run counter to the image of motherhood at the base of care ethics. Ruddick acknowledges that merely giving birth or having responsibility for a child does not ensure that the person will engage in mothering practices: "There is nothing foreordained about maternal response. Birthgivers or legal guardians may respond to children with indifference, assault, or active neglect" (xi). Ruddick's comment helps to draw a distinction between the biological mother or official caretaker and those who engage in maternal practices—the two categories can overlap but do not necessarily do so—and thus avoids idealizing or essentializing mothers. Marisa Coulter, however, defies the categories of mothering and not-mothering. She uses physical violence against her child but also sacrifices herself to save that child; she seems to have developed a deep and sincere attachment to Lyra, but she chooses to display that attachment in a "shameless" and calculating attempt to manipulate others into sympathizing with her (Pullman 700). While a maternal ethics of care helps to explain and justify what might seem to be wildly inconsistent or essentializing behavior on the part of Marisa Coulter, her character also highlights some of the gaps in this relational form of ethics. At the very least, the field may benefit from a more careful examination of the wide spectrum of mothering identities and further analysis of how mothers deploy the various images of maternity in ethical and unethical ways.

Expanding the Boundaries of Motherhood: McKinley, L'Engle, and Beyond

A thorough study of Robin McKinley's *Spindle's End* and Madeleine L'Engle's *A Swiftly Tilting Planet* exceeds the scope of this chapter, but I include brief readings of the two novels in order to demonstrate the possibility for further productive exchanges between young adult fantasy and a maternal ethics of care. *Spindle's End*, a reworking of the Sleeping Beauty tale, offers a vision of Ruddick's maternal thinking that extends, as Ruddick theorizes, beyond the biological mother. When young fairy Katriona witnesses the evil Pernicia's curse on the infant princess, she finds herself impelled to protect the baby and unaccountably drawn to her: "Katriona, with no recollection of how she got there, found herself kneeling by the cradle and snatching up the now-crying princess in her own arms and patting the little back and stroking the little head" (McKinley 43). Katriona is not Princess Rosie's mother—she has no biological connection to her at all—yet she clearly feels the demand to protect and nurture that Ruddick describes as inherent to mothering. As Katriona makes a months-long trip from the castle back to her modest home, it emerges that this ethical demand affects others as well and is powerful enough to reach even across species. Each night a different mother animal shows up to feed Rosie with her own milk, and although Katriona can talk to animals, they never ask why she is traveling with someone else's baby, because for animals, "the baby was the baby and the mother was the mother, even when she wasn't" (McKinley 60). The animals thus enact Noddings's idea of "ethical caring," which exists in order "to sustain and expand the community of natural caring" that "is practiced out of love or inclination" (*Maternal* 18, 36). According to Noddings, ethical caring "becomes morally necessary when natural caring fails in its usual settings" (34). In this case, evil acts cause natural caring to fail; the queen cannot nurse her baby because of the threat of the curse and the subsequent need to hide Rosie, while Katriona, though she is inclined to do so, cannot provide the milk herself. Located though the animals are within the "natural" realm, often associated with unthinking instinct, they exemplify the extent to which mothering is an ethical activity that requires active thought and conscious choice. When Katriona starts to wonder how it is that she always finds an animal mother to share her milk with Rosie, she realizes that "word had gone out" among the animals about Pernicia's curse and that "they didn't have to understand human language to recognise very bad news for everybody when they saw it" (McKinley 88). Acknowledging the connection among all beings, the animals make a moral decision to care in ways that go against their normal inclination, extending the community of mothers that nurture Rosie. The rest of the novel continues to redefine the relationships among biological motherhood, cultural ideas of femininity, and maternal practices as a variety of characters work together to perform Ruddick's three vital mothering tasks of protection, nurture, and training, thus enabling the princess to grow to maturity and thwart Pernicia's curse.

Unlike *Spindle's End*, *A Swiftly Tilting Planet* has a biological mother at its center—pregnant Meg Murry O'Keefe. The novel plays on the powerful mother/powerless mother duality to which Ruddick traces some of our societal ambivalence about the maternal. As Ruddick points out, mothers often seem all-controlling to young children; she posits that many of the negative associations with motherhood derive from the difficulty of reconciling the psychological force of mothering with the lack of control that many mothers experience in their relationships with other adults and with institutions (*Maternal* 34–37). *A Swiftly Tilting Planet* disrupts this antifeminist pattern by dividing the physical and sociocultural burdens of motherhood between Meg and her brother, Charles Wallace. As they work together to save the world from nuclear annihilation, both siblings engage in ethical caring, effecting a large-scale act of maternal preservation through their ability to protect and nurture the individuals they encounter during their adventure. Only Meg undergoes the physical manifestations of pregnancy and their concomitant restrictions on her range of motion, but Charles also experiences an embodied sense of interrelatedness that challenges the idea of autonomous selfhood. Moreover, he encounters an extreme level of the self-abnegation that has become associated with motherhood under patriarchy. In the interest of time, I will discuss Meg only briefly; I focus on Charles Wallace because his masculinity both expands the definition of maternal identity, as Ruddick claims is possible, and throws into high relief the difficulties of taking on a maternal role.[4]

Meg's pregnancy might at first seem restrictive; as opposed to L'Engle's earlier books about the Murry family, in which Meg quests to save Charles Wallace, this time only Charles gets to travel throughout history, while Meg stays at home. Her family seems determined to reinforce the idea of a fragile, powerless pregnant body, as they remind her at every opportunity that she should stay in the house and preferably in her bed. However, by remaining at home, Meg actually retains more freedom of movement and thought than Charles Wallace, who must relinquish his sense of autonomous selfhood as he inhabits the bodies of people from various time periods in an effort to change the timeline and avert nuclear war in the present. L'Engle's description of this process, called "going Within," evokes the pregnant woman's experience of sharing her body, in which mutuality replaces separation as the defining characteristic of selfhood. Startled to hear that he will be residing within the bodies of other people in different time periods, Charles Wallace discusses the idea with his cosmic guide, the unicorn Gaudior:

> "But . . . what happens to my own body?"
> "It will be taken care of."
> "Will I get it back?"
> "If all goes well."
> "And if all does not go well?"
> "Let us hold firmly to all going well." . . .
> "Gaudior, it's a very scary thing. . . . What happens to *me*?"
> "I'm not entirely sure. But you don't get lost. You stay you." (57)

While this exchange could apply to a woman's concerns about the emotional and physical consequences of pregnancy, there are, of course, significant differences—not just Charles Wallace's gender, but also the fact that he will be the inhabitant instead of the host. Still, Charles Wallace's participation in an ethic of care has already associated him with motherhood, an association that helps to construct his experiences of going Within as a reflection of mothering identity. By complicating the powerful/powerless maternal binary through the characters of Meg and Charles, *A Swiftly Tilting Planet* encourages readers to become more cognizant of the various power dynamics surrounding the image of the mother and the bodily experience of mothering women.

Maternal care ethics has enormous potential to help us rethink cultural attitudes toward mothers and to reshape relationships and institutions according to a model of care. Working with a topic as ideologically charged as motherhood, though, creates equally significant challenges. Fantasy literature, with its blend of the strange and familiar, provides a space where we can explore our current conceptions of motherhood, the complicated negotiations of power and identity in which mothering persons engage, and the structural and conceptual restrictions with which these persons must contend. Pullman's Marisa Coulter, McKinley's coalition of human and animal mothers, and L'Engle's Meg and Charles Wallace engage in various kinds of care for themselves and others, and in doing so they help to expand our ideas of who mothering persons are and what they can achieve.

Notes

1. Thanks are due to the students in my graduate seminar of fall 2013; our rich discussions about fantasy and feminist ethics have informed this chapter in many ways.

2. Sara Ruddick's article "Maternal Thinking" predates Gilligan by two years, but I will focus primarily on Ruddick's book, *Maternal Thinking: Toward a Politics of Peace*, since it represents a more developed version of her theories.

3. Although *Spindle's End* is based on a fairy tale, I would place it in the category of what Nikolajeva calls the "literary fairy tale," which she suggests is closer to fantasy than to traditional fairy tales (138).

4. In addition to Meg and Charles, among the intriguing maternal figures in *A Swiftly Tilting Planet* are Meg's bitter, emotionally scarred mother-in-law and the vengeful mother of the war-mongering dictator who initiates the global crisis.

Works Cited

Brennan, Samantha, ed. *Feminist Moral Philosophy*. Calgary: U of Calgary P, 2002. Print.

Gilligan, Carol. *In a Different Voice: Psychological Theory and Women's Development*. Cambridge: Harvard UP, 1982. Print.

Held, Virginia. *The Ethics of Care: Personal, Political, and Global*. Oxford: Oxford UP, 2006.

———. *Feminist Morality: Transforming Culture, Society, and Politics*. Chicago: U of Chicago P, 1993. Print.

L'Engle, Madeleine. *A Swiftly Tilting Planet*. 1978. New York, Square Fish, 2007. Print.

McKinley, Robin. *Spindle's End*. 2000. New York: Penguin, 2002. Print.

Nikolajeva, Maria. "Fairy Tale and Fantasy: From Archaic to Postmodern." *Marvels and Tales: Journal of Fairy-Tale Studies*. 17.1 (2003): 138–56. Print.

Noddings, Nel. *Caring: A Feminine Approach to Ethics and Moral Education*. Berkeley: U of California P, 1984. Print.

———. *The Maternal Factor: Two Paths to Morality*. Berkeley: U of California P, 2010. Print.

Pullman, Philip. *His Dark Materials*. 1995, 1997, 2000. New York: Knopf, 2007. Kindle Edition.

Robinson, Fiona. *The Ethics of Care: A Feminist Approach to Human Security*. Philadelphia: Temple UP, 2011. Print.

Ruddick, Sara. *Maternal Thinking: Toward a Politics of Peace*. 1989. Boston: Beacon, 1995. Print.

———. "Maternal Thinking." *Feminist Studies* 6.2 (1980): 342–67. Print.

Russell, Mary Harris. "'Eve, Again! Mother Eve!': Pullman's Eve Variations." *His Dark Materials Illuminated: Critical Essays on Philip Pullman's Trilogy*. Ed. Millicent Lenz with Carole Scott. Detroit: Wayne State UP, 2005. 212–22. Print.

Rutledge, Amelia A. "Reconfiguring Nurture in Philip Pullman's *His Dark Materials.*" *Children's Literature Association Quarterly* 33.2 (2008): 119–34. Print.

Sherwin, Susan. "The Importance of Ontology for Feminist Policy-Making in the Realm of Reproductive Technology." *Feminist Moral Philosophy*. Ed. Samantha Brennan. Calgary, AB: U of Calgary P, 2002. 273–95. Print.

PART IV
Performing Postfeminist Motherhood

Chapter 11

"I Would Never Be Strong Enough": Sarah Dessen's Postfeminist Mothers

Sara K. Day

The phrase "having it all," coined by Shirley Conran in the 1970s, has become shorthand for a large and complicated conversation regarding women's potential to find success and satisfaction in both their professional and their personal lives. Though the phrase itself has at times been replaced with other buzzwords, such as "work/life balance," the concept has remained prevalent for the past four decades. Works such as Susan Faludi's still-relevant *Backlash: The Undeclared War Against American Women* (1991) have engaged with not only the possibility of women's "having it all" but also the increasingly problematic ways in which that phrase and its implications have infiltrated American culture. In 2012, Anne-Marie Slaughter revitalized the conversation with her *Atlantic Monthly* article "Why Women Still Can't Have It All," in which she asserts that the phrase itself holds different significance for different generations of women. "Women of my generation have clung to the feminist credo we were raised with . . . because we are determined not to drop the flag for the next generation," she states. "But when many members of the next generation have stopped listening, on the grounds that glibly repeating 'you can have it all' is simply airbrushing reality, it is time to talk" (Slaughter). This gap between generations of women and their expectations for feminism, for work/life balance, and for themselves has led to confusion about the direction the feminist movement has taken and should take—and that confusion has pronounced consequences for contemporary mothers and their adolescent daughters as they try to navigate the spaces between.

It is precisely within these conversations, which investigate private and public spaces, personal and professional obligations, feminist sensibilities and postfeminist culture, that popular young adult author Sarah Dessen locates many of the mother-daughter relationships in her fiction. Throughout Dessen's eleven[1] novels, readers encounter adolescent women protagonists confronting a variety of conventional struggles: dysfunctional family relationships, evolving peer relationships, budding romances. While their specific plotlines vary, Dessen's narrators do share a number of important traits, particularly their intelligence and ambition. Most are high-achieving students with plans of attending college and pursuing careers, which suggests a general message of empowerment for adolescent women—indeed, that young women can look forward to "having it all" as they reach adulthood. Meanwhile, their mothers and stepmothers represent a complex and often problematic understanding of womanhood informed by precisely this rhetoric. Whether they are overachieving career women, distracted stay-at-home moms, or unreliable serial monogamists or alcoholics, these mothers appear to be incapable of finding a satisfying balance in their lives, which in turn complicates their relationships with their daughters.

Ultimately, the mother-daughter relationships in Dessen's novels represent not "feminist underpinnings," as Wendy J. Glenn has claimed, but *post*feminist stereotypes, particularly in their modeling of the problematic rhetoric of "having it all." Postfeminism as a concept has been defined in a number of ways and can be understood in a variety of other domains of women's lives, but in my discussion of Dessen's work I am primarily interested in the ways that her novels engage with feminism (explicitly or implicitly) within the framework of mother-daughter relationships with the ultimate, if indirect, effect of diminishing or dismissing it in favor of traditional expectations of womanhood. The struggles of Dessen's mother figures to achieve successful adulthood reinforce a belief that women must *not* achieve or even strive for the kinds of goals that these fictional women largely fail to accomplish. In turn, the conclusions of most of her novels undermine the generally positive models that the teenage characters set forth: despite their strong, capable beginnings, the young women at the hearts of Dessen's novels frequently find themselves, in the end, pursuing somewhat less ambitious paths than the novels' premises suggest. Mothers and daughters alike, then, create the impression that not only can women not balance the demands of professional and personal lives, but they should not even try.

Feminism, Postfeminism, and the Adolescent Woman

The question of feminist and postfeminist impulses in Dessen's novels requires a brief consideration of these terms (and, perhaps more importantly, their associated misconceptions), as well as their specific relevance to contemporary adolescent womanhood. It has become commonplace in the past decade or more for young women to distance themselves from the feminist movement, often using the specific phrase "I'm not feminist, but . . ." to ensure that any potentially feminist sentiment is not understood as belonging to the movement itself. The popular misconception is that feminism is code for misandry. Hence, young women often hedge their beliefs in an attempt to distance themselves from this uncomfortable perception. Although some young women do proudly identify as feminists—indeed, teenage blogger Julie Zeilinger founded the blog *The F Bomb* precisely to offer a forum for young women to engage with feminism—the larger tendency among young people is to either reject feminism or, perhaps more commonly, to express a belief that both personal and institutional equality have been achieved, rendering feminism unnecessary.

Such assertions participate in a larger system of postfeminist discourse identified by Angela McRobbie as a force that "positively draws on and invokes feminism as that which can be taken into account, to suggest that equality is achieved, in order to install a whole repertoire of new meanings which emphasise that it is no longer needed, it is a spent force" (255). In some cases, furthermore, postfeminism implicitly or explicitly accuses the feminist movement of having been harmful to women and their subjectivity. As Susan J. Douglas and Meredith W. Michaels bluntly put it, "Postfeminism, as a term, suggests that women have made plenty of progress because of feminism, but that feminism is now irrelevant and even undesirable because it supposedly made millions of women unhappy, unfeminine, childless, hairy, loony, bitter, and prompted them to fill their closets with combat boots and really bad India print skirts" (24). While such interpretations of feminism are by no means new—indeed, Faludi's *Backlash* clearly delineates the efforts of the American media in the 1980s to blame women's unhappiness on feminism—postfeminist discourse has become particularly pronounced in the twenty-first century.

The various definitions and understandings of postfeminism render it a complicated space to interrogate, particularly as critics such as Jessica Ringrose uphold it as a potentially positive cultural force that should be understood as yet another "wave" in the evolution of the women's movement. However, as Yvonne Tasker and Diane Negra, among others, have pointed out, postfeminism is far from an ideal "next step," due in no small part to its contradictory simultaneous efforts to "incorporate, assume, or naturalize aspects of feminism" even as it dismisses feminism as outdated or unnecessary (2). Postfeminism also relies heavily and often uncritically on the expectation that women have access to the resources necessary to fully explore a wide range of choices about their lives, meaning that much of postfeminist culture assumes whiteness, middle- or upper-class status, and heteronormativity. (Indeed, almost without exception, Dessen's characters meet all of these qualifications.) Furthermore, postfeminism's concerns with individual subjectivity frequently contradict its imperatives to work within specific constraints and conventions. In "Going Rogue: Postfeminism and the Privilege of Breaking Rules," for example, Marjorie Jolles asserts that "successful femininity in postfeminist terms amounts to a formula for selfhood that calls for a complex engagement with social rules, allowing for novelty to signal uniqueness though constrained by adherence to dominant norms of respectability and intelligibility" (45).

Postfeminist culture frequently turns to the rhetoric of choice—often within a larger consideration of "having it all" or "work/life balance"—in order to demonstrate that contemporary women no longer need feminism. However, as Negra and others have noted, "the choices postfeminism urges upon women are usually traditional ones" (7). One of the most prominent representations of postfeminist culture therefore relates to expectations of motherhood. In *The Mommy Myth: The Idealization of Motherhood and How It Has Undermined Women*, Douglas and Michaels argue that "the new momism"—which they define as "a set of ideals, norms, and practices, most frequently and powerfully represented in the media, that seem on the surface to celebrate motherhood, but which in reality promulgate standards of perfection that are beyond your reach" (4–5)—undermines feminism even as it claims to uphold it. Indeed, new momism highlights the degree to which postfeminism distorts the concept of choice in order to privilege a version of mothering that is "a combination of selflessness and professionalism that would involve the cross cloning of Mother Teresa with Donna Shalala," resulting in an understanding of mothering as a public and competitive activity (5).

In turn, the rhetoric of choice and "having it all" influences expectations of adolescent womanhood, a point that is reinforced by increased attention to and interest in teenage girls as citizens and consumers.[2] As Rosalind Gill asserts:

[Postfeminism's] constructions of contemporary gender relations are profoundly contradictory. On the one hand, young women are hailed through a discourse of "can-do" girl power, yet on the other their bodies are powerfully reinscribed as sexual objects; on the one hand women are presented as active, desiring social subjects, yet on the other they are subject to a level of scrutiny and hostile surveillance that has no historical precedence. (442)

For both mothers and teen daughters, such as the fictional characters featured in Dessen's novels, then, postfeminism and the concept of choice have increasingly visible connotations and consequences. Moreover, the shifting role and nature of feminism and postfeminism more generally clearly influence the struggles in many mother-daughter relationships, as both adult and adolescent women alike face standards and scrutiny that can lead to personal uncertainty and interpersonal tensions.

Having It All in Sarah-Land

In addition to their engagement with cultural discourses, Dessen's novels work within larger literary conventions regarding mother-daughter relationships. To some degree, the importance and presence of mothers in Dessen's novels are unusual in contemporary adolescent literature, a genre which tends to minimize the role of parents in order to grant its characters more independence and movement toward maturity.[3] In literature for young people in which mothers do appear, such representations tend to follow set patterns that emphasize the growth of young people's personal agency, often at the cost of their relationships with their parents. As Roberta Seelinger Trites has argued, "Mother/daughter relationships take two predominant forms in children's and adolescent novels: those traditional narratives that allow for the daughter to achieve independence from her mother in the classically Oedipal model . . . and those less traditional and less Freudian ones that allow the daughter to mature without necessarily breaking from her mother" (103). Likewise, Hillary S. Crew notes that, compared to the previous reliance on Freud, recent feminist studies of mother-daughter relationships look to other patterns of human development: "Feminists assign value to the attachment and continuity of connections that so often have been de-emphasized in explanations of the relationship between adolescent girls and their mothers. Emphasized in feminist accounts are patterns of development in which young people grow up in relationships with others" (4). Thus, the less feminist version of mother-daughter relationships in literature for young people essentially requires the diminishment or destruction of one woman to make room for another, whereas feminist models can allow for both women to exist together.

It is important to note that Dessen's novels often insist upon the possibility of mothers and daughters successfully coexisting, allowing for potentially feminist readings of her work. Likewise, Dessen's interviews and personal writings, including those about her day-to-day life with her young daughter,[4] seem to suggest that she herself engages with the question of feminism as a result of her own life experiences. In *Sarah Dessen: From Burritos to Box Office*, to date the only book-length work examining Dessen's novels, Wendy J. Glenn emphasizes the author's relationship with her feminist literature professor mother in order to establish a biographical context for Dessen's frequent treatment of mother-daughter relationships in her novels. "Dessen describes her mother as an academic, a very smart woman, and an individual who chooses not to be like everybody else," Glenn asserts, adding, "Dessen's mother instilled in her daughter these same virtues, raising her to believe that she could achieve anything she set out to do" (2). For Glenn, Dessen's apparently close relationship with her mother is evidence that the author's fiction possesses "feminist underpinnings," a point that Glenn underscores with her claim that "Dessen's women, although not always in agreement, share a common bond that unites them even in the hardest of times" (19).[5]

Glenn is certainly correct in articulating the centrality of mother figures and mother-daughter relationships in Dessen's novels. Indeed, her debut novel, *That Summer* (1996), focuses a great deal of attention on the way that a series of dramatic changes—her parents' divorce, her father's subsequent remarriage, and her older sister's impending nuptials—challenge teenage narrator Haven's relationship with her mother. Even as Haven prepares to attend her father's wedding in the novel's opening pages, her attention is focused primarily on her mother. Reflecting on their relationship, Haven notes, "It was as if I was attached to her with a tether" (*Summer* 2). This metaphor, with its echoes of the umbilical cord connecting mother and child, reappears throughout the novel, alternatively representing Haven's desire for closeness to and independence from her mother, and offers what seems in many ways to be a conventional treatment of the adolescent struggle for autonomy from parents and other authority figures. In the end, though—and standing in contradiction, I would argue, to Glenn's treatment of Dessen's fiction as feminist—the novel presents Haven as embracing a renewed sense of her childish dependence on her mother, a trend that is echoed in several of Dessen's other novels.

Although *That Summer* does establish Dessen's interest in mother-daughter relationships, its portrayal of motherhood in particular does not engage overtly with the question of "having it all": Haven's mother does not appear to have a career, for example, and she does enjoy at least a limited social life with a neighbor. However, the majority of Dessen's novels—even those that feature stay-at-home mothers, such as *Dreamland* (2000) and *Just Listen* (2006)—do directly or indirectly investigate the apparent impossibility of women achieving balance in their lives. Dessen's working mothers in particular seem to struggle between achieving career success and maintaining healthy relationships with their families, particularly their teenage daughters. *Keeping the Moon* (1999), for example, follows Colie as her famous fitness-instructor mother ships her off to stay with an aunt for the summer. In the most extreme cases—such as *Lock and Key* (2008), in which Ruby's alcoholic mother abandons her to run off with a new boyfriend—mothers' struggles to balance their personal and professional responsibilities result in catastrophic failure.

For the remainder of this chapter, I will be focusing on the mothers who best exemplify Dessen's postfeminist portrayals of the impossibility of "having it all"—the mothers who attempt and generally fail to balance successful careers and successful parenting—as well as the construction of a perpetually codependent mother-daughter relationship that frequently results. For example, in *The Truth About Forever* (2004), Macy's widowed mother, Deborah, invests all of her time in the family business, real estate, without realizing the toll it has taken on her relationship with her teenage daughter. This mother-daughter pair lives a very structured life, with scheduled dinners and extensive plans for Macy's current and future scholastic success. At the same time, Macy's mother rarely interacts in any meaningful way with her daughter, a situation that grows increasingly dire as a major new real estate development occupies more of Deborah's time. Though Macy has accepted this state of affairs in the years since her father's death, she notes with concern that her mother's stress level seems higher than ever: "She never seemed to sleep, and she was losing weight, the dark circles under her eyes clearly visible, despite her always careful application of concealer. More and more I found myself watching her, worrying about the toll her stress was taking on her body" (*Truth* 318). As her relationship with her mother grows more distant, Macy finds herself seeking connections with others, including her new boss, Delia, who runs her own catering service (poorly, at times). Delia herself has a young daughter and gives birth to her second child near the end of the novel, an event for which Macy is present. While Delia *does* seem capable of achieving a better balance than Macy's mother, her success as a mother overshadows some of her failings as a boss, suggesting that if she cannot maintain balance, motherhood should take priority.

Macy's increasing closeness with Delia adds to the strain of her relationship with her mother, who feels betrayed. Their troubled relationship comes to a head when Macy chooses to miss an event her mother has planned in order to be present at the birth of Delia's second daughter, a choice that reflects the privileging of motherhood over career. In the end, Macy and her mother do confront their problems; however, rather than resolving these issues in a forward-looking way, with an acknowledgment that their new experiences and desires are valid and worth pursuing, the novel insists on something of a regression for both of them. Indeed, the conclusion of the novel locates the mother-daughter pair in a space that literally represents the past rather than the future: the beach house they frequently visited during Macy's childhood. In the novel's final pages, as her mother relaxes on the beach, Macy is comforted by the return of the mother she remembers from her childhood, allowing their relationship to function as it did prior to her father's death—without any seeming awareness of the challenges that the future will necessarily hold.

The implicitly postfeminist attitudes present in *The Truth About Forever* find echoes in many of Dessen's other novels, in which similar struggles between mother and daughter play out and find regressive resolutions. Only in a few instances does Dessen engage with feminism in any kind of explicit way; notably, these instances further highlight the author's problematic assumptions about the feminist movement and its place in the lives of contemporary adolescent women. For example, *Dreamland* features a sort of "bonus" mother figure in Caitlin's next-door neighbor, Boo, a women's studies professor at the local college. Caitlin recounts a memory from her childhood in which Boo encouraged her to think about Barbie as more than just a fashionable girl with a boyfriend, saying, "'I think your Barbie can go shopping, and go out with Ken, and also have a productive and satisfying career of her own'" (*Dreamland* 36). Notably, this moment seems to have been inspired by Dessen's childhood experiences with Barbie dolls, which her feminist mother allowed only after protest and required to have names and backstories (Glenn 3). While as a child Caitlin wished that she could be Boo's child instead of her biological mother's—a desire that highlights the novel's larger contrast between Boo and Caitlin's traditional stay-at-home mom—Boo and her husband are frequently, if gently, mocked throughout the novel for their "eccentric" beliefs.

In *Someone Like You* (1998), Halley's renowned psychologist mother invests heavily in discourses of female empowerment often aligned with feminism. At the beginning of the novel, Halley is away at a summer camp chosen by her mother:

> The basic gist [of Camp Believe] was this: a camp with the usual swimming and horseback riding and lanyard making, but in the afternoons seminars and self-help groups on "Like Mother, Like Me" and "Peer Pressure: Where Do I Fit In?" There was a whole paragraph [in the brochure] about self-esteem and values maintenance and other words I recognized only from the blurbs on the back of my mother's own books. (*Someone* 12)

When Halley's best friend experiences a tragic loss, Halley asks her mother to come get her from camp, a decision her mother resists; their disagreement signals their larger, and growing, conflict relating to the importance of interpersonal relationships over personal growth. Over the course of the novel, Halley works to create distance between her and her mother, despite their once very close and apparently healthy relationship. Once again, tragic circumstances work to alter the trajectory of their relationship: as Halley's grandmother grows ill, the teenager observes her mother as she manages to comfort others without giving into her own grief. Near the end of her grandmother's life, Halley watches her mother cry at her own mother's bedside and realizes that "there would never be a way to cut myself from her entirely. No matter how strong or weak I was, she was a part of me, as crucial as my own heart. I would never be strong enough, in all my life, to do without her" (*Someone* 275). Rather than gaining the independence suggested by Camp Believe, Halley instead seems to return willingly to a relationship of dependence on her mother, one that she notably figures as a form of *weakness* rather than a potential space for strength.

In some of the most explicit echoes of Dessen's own experiences as the daughter of a feminist college professor, *Along for the Ride* (2009) follows Auden as she attempts to determine for herself the importance of school, romance, and friendship by examining the examples of her staunchly feminist mother and her more conventionally feminine, pink-loving young stepmother, Heidi. From the beginning of the novel, Auden explicitly compares the two women:

> Where my mother was an academic scholar with a smart, sharp wit and a nationwide reputation as an expert in women's roles in Renaissance literature, Heidi was . . . well, Heidi. The kind of woman whose strengths were her constant self-maintenance (pedicures, manicures, hair highlights), knowing everything you never want to about hemlines and shoes, and sending entirely too chatty emails to people who couldn't care less. (*Along* 2)

Although this initial impression suggests that Auden privileges her mother's accomplishments over Heidi's girlishness, the trajectory of the story undermines this comparison. Indeed, the novel positions Heidi as a threat to Auden's mother in general and her feminist aspirations for her daughter in particular, as Auden becomes increasingly comfortable with her stepmother and the "girly" world she occupies. Eventually, Auden's mother frames Heidi as the root of what she perceives to be negative changes in Auden: "'I should have known spending the summer with Heidi would do this to you,' she said. 'I spend eighteen years teaching you about the importance of taking yourself seriously, and in a matter of weeks you're wearing pink bikinis and totally boy crazy'" (*Along* 252). Despite her mother's disdain, Auden perceives her new interest in friendship and romance as a natural part of her personality that she has not been able to explore before—"'This is just me,'" she tells her mother (*Along* 252).

While Auden's mother initially perceives her daughter's shifting priorities as a mistake and a form of rebellion that will endanger her upcoming college career at a fictional Ivy League school, the novel concludes with a mother-daughter conversation that does not completely resolve their differences but does allow Auden to voice her desires for a lifestyle that diverges from her mother's expectations. Although this declaration of independence does suggest a feminist representation of mother-daughter relationships, the resolution of the novel ultimately undermines such a reading by subverting Auden's mother's independence when Auden urges her to pursue a romantic relationship rather than engaging in short-term flings. As Negra asserts, "Over and over again the postfeminist subject is represented as having lost herself but then (re)achieving stability through romance, de-aging, a makeover, by giving up paid work, or by 'coming home'" (5). Auden's mother's tentative reentry into the world of traditional romance, then, suggests that her deficiencies in interpersonal relationships can be corrected through a return to conventional feminine priorities.

Regardless of how explicitly her works engage with feminism as a concept, Dessen's representations of motherhood are distinctly postfeminist in their problematic treatment of feminism as a movement. More generally, even in works that do not engage directly with feminist discourse, the insistence upon mothers' inability to successfully navigate their personal lives, their working lives, or both relies upon an implicit rejection of the possibility of "having it all." In turn, the teenage daughters in these novels are offered models of adult womanhood that are largely unsatisfying and conflicted rather than peaceful and emotionally full, which, as I discuss in the next section, frequently leads not only to increased dependence on their mothers but also a larger unwillingness to pursue the possibility of "having it all" in their own future adult lives.

Like Mother, Like Daughter

Whereas Dessen's mothers share a struggle to achieve satisfying "work/life balance," their daughters are united by a number of admirable traits that seem to position them each for future success: they are smart, driven, and focused, with clear academic or professional goals. However, even as these characters find themselves moving capably toward promising futures that include college (including acceptances to Ivy League schools for at least three characters) and careers, the novels themselves frequently conclude with messages that focus primarily on more conventional themes of romance and family. For example, in *The Moon and More* (2013), Emaline ultimately decides not to attend Columbia despite the hard work required to secure admission; while this decision is predicated in part on her father's reneging on an offer to pay for her tuition, Emaline also expresses that she is comfortable attending a state school near home where she can remain in contact with her mother, stepfather, and the rest of her family. Even when Emaline does consider an internship with a famous documentary filmmaker that would take her to New York City after all—an opportunity she earns by ably organizing a major event in her hometown—her decision depends as much on the possibility of developing a closer relationship with her younger half-brother as it does the potential career opportunities that might be made available to her.

Dessen further undermines the potentially empowering messages in her novels by emphasizing the similarities between these struggling mothers and their adolescent daughters. In many cases, those similarities are highlighted by shared or similar names: *Lock and Key*'s Ruby is both named after and a physical dead ringer for her flighty mother, for example, and both Emaline's name and appearance are similar to those of her mother, Emily. Indeed, almost all of Dessen's daughters assert that they physically resemble their mothers, often strongly. Moreover, the novels highlight both explicit and implicit similarities between mothers and daughters in terms of temperament and other traits. Whether the characters share appearances, names, or other qualities, Dessen's mothers and daughters are tied to each other through explicit connections that reinforce sameness across generations; in turn, this sameness suggests that these daughters are destined for futures similar to their mothers' unless they actively choose simpler and thus ostensibly more satisfying paths focused on romance and family.

Even when Dessen seems most willing to challenge the narrative of love, marriage, and family, her novels ultimately privilege these personal experiences over the possibility of satisfying professional pursuits. In *This Lullaby* (2002), for example, Dessen presents narrator Remy as a cynical realist who has rejected the concept of lasting love after witnessing her mother's multiple failed marriages. Over the course of the novel, Remy helps her mother plan her fifth wedding, despite her misgivings about her newest stepfather-to-be; she then chronicles the ways in which her mother's behavior in this marriage diverges from her previous marriages, suggesting that perhaps this really is "the one"; but ultimately, the new husband is revealed to have not only a mean temper but also a cheating disposition, as he has been unfaithful to Remy's mother since before their wedding. At the same time, Remy falls into a relationship with a charismatic young musician, Dexter, who challenges her once-firm resolve to avoid romantic commitment. Even as her mother's marriage falls apart—which theoretically supports all of Remy's assumptions about love—Remy gives herself over to the possibility of a long-term relationship with Dex. Notably, the novel begins by emphasizing Remy's intelligence and focus; she is heading to Stanford in the fall, though her potential major or career goals are never fully revealed. In the end, Remy does find herself ensconced in a Stanford dorm room, but the novel's conclusion focuses primarily on her happiness at receiving a package from Dex—ignoring almost entirely the accomplishment of having been admitted to an Ivy League school and giving no indication of how Remy is faring there. Interestingly, however, Remy and Dex appear in a later Dessen novel, *Just Listen*, still happily involved in their romantic relationship.

Dessen and Postfeminist Girling

Across her eleven novels, Dessen offers a variety of mother-daughter relationships that ultimately all contribute to a shared postfeminist message regarding the challenges of adult womanhood and the impossibilities of work/life balance. The teenage daughters witnessing these mothers' struggles, in turn, frequently respond to these models by seeking to extend childish dependence on their mothers or focusing their attention on romantic or familial pursuits rather than their academic accomplishments. As a result, Dessen engages not with feminist discourses that seek to improve women's chances of "having it all" but with postfeminist sensibilities that emphasize "choice" within limited, typically conventional parameters. In the process, Dessen's novels participate in a larger "girling" discourse of postfeminist culture in which youth and girlhood are prized at the expense of the possibilities of feminist womanhood. Tasker and Negra have argued, "As postfeminism has raised the premium on youthfulness, it has installed an image of feminism as 'old' (and by extension moribund)" (11). While much of postfeminism discourse is aimed at adult women already facing questions about careers, families, and aging, Dessen's novels assert similar concerns to a younger generation of women, reinforcing the ostensibly outdated nature of feminism to adolescent women who may already reject the term (if not necessarily its associated beliefs) out of hand. As McRobbie has argued, "popular texts normalise post-feminist gender anxieties so as to re-regulate young women by means of the language of personal choice" (262). Dessen's daughters, though seemingly empowered to make choices for themselves, frequently find themselves instead avoiding the paths their mothers have trod, seemingly accepting the impossibility of "work/life balance" and abandoning the potential of "having it all."

Notes

1. A twelfth novel, *Saint Anything*, was published in 2015, after this chapter was completed.

2. See Anita Harris's *Future Girl: Young Women in the Twenty-First Century* for a more thorough discussion of contradictory expectations of adolescent womanhood in contemporary Western culture.

3. Some of the "classics" of young adult literature, such as J. D. Salinger's *The Catcher in the Rye*, S. E. Hinton's *The Outsiders*, and Robert Cormier's *The Chocolate War*, help to establish this convention, as parents are either physically or emotionally absent from their adolescent protagonists' stories.

4. Dessen maintains a visible social media presence, including her own website (www.Sarah-Land.com), blog, and very active Twitter account in which she frequently shares personal anecdotes about such topics.

5. It is worth noting that all eleven of Dessen's novels to date are located in North Carolina, many in the fictional beach town of Colby, and frequently in the same "universe." Characters from her earlier works often make cameo appearances in later novels.

Works Cited

Crew, Hillary S. *Is It Really Mommie Dearest? Daughter-Mother Narratives in Young Adult Fiction*. Lanham, MD: Scarecrow, 2000. Print.
Dessen, Sarah. *Along for the Ride*. New York: Viking Juvenile, 2009. Print.
———. *Dreamland*. New York: Speak, 2000. Print.
———. *Just Listen*. New York: Speak, 2006. Print.
———. *Keeping the Moon*. New York: Speak, 1999. Print.
———. *Lock and Key*. New York: Viking Juvenile, 2008. Print.
———. *The Moon and More*. New York: Viking Juvenile, 2013. Print.
———. *Someone Like You*. New York: Speak, 1998. Print.
———. *That Summer*. New York: Speak, 1996. Print.
———. *This Lullaby*. New York: Speak, 2002. Print.
———. *The Truth About Forever*. New York: Speak, 2004. Print.
Douglas, Susan J., and Meredith W. Michaels. *The Mommy Myth: The Idealization of Motherhood and How It Has Undermined Women*. New York: Free, 2004. Print.
Faludi, Susan. *Backlash: The Undeclared War Against American Women*. 1991. Fifteenth anniversary ed. New York: Three Rivers, 2006. Print.
Gill, Rosalind. "Culture and Subjectivity in Neoliberal and Postfeminist Times." *Subjectivity* 25 (2008): 432–45. Print.
Glenn, Wendy J. *Sarah Dessen: From Burritos to Box Office*. Lanham, MD: Scarecrow, 2005. Print.
Harris, Anita. *Future Girl: Young Women in the Twenty-First Century*. New York: Routledge, 2003. Print.
Jolles, Marjorie. "Going Rogue: Postfeminism and the Privilege of Breaking Rules." *Feminist Formations* 24.3 (2012): 43–61. Print.
McRobbie, Angela. "Post-Feminism and Popular Culture." *Feminist Media Studies* 4.3 (2004): 255–64. Print.
Negra, Diane. *What a Girl Wants? Fantasizing the Reclamation of Self in Postfeminism*. New York: Routledge, 2009. Print.
Ringrose, Jessica. "Successful Girls? Complicating Post-Feminist, Neoliberal Discourses of Educational Achievement and Gender Equality." *Gender and Education* 19.4 (2007): 471–89. Print.
Slaughter, Anne-Marie. "Why Women Still Can't Have It All." *Atlantic Monthly*. Atlantic Monthly Group, 13 June 2012. Web. 17 April 2014.

Tasker, Yvonne, and Diane Negra. "Introduction: Feminist Politics and Postfeminist Culture." *Interrogating Postfeminism: Gender and the Politics of Popular Culture*. Ed. Yvonne Tasker and Diane Negra. Durham: Duke UP, 2007. Print.

Trites, Roberta Seelinger. *Waking Sleeping Beauty: Feminist Voices in Children's Novels*. Iowa City: U Iowa P, 1997. Print.

Chapter 12

Abandoning Mothers

Lisa Rowe Fraustino

The central claim of this chapter is that the ubiquitous plot of maternal abandonment in children's literature has risen to prominence since the 1970s in service of the backlash to feminism in American culture as articulated by Susan Faludi in her 1991 bestseller, *Backlash: The Undeclared War Agaisnt American Women*. To support this claim I will examine the backlash ideology at work in three award-winning novels, two representing the backlash to feminism's second wave and one the third wave: Katherine Paterson's 1979 National Book Award and Newbery Honor winning book *The Great Gilly Hopkins*, Cynthia Voigt's 1983 Newbery Award winner *Dicey's Song*, and Kimberly Willis Holt's 2000 National Book Award winner *When Zachary Beaver Came to Town*. But first, to provide cultural context, I offer an example from real life.

In a 2007 memoir entitled *Baby Love: Choosing Motherhood After a Lifetime of Ambivalence*, the reader is told: "I've started reading children's books. The Berenstain Bears, Richard Scarry, *Goodnight Moon*. The books take me back to purity, simplicity, ease. I remember why these books were my best friends when I was a little girl. Everything gets worked out, people love each other, the world is good." Then the memoirist explains, "I am reading these to counterbalance the e-mails that have been flying back and forth between me and my mother. I ask her to apologize . . . and acknowledge the ways she has hurt me over the years with neglect, withholding, and the ambivalence she seems to have about my race, relative privilege, and birth itself" (154–55). The memoirist, Rebecca Walker, coined the term "third-wave feminism," and her mother, Alice Walker, was a prominent activist during the second wave.[1] In both *Baby Love* and her first bestselling memoir, *Black, White, and Jewish: Autobiography of a Shifting Self*—a 2002 Alex Award winner described by the Young Adult Library Services Association (YALSA) as a "poignant, sometimes angry recollection about racism, growing up, growing away, and finding oneself"—Rebecca expresses anger and resentment toward her mother's postdivorce "Feminism, with a capital F, codified Femisim, 'movement' Feminism" (*Black* 60). With the publication of *Baby Love*, Rebecca embarked on a publicity campaign that included a scathing and oft-quoted interview with the *Daily Mail* entitled "How My Mother's Fanatical Views Tore Us Apart." From its provocative lede: "Here the writer describes what it was like to grow up as the daughter of a cultural icon, and why she feels so blessed to be the sort of woman 64-year-old Alice despises—a mother."

Alice—who had despised no mothers in her widely read 1983 essay collection *In Search of Our Mothers' Gardens*[2]—kept her thoughts about her daughter's accusations to herself (at least in print) until 2013, when she published a brief post on her website: "Taking Care of the Truth: A Meditation on the Complicity of Wikipedia." Here she seeks to correct what she calls "misinformation" and "mendacity" appearing in the Wikipedia entry on her, including "some of my daughter's most distorted comments about me. Presented as legitimate information. As if they were true." Alice writes:

> I was not a perfect mother, whatever that means, but I was good enough. The pain of being unfairly and publicly accused of willful harm, by someone I gave birth to, and raised, to the limits of my ability, someone I've deeply loved, has been at times almost unbearable. For the past decade or so I have borne this injustice as well as I could, in silence, for the most part, but now, being on the other side of the trauma to some degree, I begin to see unexpected ways uncontested slander harms us. This is what I wish to share.

Alice, as all traditional "good" mothers do, has absorbed the mother blame that "is interwoven throughout our daily lives," in the words of second-wave feminist psychologist Paula Caplan in *The New Don't Blame Mother: Mending the Mother-Daughter Relationship* (42).

According to Phyllis Chesler, "Rebecca conflates feminist views of motherhood (as she perceives them to be) with her own personal experience of Alice's choice or inability to mother in a traditional way." Indeed, in her *Daily Mail* diatribe Rebecca admits, "As a child, I was terribly confused, because while I was being fed a strong feminist message, I actually yearned for a traditional mother"—one like her stepmother, Judy, "a loving, maternal homemaker with five children she doted on" and who "did all the things my mother didn't, such as attending their school events, taking endless photos and telling her children at every opporunity how wonderful they were." This, of course, is exactly the kind of mother we see in the classic children's books that were little Rebecca's best friends and that she still reads as an adult to return to "purity, simplicity, and ease," where "Everything gets worked out, people love each other, the world is good" (*Baby Love* 154–55). No doubt children's books contributed to Rebecca's confusion. How can primary narcissism reconcile a feminist mother with Mama Bear Berenstain?[3] Popular picture books, especially those about mother-child relationships,[4] contribute to the subliminal construction of desire for the traditional good mother that continues to fuel a backlash culture against women's rights—even, apparently, among third-wave feminists.

Faludi describes "backlash against women's rights" as "a recurring phenomenon: it returns every time women begin to make some headway toward equality" (46). She describes women's progress as looking "like a corkscrew tilted slightly to one side, its loops inching closer to the line of freedom with the passage of time" (46). In a detailed, close analysis of how the popular culture depicts and restricts women's roles through trends of antifeminism in the media, movies, television, fashion, politics, and—well, everywhere, though she doesn't spend time on children's books—*Backlash* convincingly shows the backward corkscrew loop of resistance that followed the height of feminism's second wave in the 1970s. Since that time, literature for young readers has contributed to the backlash culture with increasing numbers of, as I've quoted elsewhere, "what *Horn Book* editor Roger Sutton calls 'I-Love-Baby-and-Baby-Loves-Me books'" (Fraustino, "The Apple" 57). Such books cultivate myths of motherhood both in children and in the mothers who read to them. Once primed to feel entitled to ideal mothers, independent young readers are then given increasing numbers of novels about abandoned children of mothers who leave their families not through that timeless individuating plot device of the classic orphan story—a death not chosen—but through a choice made imaginable by the women's rights movement.[5]

Sharon Wigutoff first noted this emerging pattern in her 1981 article "Junior Fiction: A Feminist Critique": "More often, mothers are depicted as negative characters without redeeming values. Many literally abandon their children in search of their own self-fulfillment" (9). Marilyn Apseloff in her 1992 article "Abandonment: The New Realism of the Eighties," blames feminism, considering the pattern "a reflection on contemporary life . . . perhaps inevitable with the increasing focus on the women's movement and the right of women to be their own persons in equality with men" (101). Identifying with the abandoned child focalizer, readers of these books are rarely permitted to glimpse the mother from her own perspective; hence, unexamined representations of selfish abandoning mothers help to perpetuate backlash culture by inculcating antifeminist resentments in young readers. That significant numbers of contemporary realistic novels about maternal abandonment have received major awards virtually guarantees a large audience across decades and magnifies the impact of their backlash.

On the first page of *The Great Gilly Hopkins*, we meet Gilly, a foster child, in the back seat of her social worker's car, being transported to her "third home in less than three years," the home of Maime Trotter. Gilly carries in her suitcase all she knows of her mother: a glossy photo of Courtney Rutherford Hopkins. Perhaps it is a publicity photo, for Gilly thinks as she studies it: "She looked as though she was the star of some TV show," and Courtney, who lives in star-studded California, has dedicated the photo: "For my beautiful Galadriel, I will always love you" (Paterson 9). These words, though taken to heart by Gilly as fuel for her false belief that one day her mother will come for her and take her away to live happily ever after, can also be read as the words of an actress playing a part—the part of the loving mother that society has scripted for women. While it is realistic that a mother can be motivated by love to give up her child to someone better able to provide adequate care, there is no evidence in the text that Courtney loves anyone but herself. In fact, there is little evidence about what motivates Courtney at all; she is defined primarily by her absence, leaving both the other characters and the book's readers to define and judge her based on stereotypical assumptions about motherhood and, eventually, hippies. When the social worker says, "God help the children of the flower children" (119), we presumably know all we need to know about Courtney. She probably conceived Gilly in the Summer of Love and doesn't even know who the father is.

But to understand the backlash ideology of the book, it doesn't matter what Miss Ellis believes about flower children. It matters what Gilly believes about mothering. Comparing her own "straw-colored hair" with her mother's beautiful black hair and considering her perfect teeth, Gilly thinks: "Weren't girls supposed to look like their mothers? The word 'mother' triggered something deep in her stomach" (9). Somehow, Gilly has absorbed certain ideas about what mothers are "supposed" to be like. Ideology dictates it as natural that women need to be mothers, mothers need their children, and children need their mothers. By age ten Gilly Hopkins takes it as given that mothers are "supposed to" love their children and take care of them, and this makes it impossible for her to understand, despite her gifted intelligence, that Courtney's expressions of motherly love are mere show, as in the postcard Gilly receives soon after arriving at Maime Trotter's home:

> *My dearest Galadriel,*
> *The agency wrote me that you had moved.*
> *I wish it were here. I miss you.*
> *All my love, Courtney* (28)

No doubt, several members of the U.S. Postal Service as well as Gilly's foster mother were able to provide an audience for Courtney playing the part she's supposed to play, though Trotter surely sees through the disconnect between words and actions. Gilly, however, does not—cannot, because she wants her own mother so much. "I don't need help from anybody except from you," she says in an imaginary speech directed to Courtney. "If I wrote you—if I asked, would you come and get me? You're the only one in the world I need" (30). Later, after Gilly is caught attempting to buy a bus ticket to California with stolen money and Trotter comes for her, the police officer asks, "Don't you want to go home?" and Gilly thinks, "Where the hell do you think I was headed?" (91), reinforcing Gilly's—and society's—view that home is where the biological mother is. Despite all evidence to the contrary, Gilly stubbornly believes that her own mother is the only one who can provide the home and the love she yearns for.

In contrast, why doesn't Gilly ever wonder about her father? Why doesn't she fantasize about him riding in on his white horse to save her from the foster care system? Indeed, why doesn't this brilliant young girl resent and hate the mother who abandoned her instead of yearning for an ending that doesn't even happen in the fairy tales Gilly often alludes to? Where did she learn to idealize mothers when a quick look around proves she's not the only one without a perfect home? She even thinks: "Other kids could be with their mothers all the time. Dumb, stupid kids who didn't even like their mothers much" (29). The closest thing to a friend that Gilly has is Agnes Stokes, who has been abandoned by both parents and lives with her grandmother. In fact, the foster mother, Maime Trotter, is the only "good mother" depicted in the text, so where does Gilly get the idea that life with her own mother would be so glorious? We know that

Gilly is a reader. Did she absorb maternal yearnings from the children's books that Rebecca Walker remembers as her best friends, or was she simply implanted with unquestionable views and values held by her figurative mother, the author?

Readers of *The Great Gilly Hopkins* cannot help but sympathize with Gilly's desires. But where do these sympathies come from? "Motherhood is utterly sentimentalized" in our culture, which demands "the mother who is always loving, selfless, tranquil; the one who finds passionate fulfillment in every detail of child rearing," claims Shari Thurer in *The Myths of Motherhood* (xii). The idea that raising a child is the natural responsibility of culture's sentimentalized mother—not the father, and certainly not the state—is deeply engrained in our society and leads to the very distress that Gilly feels because she lacks what she's "supposed to" have. The dominant ideology is loath to admit that not all women make good mothers, that not all women should be mothers, and that not all children need to be with their mothers. Of course, Paterson does somewhat challenge the "birth mother is best" assumption by demonizing Courtney while depicting Trotter as "the world's greatest foster mother," as the author called her in her National Book Award acceptance (*Gates* 110). Wigutoff concludes, "It is extremely revealing that the 'best' mothers in junior fiction are the foster mothers. Few biological mothers can hold a candle to Trotter . . . when it comes to genuine love and understanding. These women, whose job it is to mother, devote themselves to it one hundred percent" (9).

Yet, importantly, Gilly does not get to stay with Trotter in the end, but must live with her maternal grandmother, because when faced with an unfit and unwed mother, the backlash culture's next best choice is the mother's mother. We see this idea again in Cynthia Voigt's *Dicey's Song*, in which Gram adopts the four children their mother abandoned in a parking lot back in Voigt's 1982 Newbery Honor book *Homecoming*. Unlike Gilly, Dicey knows who her father is. He left when Momma was pregnant for the fourth time, presumably because he didn't want more children. Fathers are allowed not to want children, often even allowed to leave without being demonized for it, in children's literature as in other areas of popular culture.[6] Momma, of course, chose to abandon her children for the only socially acceptable reason a mother could do such a thing: she lost her mind. Liza Tillerman, because she didn't leave her children to pursue her own fame and fortune, can be called an affectionate name like "Momma" and can be sympathetically developed, loved, and forgiven, unlike Courtney Rutherford Hopkins, whom we cannot afford to know and understand or else perhaps we might empathize with her situation—something the backlash cannot allow us to do.

Gilly's longing question to Courtney's photo, "Why did you go away and leave me?" is never answered. Only by interpreting the few clues we get about Courtney in her youth can we attempt to read the situation. When Gilly moves in with her grandmother, Nonnie, we see Courtney's bedroom exactly as she had left it: "Everything was pink with a four-poster canopied bed complete with stuffed animals and dolls" (132). How much more "feminine" can a room get? This is the room of a sheltered and pampered child. When Courtney got pregnant and decided at first to keep the baby, did she believe her child would be like her dolls, traditionally given to girls in training for motherhood? Did Courtney the flower child fantasize about loving a baby named Galadriel after a fantasy queen, and being loved in return? Was she unprepared for the unrelenting responsibility of diapers, feedings, and constant demands on her attention, the lack of freedom to do her own thing? We can only speculate because Paterson shows us so little of Courtney, the "flower child gone to seed" who shows up for Christmas, and even then only because she was paid by Nonnie. "Don't start pushing me before I'm hardly off the plane," Courtney tells her mother. "My god, I've been gone thirteen years, and you still think you can tell me what to do" (146).

According to Alice Blint, one of the reasons for the idealized social ideology of motherhood is people's tendency to retain "a naïve egoistic attitude throughout their lives"—continuing to view mothers as they did during childhood rather than identifying with the adult mother's perspective (qtd. in Chodorow 81). Naïve, egoistic Courtney still acts like an adolescent, and Gilly finally realizes what the reader knew all along: She's better off without this mother. Of course, keeping both of her children's rooms intact after their leaving suggests that Nonnie never moved on due to another side effect of cultural ideology, the one requiring that "the mother sacrifices herself to the child. She sacrifices her self. Her self is lost. The child becomes the center of her life; the child's needs placed before her needs, until often she lives in her child, through her child. . . . Her love devours the child. Her value becomes repression, her protection, dominance" (Griffin 37). We see signs that this is what happened to alienate Courtney when, after only a few days of living with Nonnie, Gilly thinks: "Stop hovering over me. I'll smother" (134). Every time I close the book I hope Nonnie has learned her lesson about that.

The ambivalence of motherhood that Paterson avoids in *Gilly* comes across clearly along with a subtle critique of motherhood's societal burdens in Voigt's richly characterized *Dicey's Song*. As the eldest child and a girl, Dicey has already served as a stand-in mother by leading the children on their journey to Gram's house, providing for them and protecting them, a role she continues. Only thirteen herself, Dicey gets a job to pay for Maybeth's piano lessons and give the two boys an allowance, and her worries include the motherly self-sacrificial question of "how much Dicey should give up for her brothers and sisters in order to have any kind of home together" (3–4). One day, when her youngest brother is causing mischief in the barn, she feels "anger spurt up her spine," and she yells, "Wherever you are, get back where I can see you. . . . I've about had it, you hear me? There's almost no time for me to work on the boat, and you're interrupting me. You know the lofts aren't safe to play in" (29). Like a true-to-life ambivalent mother, she can't focus on her own task, her own goals, her own pleasure, because she has a child to worry about.

Besides revealing her own ambivalence toward responsibility for children, Dicey is able to depict her absent mother with empathy through the character sketch she writes for English class. Disguising her mother's identity by calling her "Mrs. Liza," Dicey is accused by her teacher of plagiarism. Mr. Chappelle has seen Dicey's work before and must know of her excellent writing ability, so perhaps he finds it impossible to believe the circumstances of the story she tells rather than her skill in telling it. How could a child in his class bear witness to the life of a woman who breaks under the strain of single motherhood unsupported by the children's father or by society? The reader can infer that the heavy financial burden of supporting the children and the social problems associated with being an unwed mother led to good-natured and lovely Liza's retreat to a catatonic state (119). One student in the discussion of Dicey's essay remarks, "And it's a mental hospital at the end? But it sounded like a jail picture" (120). The jail image is pertinent. Motherhood, after all, is a life sentence. Any "parole" allowed in our culture comes only with stigma—the "bad mother" label of the deserter who breaks free by giving her child over to Social Services like Courtney, or the "crazy" label of one who escapes into mental illness like Liza. Somehow, the unwed father of children escapes accountability.

But that doesn't mean the accountability stops with the mother. It follows a matrilineal line—the grandmother reaps what she sows. The family discussion later about Dicey's essay leads Gram to say, "I've made a lot of mistakes in my life," and she explains: "I married John, and that wasn't a mistake. But the way we stayed married, the way we lived, there were lots of mistakes. He was a stiff and proud man, John—a hard man" (127). In the years after his death, Gram admits, she has realized that she should have done things differently. "He wasn't happy to be himself. And I just let him be, let him sit there, high and proud, in his life. I let the children go away from him. And from me. I got to thinking—when it was too late—you have to reach out to people" (128). This is the turning point where we start to see Gram surrendering to the myths of motherhood. Before now she's come across as fiercely independent, but now she's taking the blame for her children's reactions to their father. The backlash culture is getting across its message that the woman is supposed to be the negotiator, the reconciler, the conciliator. So, though Voigt shows that real-life motherhood isn't a happily-ever-after fantasy, the old myths are allowed to resurface.

When Gram takes her to visit her mother at her deathbed, Dicey admits to herself that she hadn't "ever expected to see Momma again, not after the way Momma had wandered off and forgotten them" but she feels "sad and hurt" now because "this was really Momma, not some idea of her. All the time Momma had been gone, Dicey had carried around an idea of her. The idea was of Momma sleeping, and behind that were all the ideas of Momma that Dicey had saved up over her life. But the idea wasn't the same as real, and real hurt" (177). This is the same lesson that Gilly learns. Gilly has carried an idea, and an ideal, of Courtney, and only in the moment of facing her real mother does she understand the truth of the matter. Through Dicey's reflections, we're convinced that "Momma loved her children. You could tell in the way her hands rested on their heads. . . . And in her voice when she talked to them. You could tell in how long she tried, how hard she worked" (177). Now, in her moment of death, the mother is utterly sentimentalized. She loved her children. "Momma was good, and she didn't deserve to be dying here. She deserved to be with her family, at Gram's house, seeing how things were working out all right. There was no call for Momma to die, no reason for it, no good to come of it" (177). It doesn't matter that she irresponsibly gave birth to not just one but four unplanned children with an unreliable partner and insufficient job skills to support a family. It doesn't matter that she abandoned them in the only socially acceptable manner possible, mental illness. As she lost her grip, she could have reached out to her own mother, and perhaps even to the father's family, but she chose not to.

Why is Liza idealized as a loving mother? Why is her story a tragedy rather than a condemnation? I suggest the answer comes from Dicey herself earlier in the story when she says it's not Momma's fault, it's not anybody's fault. Rather, it's the fault of a culture that scripts women into the role of motherhood without providing all the necessary props. Unfortunately, though, that revolutionary message gets lost in the end, coopted by the death of Liza—because the only "good" abandoning mother is a dead one, and her death leaves room for the adoption of the children by the best possible replacement mother, the maternal grandmother. Despite her rugged independence and "crazy" ways, Ab Tillerman is reclaimed by the ideology of motherhood when she takes responsibility for the children, reaching out to the community to rid herself of her reputation as crazy or eccentric, applying for welfare despite her pride, and accepting the blame along with the responsibility of the abandoned children. If only she had been a better mother, she seems to feel, perhaps Liza would still be alive. With Susan Griffin in "Feminism and Motherhood," we might ask: "And why is it in the case of women that we always blame the individual and not the social structure. That we see failure in discrete lives and do not question 'the way things are'" (37)?

Faludi's corkscrew metaphor for women's progress amidst backlash aptly applies as we move past the rising of feminism's third wave to Kimberly Willis Holt's more superficial treatment of the absent mother in *When Zachary Beaver Came to Town*. Set in 1971 though published in 1999, *Zachary Beaver* takes us backward in more ways than one. In the beginning of the book, as "half of Antler is standing in line with two dollars clutched in hand to see the fattest boy in the world," 643-pound Zachary Beaver, we learn that narrator Toby Wilson is not happy that his mother, Opalina, has won a singing contest and gone to Nashville to compete at the Grand Ole Opry for a record contract. His biggest problem: "My stomach's been growling all the time now because I haven't had a decent meal since Mom left a few days ago" (5)—a recurrent complaint. Toby recalls that "Mom sang 'Hey, Good Lookin' as she packed, and the entire time I couldn't help wondering if moms were supposed to be that happy to get away. Mrs. McKnight doesn't go on trips without her family" (21). Like Gilly Hopkins (and Rebecca Walker), Toby Wilson has a firm idea about what mothers are "supposed to" be and do, only his idea is based on the mother of his best friend down the street, the always-present Mrs. McKnight wearing "a floral apron tied around her waist" and her natural hair blowing "wildly in the breeze" as she prunes roses (19). Like so many aproned mothers in movies, television, and literature, Mrs. Knight, whom Toby calls "the nicest person I've ever known" (87), helps to maintain an idealized image of the mother that nobody ever really had but everyone feels entitled to. Toby, however, has the mother that nobody wants—one whom the editors of *Representations of Motherhood* might call "a subject with her own needs and interests" (Bassin 2), who claims her teased and sprayed "big hair helps her hit the high notes" (Holt 19). We see the community's ingrained chauvenistic attitudes when Dad takes Toby to lunch at the Bowl-a-Rama Café, where Mom works as the town's favorite singing waitress. Though her boss, Ferris, has hung a "Good Luck, Opalina!" sign, he tells Dad, "Sure do miss your woman" (45), as if a wife is a possession belonging to the husband. Antler is the kind of small town where everyone knows everyone else, and during lunch Earline Carter, the Real Estate Lady, says, "I guess this is her shot at the big time, isn't it? She's a brave woman, going all the way to Nashville. Alone at that. You're mighty brave to let her." And, we're told, "She raises her eyebrows, waiting" (46). In the hush that falls while everyone waits to see how Dad responds to this questioning of his patriarchal control, we hear Elvis singing "The Old Rugged Cross," as if reminding Dad and the reader to think about traditional Christian attitudes toward a wife and mother's role.

The conversation turns to the abandonment of Zachary Beaver by his manager, Paulie Rankin:

> "Well," Earline says, walking out the door, "decent people don't leave a child unattended for days on end." She turns and looks at Miss Myrtie Mae. "Do they?"
>
> Ignoring Earline, Miss Myrtie Mae picks up her cracker and takes a bite. Her mouth chews in exaggerated circles.
>
> Ferris chuckles. "If Opalina had been here, she would make up a song about it. Probably something like 'The Ballad of Zachary Beaver.'"
>
> Everyone laughs but Dad. (49)

Though purportedly about Zachary Beaver, this conversation can be read as a veiled criticism of Opalina. In fact, throughout the book the reader is distracted from thinking very long about Opalina by the Zachary Beaver plotline, along with interweaving plots about Toby's unrequited romance and the death of his best friend's brother in Vietnam. Fundamentally, all of these subplots are about a child having to cope with loss, and most fundamental of these losses is that of Toby's mother as primary caregiver. Despite its spoken well wishes, the community makes its disapproval clear between the lines. "Because women who leave children go against the grain of the selfless, masochistic and self-sacrificing function that our culture expects of mothers, they invariably invite censure from the system they seem to offend," according to Rosie Jackson (41), and Antler's Real Estate Lady might just as well be asking the lunch crowd if a decent mother would leave for Nashville for a week. Ferris inadvertently points the reader's attention straight at the parallel between Zachary Beaver and Toby by saying, "If Opalina had been here . . ." They all know she's not here, and the sense is that she ought to be.

No wonder Dad doesn't laugh. He knows something that nobody else does: Opalina isn't coming back. She's leaving him, which she apparently knew before she left but chose not to tell her son. Along with the rest of the town, Toby thinks she's coming back after the contest. When she is named the runner-up, Dad rather bitterly tells Toby that she has decided to stay on in Nashville because "apparently some hotshot manager in the audience thinks he can get her a record deal" (75), and when Toby asks how long she's going to stay, Dad says, "Toby, I'm not the person to answer that question. I'll give you her phone number and you can ask her yourself" (75). Strangely, she's been gone a week and we haven't yet witnessed direct contact between Opalina and her son, which seems unrealistic given the caring attention this mother has shown for all of Toby's life up until now, piling up sentimental memories of good food, trips to the library, and warm jackets, not to mention church every Sunday. Wouldn't she have called him? In fact, if such a mother knew she wasn't coming back, wouldn't she have explained to her son before she left and sought his understanding? Most likely she would, but Holt could not risk providing that conversation for the reader. What if we were to empathize with Opalina?

The backlash needs us to rely on our stereotypes of mothers who leave as selfish and bad, so instead of writing honestly, Holt has Dad renege all responsibility in informing his son about the broken marriage and waits until pages 115–16 for Mom to inform Toby in a letter:

> Critter, what I'm about to write is pretty darn hard for me. And I'm writing it before the contest because I wanted you to know this has nothing to do with whether I win or not. Me and your dad have been having a rough time of it lately. You've heard us arguing. Or I guess you've heard me hollering and seen your dad stomping off. I guess I need some time to figure everything out.
>
> And don't you go blaming yourself. You've been the best son a mother could have. I'm not leaving you, Critter. Your dad has my phone number, and I'm only a dime away. Come to think of it, that would make a good title for a song—"Only a Dime Away from Your Love." I know this will take some getting used to. Please don't hate me. It would tear my heart to shreds. I'll write to you soon with my new address.
>
> Love always,
> Mom

The letter would be a cowardly way to handle this situation in real life, and it's a cowardly fictional device as well, designed to build suspense in the novel, to keep the reader hanging about whether Mom is coming back or not rather than to create verisimilitude. It also allows the reader to view Opalina as extremely self-absorbed, with her schmaltzy song title trivializing a subject that she knows will be devastating to the child reading it. To him, her love has been food every day, stories at night, constant care and concern up until the moment she left the pantry overflowing with groceries. It's impossible to be a dime away from that kind of love, and she has to know this. Besides: If she's only a dime away, why hasn't she used the pay phone? She's the adult. Why must he call her? The letter simply doesn't ring true, but its falsity passed by the National Book Award Committee and other reviewers unnoticed, probably because it reproduces the popular image of mothers who leave. As Jackson describes, "The mother herself is a vague, inaccessible figure, sensed only in the distance," and we, the audience, "are placed on the side of the child" (38).

Holt does provide a scene with strong potential to turn the backlash around. In a conversation between Toby and Mrs. McKnight as she trims her roses, she talks about how much he must miss Opalina, which she does, too. "It takes a brave woman to go after her dreams these days. You should be proud of her. . . . Sometimes people don't feel complete until they go after their dreams. Even I have a few dreams of my own" (158). Toby is surprised, and she confesses, "It's nothing glamorous like your mom's. I've always wanted to travel around the southeastern part of the country, searching for old roses" (158). And this is when the military officers show up to tell her that her son Wayne has been killed in Vietnam. As they approach, Mrs. McKnight chops apart her rose bush, symbolically cutting her dream down to nothing. The news of Wayne's death overcomes the message that Toby should be proud of Mom for following a dream. In what may be the most affecting scene in the novel, a mother's inconsolable grief over her absent son overshadows a son's grief over his absent mother. The news of Wayne's death causes the whole town to act depressed. There's no laughter, and "little kids haven't played outside, as if their moms are afraid someone might snatch them out of their yards and send them off to war" (163). After allowing one classic mom in an apron to admit she understands and admires the liberated Opalina, the backlash requires all moms to hunker down and keep their kids close. How can you go out in the world and sing when your son might be snatched away and killed in war? Keep them close, keep them safe, mothers.

Near the end of the novel, Holt finally provides a father-son heart-to-heart in which Dad answers Toby's question about why he married Mom:

"That tiny little thing was filled with so much life. . . . Passionate about her dreams, even back then. I guess I thought like me, her dreams belonged to her youth and that she'd be happy with the simple life. But that was my dream. It wasn't right for me to expect her to change. . . . So if there is any blaming to do, aim it my way." (195)

Toby doesn't blame him, and Dad says, "Then don't blame her either. She loves you, Toby. You need to let her love you" (195). This speech is a step in the right direction of understanding mothers as separate individuals with dreams outside of having a family, and with equal rights to self-actualization, but it happens too little, too late, and too easily. Dad sees the light just in time to tie the book up in a bow in the end. One would think that nearly thirty years of perspective on the second wave of feminism would allow an author to transcend stereotype in historical fiction, but interestingly, the treatment of the abandoning mother in *When Zachary Beaver Came to Town* is less complex and insightful than in Paterson's and Voigt's texts, both written *in medias res* of the late 1970s. But another way of looking at it, of course, is that Holt, born in 1960, was a child during the women's movement and doesn't remember it from an adult perspective; rather, in the time between the setting and the writing of the book, she has had nearly thirty years of being "steeped in the lore of backlash" of *Kramer vs. Kramer* and other stories. To Holt as well as to reviewers and award committees, her false rendition of the mother who leaves "rings true because we've heard it so often," as Susan Faludi might say (45).

Faludi concludes: "The backlash could never mold America into the backward-looking, dad-hailing, nuclear family fantasy it promoted. But it could implant that image in many women's minds and set up a nagging, even tormenting dissonance" (452). A field dominated by women as writers, editors, critics, librarians, and teachers cannot help but embody this dissonance. All three of the novelists discussed here are women—all mothers as well as daughters, in fact—and are representing motherhood in their texts, but not from a mother's viewpoint. Feminist psychoanalytic critics suggest that "the writer or artist always speaks from her position as child rather than mother" (Davey xiv). The child of Alice Walker seems to be a case in point, tormented in the dissonance of motherhood myths despite the likelihood that Rebecca even read and agreed with Faludi's book when it came out;

early in "Becoming the Third Wave" she writes: "The backlash against U.S. women is real" (39). Sara Ruddick points out that adults "may still hate a punishing or neglecting mother or fear maternal power or share the culture's contempt for mothers, perhaps especially their own. No adult simply outgrows childish feelings, but mothers who live in the midst of childhood passion are particularly susceptible to a return of their own childhood needs and fantasies" (194). Susan Rubin Suleiman argues that any mother "who wants to do serious creative work—with all that such work implies of the will to self-assertion, self-absorption, solitary grappling—must be prepared for the worst kind of struggle, which is the struggle against herself," for the social ideology of motherhood presents "conflicts [that] are *inside* the mother, they are part of her most fundamental experience" (122). Perhaps this explains Rebecca Walker's *Baby Love*. Becoming a mother herself brought out her childhood resentments.

These largely subconscious perceptions can show themselves, often unintentionally, in creative writing. "Thus separation and guilt often emerge as the axis of conflict for contemporary women writers," claims Jessica Benjamin. The conflict felt by the mother-author, the mother-editor, the mother-critic, is projected into award-winning children's fiction about mothers who leave and becomes part of the backlash that serves to perpetuate the conflict itself. Although Jacqueline Rose has argued the impossibility of representing a child's viewpoint in fiction written by adults, the use of a child's focalizing perspective defines the genre. Perhaps that makes representing mothers in children's fiction a double impossibility.

Abandoning mothers, indeed.

Notes

1. Rebecca claimed the term in her 1992 *Ms. Magazine* article, "Becoming the Third Wave," in response to the Clarence Thomas/Anita Hill trial. Her mother had been a contributor to *Ms. Magazine* from 1974 through 1986.

2. See especially "A Writer Because of, Not in Spite of, Her Children" (66–70) and "One Child of One's Own: A Meaningful Digression within the Works" (361–83).

3. For a discussion of how Mama Bear reinforces traditional gender role patterns and "holds back women's progress from within, and without question" (259) see my "The Berenstain Bears and the Reproduction of Mothering."

4. For a discussion of how popular picture books contribute to the reproduction of traditional mothering, see my "The Apple of Her Eye: The Mothering Ideology Fed by Best-selling Trade Picture Books."

5. During the first wave of the women's movement in the late nineteenth century, some examples of the independent "New Woman" character began to leave the traditional family, as, for instance, in Henrik Ibsen's play *A Doll's House* (1879)—viewed at the time as scandalous. However, a mother leaving "to find herself" was virtually unthinkable in children's literature until the second wave.

6. However, Karen Coats has noticed a recent trend of absent fathers being increasingly demonized in the books she reviews. In an editorial comment she suggested this explanation to me: "It seems more the case that the fathers are irrelevant in these 70s texts, which may also be considered in the context of those 'a woman needs a man like a fish needs a bicycle' days, while the mothers never are [seen as irrelevant]."

Works Cited

Apseloff, Marilyn. "Abandonment: The New Realism of the Eighties." *Children's Literature in Education* 23.2 (1992): 101–6. Print.

Bassin, Donna, et al., eds. *Representations of Motherhood*. New Haven: Yale UP, 1994. Print.

Benjamin, Jessica. "The Omnipotent Mother: A Psychoanalytic Study of Fantasy and Reality." *Representations of Motherhood*. Ed. Donna Bassin et al. New Haven: Yale UP, 1994. 127–46. Print.

Caplan, Paula J. *The New Don't Blame Mother: Mending the Mother-Daughter Relationship*. New York: Routledge, 2000. Print.

Chesler, Phyllis. "The Mother-Daughter Wars." *Salon.com*. Salon Media Group, Inc., 10 June 2008. Web. 3 Dec. 2014.

Chodorow, Nancy J. *The Reproduction of Motherhood: Psychoanalysis and the Sociology of Gender with a New Preface*. 1978. Los Angeles: U of California P, 1999. Print.

Davey, Moyra, ed. *Mother Reader: Essential Writings on Motherhood*. New York: Seven Stories, 2001. Print.

Faludi, Susan. *Backlash: The Undeclared War Against American Women*. New York: Crown, 1991. Print.

Fraustino, Lisa Rowe. "The Apple of Her Eye: The Mothering Ideology Fed by Bestselling Trade Picture Books." *Critical Approaches to Food in Children's Literature*. Ed. Kara K. Keeling and Scott T. Pollard. Children's Literature and Culture 59. New York: Routledge, 2009. 57–72. Print.

———. "The Berenstain Bears and the Reproduction of Mothering." *The Lion and the Unicorn* 31.3 (2007): 250–63. Print.

Griffin, Susan. "Feminism and Motherhood." *Mother Reader: Essential Writings on Motherhood*. Ed. Moyra Davey. New York: Seven Stories, 2001. 33–45. Print.

Holt, Kimberly Willis. *When Zachary Beaver Came to Town*. New York: Holt, 1999. Print.

Jackson, Rose. *Mothers Who Leave: Behind the Myth of Women Without Their Children*. London: Pandora, 1994. Print.

Paterson, Katherine. *Gates of Excellence: On Reading and Writing Books for Children*. New York: Puffin, 1992. Print.

———. *The Great Gilly Hopkins*. New York: Harper, 1978. Print.
Rose, Jacqueline. *The Case of Peter Pan: Or the Impossibility of Children's Fiction*. U of Pennsylvania P, 1992. Print.
Ruddick, Sara. "Talking About 'Mothers.'" *Mother Reader: Essential Writings on Motherhood*. Ed. Moyra Davey. New York: Seven Stories, 2001. 187–98. Print.
Suleiman, Susan Rubin. "Writing and Motherhood." *Mother Reader: Essential Writings on Motherhood*. Ed. Moyra Davey. New York: Seven Stories, 2001. 113–37. Print.
Thurer, Shari L. *The Myths of Motherhood: How Culture Reinvents the Good Mother*. New York: Penguin, 1994. Print.
"2002 Alex Award Winners." *Young Adult Library Services Association*. American Library Assoc., 2002. Web. 6 Jan. 2014.
Voigt, Cynthia. *Dicey's Song*. New York: Atheneum, 1982. Print.
Walker, Alice. *In Search of Our Mothers' Gardens*. New York: HBJ, 1983. Print.
———. "Taking Care of the Truth—Embedded Slander: A Meditation on the Complicity of Wikipedia." *Alicewalkersgarden.com*. 2013. Web. 3 Dec. 2014.
Walker, Rebecca. *Baby Love: Choosing Motherhood After a Lifetime of Ambivalence*. New York: Riverhead, 2007. Print.
———. "Becoming the Third Wave." *Ms. Magazine*. Jan.-Feb. 1992: 39–41. Print.
———. *Black, White, and Jewish: Autobiography of a Shifting Self*. New York: Riverhead, 2001. Print.
———. "How My Mother's Fanatical Views Tore Us Apart." *The Daily Mail*. Associated Newspapers Ltd, 23 May 2008. Web. 3 December 2014.
Wigutoff, Sharon. "Junior Fiction: A Feminist Critique." *The Lion and the Unicorn* 5 (1981): 4–18. *Project Muse*. Web. 18 Dec. 2014.

Chapter 13

"A Mom-Shaped Hole":
Psychoanalysis and the Dystopian Maternal

Jennifer Mitchell

Violet Durn, the symbol of failed resistance in M. T. Anderson's technological dystopia, *Feed*, has a significantly more complicated relationship with her parents than her boyfriend, Titus, has with his. While Titus's parents are a single unit, employing the term "we" to explain their collective decision making (118), Violet's parents warrant delineation into their corresponding components: father and mother. Importantly, Mr. Durn is a single father, which prompts Violet's initial awkward but telling explanation of her seemingly atypical family dynamic:

> "Where's your mom?" [Titus] asked.
> "Probably South America," Violet said. "She likes it warm."
> "Are they divorced?"
> "They never married."
> "Your life. . . . It must be kind of strange?"
> "Meaning what?"
> "Just . . . it's not . . . the things that most of us . . . do?"
> "No," she said, like she wanted to change the topic. (138)

Titus's equation of unmarried parents with strangeness is significant as Titus's voice in the novel is indicative of more widespread and generally accepted experiences, concerns, and identities. Violet, given the baggage that accompanies her parents, is not at all the "most of us" to whom Titus refers. Subsequently describing the "romance" between her parents as "an experiment in lifestyle" (139), Violet has little to say about her mother throughout the text. When Titus asks Violet "what's doing . . . ?" during a routine chat session, she explains, "Dad's off at work. Mom's just a mom-shaped hole in the front door. I'm eating cereal, putting on my stockings, and reading ancient Mayan spells" (187). Utterly clueless, Titus misses the covert content of this response, focusing on the mind-blowing insinuation that Violet knows Mayan rather than on the weight of her description of her mother as simultaneously present and absent. The "mom-shaped hole" that Violet identifies is a testament to the impact that her physically absent mother has on her.

Violet's mother's absence, which predates the earliest action in the book and is a consistent component throughout, consequently celebrates Violet's father as a single parent. Without a viable, present maternal influence, Violet grows up by consciously and unconsciously mimicking the behaviors and characteristics of her father, which deliberately position him outside of conventional society. Much like her father, Violet finds herself marginalized from the system, no longer deserving of the help that only the system itself can provide. Ultimately doomed by her overt attempts to resist consumer culture, Violet "dies" a slow, painful death with only her father to grieve.[1] Just as Violet's mother physically disappears, so too Violet disappears within her failing body. The fleeting references to Violet's mother allude to the possibility that Violet might have lived a different, longer life had her father not been her only parental influence—had Violet not internalized his reactionary resistance. Instead of hoping for a hypothetical, more positive alternative for Violet through her absentee mother, though, readers empathize with Violet's father, further condemning her missing mom and celebrating the heroic, if ultimately futile, resistance that Violet "inherited" from her father.

Although Violet is presented as singular within the narrative of *Feed*, she is far from alone in the realm of young adult dystopian fiction, which has recently focused on adolescent characters that are defined, in one way or another, by a great parental lack. Julie Just writes in "The Parent Problem in Young Adult Lit," "Judging from *The New York Times* children's bestseller list and librarian-approved selections like the annual 'Best Books for Young Adults,' the bad parent is now enjoying something of a heyday." Just continues by claiming that "what's striking [is] that some of the most sharply written and critically praised works reliably feature a mopey, inept, distracted or ready-for-rehab parent, suggesting that this has become a particularly resonant figure." Arguing that parents in recent adolescent fiction cannot quite figure out what parenting entails, Just identifies what she sees as a trend in the rise of literary parents who are "very, very busy" or who have "simply checked out." What Just declares a trend has, of course, a much longer history, with neglectful parents a staple in fairy tales from the Brothers Grimm and Charles Perrault to more contemporary "fairy tales" by Roald Dahl and J. K. Rowling. That "trend" is a foundational element in other significant texts about adolescent marginalization such as S. E. Hinton's *The Outsiders*, Robert Cormier's *The Chocolate War*, and even the canon of *Nancy Drew* mysteries. Indeed, much of the agency ascribed to adolescents in literature dating back further than the contemporary arsenal that Just dissects is indebted to an express lack of parental presence.

In this chapter, I explore a more complex trend in contemporary young adult literature: dystopian mothers like Violet's, who, through both their presence and absence, fundamentally shape the nature of heroic possibilities available to young protagonists. I focus primarily on the first novels in two different trilogies: Suzanne Collins's *The Hunger Games* (eponymous with the series title) and Patrick Ness's *The Knife of Never Letting Go* (from the Chaos Walking series). Both texts, which build the logical infrastructure of the rest of the series, experiment with the importance of motherhood within a psychoanalytic framework and highlight its relation to dystopian heroics. In Collins's series, Katniss vilifies what she sees as her mother's useless maternal instincts, ultimately failing to adequately perform any version of the Oedipal complex. Instead, she becomes a dystopian heroine by rejecting her mother, mimicking the role of her dead father, and as a result of her detachment from normative feminine trajectories, developing a keen awareness of gender performativity. In the more complicated framework of Ness's Series, Todd's society is predicated on a theoretical Oedipal complex, where developing masculinity is most legibly and literally read into the act of killing one's father. Yet, that complex can never be fulfilled because of the overwhelming absence of mothers within the system that his adversary, Mayor Prentiss, constructs. Todd's heroics, though, are contingent upon his singular recuperation of a female legacy—by discovering and embracing his mother's journal. Whereas Katniss necessarily rejects the maternal, Todd unexpectedly reclaims it. Both Katniss and Todd eventually become heroes within their respective narratives because their gendered development, gauged psychoanalytically in terms of the mother, is fundamentally compromised.

When Electra Can't: Katniss Everdeen's Masculine Heroism

On the first page of *The Hunger Games*, even before readers are formally introduced to her as the main character, Katniss Everdeen describes her young sister, Prim, whose "face is as fresh as a raindrop, as lovely as the primrose for which she was named" relative to her mother who "was very beautiful once, too" (3). Katniss follows this comparison with a deliberate caveat: "or so they tell me" (3). This jab iterates Katniss's unwillingness to acknowledge anything positive about her mother. From the Reaping to the Games to the aftermath of victory, Katniss's adamant disavowal of her mother is a consistent part of her character in the first book in the trilogy. That denial is tied significantly to Katniss's memories of her father's death and the way that her mother reacted to the tragedy:

> The district had given us a small amount of money as compensation for his death, enough to cover one month of grieving at which time my mother would be expected to get a job. Only she didn't. She didn't do anything but sit propped up in a chair or, more often, huddled under the blankets on her bed, eyes fixed on some point in the distance. Once in a while, she'd stir, get up as if moved by some urgent purpose, only to then collapse back into stillness. No amount of pleading from Prim seemed to affect her. (26–27)

From this description, the most thorough explanation of the roots of her disdain, it is clear that Katniss dismisses her mother as weak and ineffective. Even when she attempts to credit her mother with a stifling abundance of emotion, Katniss's words are filled with scorn: "She must have really loved him....I try to remember that when all I can see is the woman who sat by, blank and unreachable, while her children turned to skin and bones" (8). The notion of love is buried in this sentence underneath the dehumanizing description of her mother as "blank and unreachable." Even her chronicled attempt at forgiveness is filled with her disregard for her mother: "I try to forgive her for my father's sake. But to be honest, I'm not the forgiving type" (8). Clearly, her father's abrupt death and her mother's debilitating grief catalyze Katniss's worship of the masculine and rejection of the feminine.

Holding onto the same immediate frustrations and disappointments, Katniss, years later, still refuses to acknowledge the intensity of her mother's loss: "I was terrified. I suppose now that my mother was locked in some dark world of sadness, but at the time, all I knew was that I had lost not only a father, but a mother as well" (27). Katniss's dismissal of her mother's feelings is evident in her use of the phrase "I suppose now," with its condescending detachment. Regardless of how many years have passed, or how much she has matured since the death of her father, Katniss is unwilling and, therefore, unable to empathize with her mother. Katniss's final rejection of her mother as responsible and responsive caregiver comes with the conclusion of this particular flashback: "At eleven years old, with Prim just seven, I took over as *head of the family*. There was no choice" (27; emphasis added). Notably, Katniss neither takes over for her mother nor identifies as a kind of hybrid parental figure that would bridge the gap between lost father and "lost" mother. Rather, she self-identifies entirely with the attributes that she wholly ascribes to her father: protector and provider. Previously, in "Of Queer Necessity: Panem's Hunger Games as Gender Games," I argued that Katniss's actions suggest that she has become a surrogate parent—both mother and father—for Prim, yet that argument is contingent upon cultural myths about motherhood and a reading of the instinctive, sacrificial gesture of her taking Prim's place in the games as more maternal than paternal. Such a reading, though, comments more on general social expectations than on Katniss's own consciousness. Certainly, Katniss's inability to ascribe any protective maternal instinct to her mother suggests that her immediate decision to replace Prim as the female tribute is indebted, once again, to a notion of father as protector.

Katniss did, however, make a choice, whether conscious of it or not, when she chose to associate completely with her father as "head of the family." The arc that is set up, then, is a play on Freud's understanding of childhood development. As Juliet Mitchell explains, "In the situation of the Oedipus complex . . . the little boy learns his place as the heir to this law of the father and the girl learns her place within it" (403). Even though she acknowledges the Oedipal complex as a "patriarchal myth," Mitchell still explains the pervasiveness of the myth itself in Freud's understanding of gender development: "At first both sexes want to take the place of both the mother and the father, but as they cannot take *both* places, each sex has to learn to repress the characteristic of the other sex. But both, as they learn to speak and live within society, want to take the father's place, and *only the boy will one day be allowed to do so*" (404). Obviously, in the Everdeen family, there is no boy to take the father's place, but Katniss appraises herself as overwhelmingly up to the task—presenting an overt challenge to Freud's female Oedipal complex.

According to Freud as interpreted through Juliet Mitchell, girls are forced to acknowledge that they will never be able to take their father's place, ultimately acquiring their "secondary feminine identity" only through seduction/rape, regardless of whether they are the temptresses or the victims (404).[2] Judith Butler elaborates on the implications of this development: "The daughter's incestuous passion is less fully explored in the Freudian corpus, but her renunciation for her desire for her father culminates in an identification with her mother" (*Undoing Gender* 152). Given her father's premature demise, Katniss loses the opportunity to perform this "symbolic seduction," and her "feminine destiny" is ultimately compromised (Mitchell 404). Rather than the "necessary" trajectory of objectifying her father and replacing her mother, Katniss actively seeks to fill the position left unoccupied by her lost father, making the aforementioned "choice." Moreover, as Freud explains in "The Ego and the Id":

> a little girl, after she has had to relinquish her father as a love-object, will bring her masculinity into prominence and identify herself with her father (that is, with the object which has been lost), instead of with her mother. This will clearly depend on whether the masculinity in her disposition—whatever that may consist in—is strong enough. (640)

Katniss's father, as the love object, is indeed lost to her, and the masculinity in her disposition is indeed strong. In fact, Katniss internalizes the masculine characteristics that represent her father—including what sociologist Allan Johnson identifies with masculinity: "control, strength, competitiveness, toughness, coolness under pressure, logic, forcefulness, decisiveness, rationality, autonomy, self-sufficiency, and control over any emotion that interferes" (7)—which, for her, triumph over the feminine characteristics that she performs.

What catalyzes and solidifies this identification, though, is that the loss itself is made visible through death. In many ways, the process by which Katniss mourns her father underscores much of the backstory of the first novel. In "Mourning and Melancholia," Freud writes of mourning, "[The libido] served to establish an *identification* of the ego with the abandoned object" (586). Katniss's encompassing rejection of her mother and exaggerated valorization of her father elucidate her identification with the male influence of her childhood. Butler further articulates: "In the experience of losing another human being whom one has loved, Freud argues, the ego is said to incorporate that other into the very structure of the ego, taking on attributes of the other and 'sustaining' the other through magical acts of imitation" (*Gender Trouble* 73). As Katniss chooses to become a stand-in for her father, she works to imitate his role as "head of the family" (Collins 27). Importantly, Butler explains that "this identification [with the lost loved one] is not simply momentary or occasional, but becomes a new structure of identity" (*Gender Trouble* 73). Katniss solidifies the intimate connection between herself and her father when she thinks about her name: "'Katniss,' I said aloud. It's the plant I was named for. And I heard my father's voice joking, 'As long as you can find yourself, you'll never starve'" (Collins 52). Finding herself, for Katniss, is about embodying her father.³

Katniss's victory in the games is indebted to both her transformation into a surrogate for her father—in the woods, hunting, with a bow and arrow—and her detachment from seemingly authentic gender identities as they develop within the psychoanalytic model of the Oedipal complex. Indeed, constructing what Butler theorizes as this new structure of identity, Katniss's association of her father with survival, both before his death and in his wake, becomes both her motivation and her means of success: "A bell went off in my head. I thought of the hours spent in the woods with my father and I knew how we were going to survive" (32). The "we" in this sentence clearly refers to Katniss, her mother, and her sister, but the grammatical structure of the sentence invokes the possibility that her father is implicated as well. Turning to the woods for the first time alone—acting as a new version of her father, "sustaining" her father, in other words—Katniss not only feeds her mother and her sister but also recharges her mother: "The sight of the rabbit seemed to stir something in my mother. She roused herself, skinned the carcass, and made a stew" (51). In this instance, Katniss practically *becomes* her father, providing for her family while simultaneously recuperating her mother from her "dark world of sadness." While Katniss is willing to explicitly acknowledge that she has "put up a wall to protect [herself] from needing her [mother]" (53), she does not—and maybe cannot—recognize the broader implications of her overt emulation of her father.

The developmental significance of this mimicry is magnified in Katniss's performances within the Hunger Games themselves. As I have suggested elsewhere, "for Katniss, 'male' and 'female' or 'masculine' and 'feminine' become circumstantial parts that she plays," and Katniss's disavowal of normative gender identity allows her to perform particular genders when she deems necessary ("Of Queer Necessity" 129). While Katniss is able to identify moments within the games when it seems crucial for her to play a particular part, she is unwilling to relinquish control of that performance and, accordingly, is furious at Peeta's declaration of love and shocked by Haymitch's explanation that such a declaration renders her usefully "desirable" (Collins

135). For Katniss, desirability is tied to femininity, which, as manifested in her mother, is intrinsically tied to weakness. As such, she is only willing to put on such femininity when she is able to make the performance itself clear as performance and when it works to her advantage. When Katniss first arrives at the aptly titled "Remake Center," she is "plucked and "scrub[bed]" (61) in order to make her more overtly identifiable as a girl. While Flavius explains that Katniss "almost look[s] like a human being now" (62), Cinna's stylistic intention is to more expressly gender her, to turn her into "the *girl* who was on fire" (67; emphasis added). For Katniss, all gestures of femininity are performative as she frames her experiences in the capitol before the games entirely as affected. She explains, "Presenting ourselves not as adversaries but as friends has distinguished us as much as the fiery costumes" (79). Because she identifies with her father rather than her mother, as a direct result of the interrupted Oedipal complex, she interprets any presentation of herself as feminine, weak, and romanticized as a staged performance.

When Katniss is rewarded for the femininity that she projects—"Haymitch couldn't be sending me a clearer message. One kiss equals one pot of broth" (261)—she carefully constructs a sexualized identity that is meant to appeal to "the audience" (261). Katniss is explicit when she explains that these displays of femininity are performative, which makes them distinct from her less conscious adoption of traits that remind her of her father—her necessarily lethal skills with a bow and arrow, for instance. Ultimately, Katniss embodies the characteristics that she associates with her father in an attempt to compensate for what she feels is her mother's inability to survive. The games, however, as expressly embodied in Haymitch's "message," demand that Katniss perform femininity as much as she embraces masculinity. Even after she and Peeta prove victorious, Katniss is forced into an artificially feminized body, a dress that contains "padding over [her] breasts, adding curves" (354). Frustrated by the decision to alter what the games did to her body, she finally accepts the performed alterations as Cinna explains the padding as a "compromise" (354) to avoid surgical enhancements. The decision to make Katniss appear more womanly after the games reminds readers that her success in them had much to do with her performance of femininity. Katniss's disappointment in that fact reminds readers that she credits the survival instincts she associates with her father for that same success. Ultimately, though, Katniss's disappointment is trumped by the success of such a gendered performance, as she continues to perform femininity in *Catching Fire* by pretending to be pregnant to protect herself and Peeta. Part of Katniss's dystopian coming-of-age story is contingent upon her ability to perform external signifiers of developing womanhood.

Complicating the Oedipal Complex: Todd Hewitt's Impossible Future

Patrick Ness's *The Knife of Never Letting Go* follows its protagonist, Todd Hewitt, as he eagerly awaits his initiation into manhood. Prentisstown, Todd's home, has a population of 147— including 146 men, and with Todd himself on the cusp of adulthood, one last boy. As the only "almost-man" (19) left, Todd is both within and outside of the boundaries of Prentisstown. A society whose womenfolk no longer exist, Prentisstown has experienced a steadily dwindling population of in-the-know men and uninitiated boys. While Todd does not quite know the details of what it means to be a "man," he is especially eager to be enveloped into the fold.[4] At this point, it should be clear that we are dealing not only with the absence of a singular mother, as was the case in *The Hunger Games*, but with the absence of the entire concept of motherhood. Early in the novel, with telling nonchalance, Todd explains the absence of his "ma" in light of the overarching absence of all mothers due, as the men of Prentisstown claim, to a gendered epidemic that left all of the females dead and all of the males with the ability to hear one another's thoughts: "Ben says my ma was the last of the women but everyone says that about everyone's ma. Ben may not be lying, *he* believes it's true, but who knows?" (9). The missing mothers and the failed Oedipal development that ensues result in a destructive notion of masculinity, one that relies on actual murder rather than its symbolic enactment as in Freud's version of the family dynamic.

As the youngest boy/soon-to-be-man in Prentisstown, Todd is desperate to be let into the inner circle of manliness: "Boys become men and they go to their men-only meetings to talk about who knows what and boys most definitely ain't allowed and if yer the last boy in town, you just have to wait, all by yerself" (10). Todd's isolation is particularly important in the way that he frames his transition from boy to man; left out of all the action of Prentisstown, without an ally or comrade in the same position, Todd can only wait for his mysterious initiation even though the details of the process are kept secret from all the boys. This secrecy is particularly impressive given one of the most significant features of New World—the Noise. Made explicit by the change in fonts within the book itself, Noise is the stuff "that men spill outta theirselves, all their clamor and clatter that never lets up, even when they sleep, men and the thoughts they don't know they even think when everyone can hear" (4–5). New World is filled with Noise rather than women. Todd has been told over the course of his entire life that the Noise itself killed off the women, which makes it incredibly difficult for men in Prentisstown to keep anything a secret, hence Todd's ability to "hear every ruddy last one" (20). The men of Prentisstown are overwhelmingly involved with each other, but readers must not mistake that intimacy for honesty, as Todd is quick to point out that Noise is filled with "lies, lies, lies" (22). It should come as no surprise, given these explanations of the complexity of the Noise and given the deliberate isolation of the boys whenever possible, that the men of Prentisstown are able to keep the means of initiation into manhood a secret.

Of course, the biggest reveal of the book—among many other substantial and dramatic reveals—is the exact nature of that initiation. Before Todd "earns" the right to participate in the process, simply by reaching a certain age, his parents, Ben and Cillian, force him to flee Prentisstown.[5] Ben explains that he and Cillian promised Todd's mother that they would protect him, that they tried to hide their plan from their Noise in order to prevent anyone from accessing it while they waited until Todd was "old enough" (52) to make it on his own. In order to kick-start Todd's willingness to leave his home and to give up all he thinks he "knows" about the world in which he lives, Ben opens up his Noise, letting Todd in and showing him what will happen when he "becomes" a man:

> And there it all is—
> What happens—
> What the other boys did who became men—
> All alone—
> All by themselves—
> How every last bit of boyhood is killed off—. . . .
> I look at Ben and he's a different man than he always was . . .
> "It's why no one tells you," he says. "To keep you from running." (52–53)[6]

Todd's innocence, the characteristic that Ben deems crucial to the getaway that he and Cillian plan and that proves, over and over, to be Todd's saving grace, is implied in his unwillingness to entertain the bits and pieces of what he sees in Ben's Noise.

It takes the better part of the narrative for readers to finally have access to the process by which boys become men, though it is significant that readers learn the secret from Todd, who "makes" himself say it in order to render it real; boys become men by

> killing another man.
> All by theirselves.
> All those men who disappeared, who *tried* to disappear.
> They didn't disappear after all. (448)

Although Todd clearly has access to this information early in the novel, he is unwilling to really consider its implications until close to the book's conclusion, finally settling on the thesis of the initiation: "Men I knew killed by boys I knew to become men theirselves" (448). Todd acknowledges that this process makes the boys retroactively "complicit" (448) in the war waged on the women, turning them into the men that waged the war initially. This process literalizes the Oedipal complex. As Freud explains in "An Autobiographical Study," "boys concentrate their sexual wishes upon their mother and develop hostile impulses against their father as being a rival" (22). Freud also frames the complex as "a wish to get rid of his father in order to take his place with his mother" ("The Ego and the Id" 640). Brad Buchanan speaks to the universality of the Oedipus complex: "Oedipus' story is potentially every boy's, according to Freud, because all boys see their mothers as love-objects and their fathers as rivals" (76).

Indeed, this story, or part of it, applies to every boy in Prentisstown. Accordingly, it becomes necessary to shift from the individual to the collective in order to account for what is happening in Prentisstown. Freud's explanation of the primal horde is crucial:

> One day the brothers who had been driven out came together, killed and devoured their father and so made an end of the patriarchal horde. United, they had the courage to do and succeed in doing what would have been impossible for them individually.... They hated their father, who presented such a formidable obstacle to their craving for power and their sexual desires; but they loved and admired him too. After they had got rid of him, had satisfied their hatred and had put into effect their wish to identify themselves with him, the affection which had all this time been pushed under was bound to make itself felt. (*Totem* 176–77)

Mayor Prentiss makes real the component of the Oedipal complex that involves theoretically killing one's father in much the same way as he utilizes the trajectory of the primal horde as *the means* by which boys are "turned into" men. They are permitted, encouraged, even forced to kill their "fathers," though Mayor Prentiss as *the* patriarch in question is off limits in that regard. Notably, there are no mothers left to desire and acquire, so the anticipated end within the Oedipus complex does not exist. Mayor Prentiss, at whose behest the women were eliminated, clearly believed that the removal of the mothers—of all women, in fact—would dissipate the rivalry between the men. Initially, the unity of the army that he is building bolsters his revision of the Oedipus myth.[7]

The question of women—of mothers—is vital here to understand both Mayor Prentiss's success and Todd's complex ethical rebellion. Ben reveals that the Noise, afflicting only the men of Prentisstown, exploited a tension between the sexes: "[Men] couldn't stand women knowing everything about them and them knowing nothing about women" (392). The problematic power dynamic here is clear; the authority of the men is undercut by the unrestricted and imbalanced access that *all* women had to their thoughts, feelings, and plans. Mayor Prentiss exploited the men's insecurity until, at the height of this conflict, he and most of the men worked together to kill off the women.

The removal of outlets for what is presumed to be heterosexual desire bolsters the aims of the primal horde. Freud cites Atkinson's *Primal Law* about the sole enemy of the patriarch: "a youthful band of brothers living together in forced celibacy. . . . A horde as yet weak in their impubescence they are, but they would, when strength was gained in time, inevitably wrench by combined attacks, renewed again and again" (*Totem* 176). Such forced celibacy, according to Freud, heightens the aggression of the "youthful band of brothers" until an inevitable breaking point. What Mayor Prentiss has created, then, is an army forced to recast its singular sexual desires into communal violence. This revision of the primal horde reveals that Mayor Prentiss, fascinatingly, is both the patriarchal father as well as the leader of the primal horde, which situates itself against that father. Indeed, once Mayor Prentiss has an entire society comprised of men whose thoughts he has constant access to and men whom he has made complicit in the genocide that has been committed, the remaining boys are the only unknown: too young to participate, too young to realize what has happened, and, as a result, a hypothetical threat to the order that he has constructed. Thus, the process by which boys become men, granted access to the secret history of Prentisstown and thus made complicit in its crimes, binds the newly "made" men to their leader. Mayor Prentiss inducts the boys into his army—his primal horde—by way of simultaneously eliminating one father and adhering themselves to an even greater father, a hypothetically divine father, in fact. Ben concludes, "If [Mayor Prentiss] could make every single boy in Prentisstown a man by his own meaning, then he's God, ain't he? He's created all of us and is in complete control.... That's why he wants you. Yer a symbol. Yer the last innocent boy of Prentisstown. If he can make you fall, then his army is complete and of his own perfect making" (Ness 397). Todd is the ultimate prize; if he "falls"—if, reminiscent of biblical language, he becomes a man like the other boys before him—he is the quintessential testament to Mayor Prentiss's ability to create his own race nonbiologically, given the missing mothers.

Systematically, under Mayor Prentiss's orders, the boys of Prentisstown attempt to recreate the Oedipal complex in their singular albeit public killings of older "fathers" in order to replace them as men in the community. Their masculinity, both individualized and collective, is contingent upon the fulfillment of one component of the Oedipal complex. Given the gruesome nature of this transformation, readers are quick to condemn this particular breed of masculinity. Additionally, the missing component—the promised mother—carves out a space for Todd's specific heroism: a reclamation of forbidden maternal influence. Throughout *The Knife of Never Letting Go*, Todd is surrounded by many powerful influences: Ben and Cillian, who affect Todd when they are present *and* when they are absent; Viola, the first girl Todd has ever seen and who partners with him in this dystopian journey; the men of Prentisstown, against whom Todd is actively working; and finally, Todd's mother, of whom he has no real memory but a tangible representation in the form of her journal.

Early in the novel Todd narrates, "Before I was born, boys were taught by their ma at home and then when there were only boys and men left, we just got sat down in front of vids and learning modules till Mayor Prentiss outlawed such things as 'detrimental to the discipline of our minds'" (18). Even though Ben tries sporadically to teach Todd to read, Todd explains that he "never ended up reading too good. Don't matter. Ain't nobody in Prentisstown ever gonna write a book" (19). Keeping his army illiterate enables Mayor Prentiss to control their understanding of the world around them. Todd's ma's journal, though, helps to reconstruct the history of Prentisstown for Todd and readers alike by reconstructing women and mothers, even in their absence.

Introduced as "my ma's own book" (50), the journal itself represents a past that has been literally erased through the murders of the women and the book burnings sanctioned by Mayor Prentiss. References to his "ma's book" resurface in the novel as a form of support and inspiration for Todd and Viola. Ben says that his ma's book has "all the answers" (108) that Todd will need as he escapes from Prentisstown, and, as it turns out, the book *becomes* the answers that Ben presumes that it contains. First, it protectively shields Todd from a stabbing (286). Second, it allows Todd to imagine his mother in tangible terms, as Viola "took on my ma's voice and made the whole world change, just for a little while" (443). Finally, it becomes the symbol of what New World, and Prentisstown by proxy, was supposed to have been when they were settled: "*a whole planet made entirely of hope*" (414). Todd's eventual willingness to hear the words that his ma has written down signifies his ultimate condemnation of Prentisstown, its masculinity, and its violence. Indeed, Todd's ma's words speak directly to the way that Todd reconceives his own notion of masculinity: "*But I will say also on yer first day that the attractiveness of power is something you should learn about before you get too much older, it's the thing that separates men from boys, tho not in the way most men think*" (417). These words articulate Todd's struggle with power and with the governing infrastructure of Prentisstown. Further, they speak to "the most amazing thing [Todd] ever did" (471): ignoring an opponent in the face of conflict, choosing to implicitly challenge Mayor Prentiss's destructive notion of masculinity. Todd, consciously or not, embraces the latent content in his mother's explanation of power. Rather than dismissing his ma's book as meaningless or as a threat to his status as boy or man, especially considering his immediate rejection of it given his inability to read, Todd solidifies the connection that his mother initiates when she first addresses the book to him.

Todd's ultimate unwillingness to participate in the performance of masculinity sanctioned by the Prentisstown men is tied explicitly to his recognition and acceptance of the legacy of his mother in ways that are remarkably parallel to the connection between Katniss's successful heroism and the legacy of her father. For Katniss, her survival and her heroics are tied to her rejection of the maternal as organic; for Todd, his survival and his heroics are tied to his reclamation of the maternal as necessary. As a result, both *The Hunger Games* and *The Knife of Never Letting Go* experiment with the role of absent mothers within the Oedipal complex. Katniss, the girl on fire, and Todd, the boy who refuses to become a man, are heroes in their respective dystopias precisely because of the overwhelmingly complicated relationships that they have with their mothers. While the paradigms specific to each character and corresponding text vary substantially, their collective engagement with questions about the intersection between Freudian psychoanalysis and developmental gender dynamics speak to a contemporary trend in dystopian fiction much more telling and significant than bad parenting. Indeed, the list of recent dystopian texts that feature absent mothers is extensive: for instance, Veronica Roth's Divergent series; Lauren Oliver's Delirium series; Leigh Bardugo's Grisha series; Neal Shusterman's Unwind series. These works, among many others that employ similar tropes, reconfigure what Just identifies as the "mopey, inept, distracted" parent. The absent mother enables texts like these to experiment with evolving mechanisms that shape gender identity, all of which testify to the significance of mothers, both present and absent, in the development of adolescent heroics.

Notes

1. I put "dies" in quotation marks because the second half of the book measures Violet's life in terms of percentages, much like an operating system. As a result, she does not traditionally die at the end of the novel; instead, her last recorded percentage is 4.6.

2. While Carl Jung rejects Freud's conception of the Oedipus complex and its universality, ultimately identifying the Electra myth as "the symbol of a girl in her relations to her father and mother" (Willner 66), the "positive Oedipus complex" as further explained by Juliet Mitchell is more applicable to Katniss's situation (641).

3. Interestingly, knowledge of plants and herbs belongs to Katniss's mother rather than her father. Yet, Katniss refuses to acknowledge her mother's potential influence, choosing instead to associate her name and its botanical origins with her father.

4. The process by which boys become men remains a mystery until the exact moment of transformation, but Todd is keenly aware of his disenfranchised status as boy: "I am the youngest of the whole town, tho. I used to come out and throw rocks at field crows with Reg Oliver (seven months and eight days older) and Liam Smith (four months and twenty-nine days older) and Seb Mundy who was next youngest to me, three months and a day older, but even he don't talk to me no more now that he's a man" (9). Readers are encouraged to acknowledge the arbitrariness of the designation because it is based entirely on a calendar that does not at all line up with ours; boys *"officially"* (4) become men at age thirteen, but years on New World are thirteen months apiece.

5. Todd provides readers with the story of how Ben and Cillian become his family: "My pa died of sickness before I was born and then my ma died, of course, no surprises there. Ben and Cillian took me in, raised me" (9). The all-male population of Prentisstown hypothesizes implicitly that same sex romantic partnerships exist. Yet, also implicit is

the notion that Ben and Cillian become a couple long before the demise of the female population. The love that Ben and Cillian feel for each other is clear throughout the text, and Todd's understanding of them as his family—as his parents—is equally consistent.

6. The significance of Noise in Prentisstown is manifest in the formatting changes associated with Noise in the actual text. I cannot recreate the distinct font changes in this chapter, though.

7. Yet, as Adrienne Kertzer argues, "the male settlers appear to be suffering a collective trauma produced by a lack of boundaries between the self and the group as a whole" (11). While Kertzer focuses more on a character who surfaces in the second book in the series, her claims about "collective trauma" seem apt when considering the problems inherent in this particular type of ritualized masculine group identity.

Works Cited

Anderson, M. T. *Feed*. Somerville, MA: Candlewick, 2002. Print.
Benjamin, Jessica. *The Bonds of Love: Psychoanalysis, Feminism, and the Problem of Domination*. New York: Pantheon, 1988. Print.
Buchanan, Brad. "Oedipus in Dystopia: Freud and Lawrence in Aldous Huxley's *Brave New World*." *Journal of Modern Literature* 25.3–4 (2002): 75–89. Print.
Butler, Judith. *Gender Trouble: Feminism and the Subversion of Identity*. 1990. New York: Routledge, 1999. Print.
———. *Undoing Gender*. New York: Routledge, 2004. Print.
Collins, Suzanne. *The Hunger Games*. New York: Scholastic, 2008. Print.
Freud, Sigmund. "An Autobiographical Study." 1925. *The Freud Reader*. Ed. Peter Gay. New York: Norton, 1989. 3–41. Print.
———. "The Ego and the Id." 1923. *The Freud Reader*. Ed. Peter Gay. New York: Norton, 1989. 628–58. Print.
———. "Mourning and Melancholia." 1917. *The Freud Reader*. Ed. Peter Gay. New York: Norton, 1989. 584–89. Print.
———. *Totem and Taboo: Some Points of Agreement between the Mental Lives of Savages and Neurotics*. 1913. New York: Norton, 1989.
Johnson, Allan G. *The Gender Knot: Unraveling Our Patriarchal Legacy*. Philadelphia: Temple University Press, 1997. Print.
Just, Julie. "The Parent Problem in Young Adult Lit." *New York Times*, 1 Apr. 2010. Web. 9 May 2014. http://www.nytimes.com/2010/04/04/books/review/Just.
Kertzer, Adrienne. "Pathways' End: The Space of Trauma in Patrick Ness's Chaos Walking." *Bookbird: A Journal of International Children's Literature* 50.1 (2012): 10–19. Print.
Mitchell, Jennifer. "Of Queer Necessity: Panem's Hunger Games as Gender Games." *Of Bread, Blood and* The Hunger Games: *Critical Essays on the Suzanne Collins Trilogy*. Ed. Mary F. Pharr and Leisa A. Clark. Jefferson, NC: McFarland, 2012. 128–37. Print.

Mitchell, Juliet. *Psychoanalysis and Feminism: A Radical Reassessment of Freudian Psychoanalysis*. 1974. New York: Perseus Books, 2000. Print.
Ness, Patrick. *The Knife of Never Letting Go*. Somerville, MA: Candlewick, 2008. Print.
Willner, Dorothy. "The Oedipus Complex, Antigone, and Electra: The Woman as Hero and Victim." *American Anthropologist* 84.1 (1982): 58–78. Print.

Contributors

Robin Calland teaches children's and young adult literature at Colorado Mesa University in Grand Junction, Colorado. In her research, she explores the representation of evolutionary biology in children's and young adult fiction and narrative structures in children's nonfiction.

Lauren Causey earned a PhD in education, curriculum and instruction: literacy education from the University of Minnesota—Twin Cities. Her primary research focus is the set of issues surrounding diversity in children's and young adult literature. She holds an EdM from the Harvard Graduate School of Education, with a focus in language and literacy and a BA from Howard University. She is a reviewer for the *Horn Book Guide*, is a recipient of a Carnegie-Whitney grant from the American Library Association, and previously worked at the global headquarters of Scholastic Inc.

Karen Coats is professor of English at Illinois State University, where she teaches children's and young adult literature. She is author of *Looking Glasses and Neverlands: Lacan, Desire, and Subjectivity in Children's Literature* and *Children's Literature and the Developing Reader*. She is also coeditor of the *Handbook of Research on Children's and Young Adult Literature* and *The Gothic in Children's Literature: Haunting the Borders*.

Sara K. Day is an assistant professor of English at Southern Arkansas University and the author of *Reading Like a Girl: Narrative Intimacy in Contemporary American Young Adult Literature* (University Press of Mississippi, 2013). Her research frequently focuses on representations of gender and identity in literature and popular culture for adolescent audiences. Currently, she is developing projects relating to contemporary retellings and adaptations of Victorian literature for children and young adults.

Lisa Rowe Fraustino is a professor and chair of the Department of English at Eastern Connecticut State University and on the visiting faculty in the Graduate Program in Children's Literature at Hollins University, teaching both literature and creative writing courses. She has published on a range of scholarly interests such as publishing, anthropomorphism, Disney, and, of course, mothers in children's and young adult literature. She has also edited three collections of short fiction for young adults and authored several critically acclaimed books for young readers, including the 2010 Milkweed Prize winner, *The Hole in the Wall*.

Dorina K. Lazo Gilmore teaches children's literature at California State University, Fresno. She has published three picture books, including *Cora Cooks Pancit*, which was named the Asian American Librarian Association's Picture Book of the Year, featuring a mother-daughter team cooking up stories and a traditional Filipino dish in the kitchen. Dorina is the mother of three active girls who love to read and create stories of their own.

Anna Katrina Gutierrez teaches English and literature at the Ateneo de Manila University in the Philippines. Following a PhD in children's literature at Macquarie University in Sydney, she has been granted fellowships at several international research centers, including the Hans Christian Andersen Centre and the Swedish Institute for Children's Books. Her publications include articles in *International Research in Children's Literature* and the *Journal of Graphic Novels and Comics*. Her doctoral thesis was awarded the Vice Chancellor's Commendation and is the basis of her forthcoming book on glocalization, conceptual blending, and fairy tale and folktale retellings. She has also edited picture books for children's book publishers in the Philippines and is a consultant for Lantana Publishing.

Adrienne Kertzer is a professor emerita of English at the University of Calgary. She is the author of *My Mother's Voice: Children, Literature, and the Holocaust* (Broadview 2002), which received the Canadian Jewish Book Award and the Children's Literature Association Honor Book Award. Her recent publications include "'Don't You Know Anything?': Childhood and the Holocaust," *The Bloomsbury Companion to Holocaust Literature*, ed. Jenni Adams; "'Does Not Happen': M. T. Anderson and Terry Pratchett Imagine the Nation," *Children and Cultural Memory in Texts of Childhood*, ed. Heather Snell and Lorna Hutchison; and "Not Exactly: Intertextual Identities and

Risky Laughter in Sherman Alexie's *The Absolutely True Diary of a Part-time Indian*," *Children's Literature*.

Koeun Kim is currently a PhD candidate in English literature at the University of Exeter. In her research, which is titled "Going beyond the Domestic Sphere: The Child as the Vehicle for Expansion in Female Children's Literature of the Nineteenth Century," she explores the various ways Victorian female children's writers such as Charlotte Yonge, Juliana Ewing, and Mary Louisa Molesworth used the figure of the child and children's literature to expand their literary sphere and realm of activity. She is also interested in examining how the motivations of women children's writers to widen their literary sphere and readership were integral to the development of children's and women's literature.

Alexandra Kotanko graduated from the University of Texas with a BA in English and is currently working on an MFA in Creative Writing and Children's Literature at Hollins University. She also teaches Language Arts and Reading to middle school students, is an Army wife, and is the mother of four young children.

Jennifer Mitchell is currently a visiting assistant professor at Union College. Her scholarship, which has appeared in *Bookbird*, *The Journal of Bisexuality Studies*, *The Journal of the Fantastic in the Arts*, and various edited collections, focuses on popular culture, queer theory, gender and sexuality, children's and young adult literature, and modernism. With Elwood Watson and Marc Edward Shaw, she coedited the essay collection *HBO's Girls and the Awkward Politics of Privilege, Gender Race* (Rowman & Littlefield, 2015).

Mary Jeanette Moran is an associate professor of English at Illinois State University, where she teaches courses on children's and adolescent literature at the undergraduate and graduate levels. She has published articles on Madeleine L'Engle's fiction, the Anne of Green Gables series, and the Judy Bolton mystery series, and she has presented papers on children's literature, narrative, and feminist ethics at conferences including ChLA, MLA, and the symposium on ethics and children's literature at the Janet Prindle Institute. Her current project investigates the intersections between feminist ethics, particularly ethics of care, and fantasy for children and young adults.

Julie Pfeiffer is an associate professor of English at Hollins University, where she teaches children's literature, Milton, and the novel. The chapter included in this text is part of a larger project on nineteenth-century novels for girls.

Donelle Ruwe, a professor of English at Northern Arizona University, teaches children's literature, poetry, and British literature of the eighteenth and nineteenth centuries. She is the author of *British Children's Poetry in the Romantic Era: Verse, Riddle, and Rhyme* (Palgrave 2014) and the editor of *Culturing the Child 1690–1917: Essays in Memory of Mitzi Myers* (Scarecrow 2005). She is co-president of the 18th- and 19th-Century British Women Writers Association, chair of the Children's Literature Association Edited Book Award Committee (2012–15), and a member of a committee awarding the *Lion and the Unicorn* Award for Excellence in North American Poetry for Children (2012–2014). Her chapbook, *Another Message You Miss the Point Of*, won the Camber Press Poetry Prize in 2006. She is currently coediting with James Leve an essay collection for Ashgate about American musical theater and the child.

Index

abandonment, maternal, 15, 18–19, 153, 161, 187, 216–32. *See also* absent mother
Abate, Michelle, "A Womb with a Political View," 12
Abraham-Podietz, Eva, 92n3
Abrams, Lynn, "Ideals of Womanhood in Victorian Britain," 171–72
absent mother, 3, 11, 18, 134, 137, 213n3, 219, 223, 234, 241, 246. *See also* abandonment
Ackroyd, Meredith R., "Mothers of Misselthwaite," 11
Adams, Matthew, 166n1
Adèle et Thèodore, ou Lettres sur l'éducation (Genlis), 28
adolescent girls, 60, 61; as narrators, 14, 50, 51, 55, 56, 57n5, 62, 87, 119, 202, 206, 212; as othermothers, 69–70; *shōjo*, 136, 147n3
Aesop's Fables, in Words of One Syllable (Aikin), 35
African American (black) mothering, 16, 61, 106–8, 113, 123, 126–30
agency, 134, 136, 142, 144, 146, 235
Aikin, Lucy, 35
Al Capone Does My Shirts (Choldenko), 16, 135, 139–42
Along for the Ride (Dessen), 209–10
Althusser, Louis, "Ideology and Ideological State Apparatuses," 41n2

Altman, Jeanne, 157–58
ambivalence toward motherhood, 5, 9, 17, 137–38, 171, 172, 194, 216, 222, 223
American Kindertransport Association, 79
Anderson, David A., 166n1
Anderson, M. T., 19, 233
Angelou, Maya, 110; "Great Expectations," 109
animal babies, 153–69; books about, 166n3; as focalizers, 161; kangaroos, 153–54; koalas, 162; opossums, 162; pandas, 161–62
Animal Families (Mack), 156, 157
animal mothers, 16, 153–69, 193–94, 195; alligators, 159; baboons, 157; behavior, 159; books about, 166n3; dung beetles, 158; frogs, 158; giraffes, 157; hares, 162; hero myth, 162–63; hippos, 157; hyenas, 158; intraspecies differences, 159; kangaroos, 153–54; lack of intraspecies variation, 156–58; lack of scientific accuracy, 154; "laissez-faire," 158; lemmings, 157; manatees, 163, 164; mergansers, 159; mice, 158; mountain lions, 163; opossums, 162; owls, 157; pandas, 153, 160–62, 164; penguins, 157, 163; pigs, 157; raccoons, 159; rats, 158; reproduction, 153–54; "restrictive," 158; sea lions, 157;

survival strategies, 159–60; turtles, 159
Anne of Green Gables, 66
anthropocentrism, 164–65
anthropomorphism, 16–17, 155; as harmful pedagogy, 163–66
Apseloff, Marilyn, "Abandonment," 218–19
Arendell, Terry, 4–5
Armour, Michael C., 156, 157, 160, 163
Arnosky, Jim, 156, 157, 159, 160
Aunt Judy's Letters (Gatty), 47
Aunt Judy's Magazine (Gatty), 47
Aunt Judy's Tales (Gatty), 47
autobiographical fiction, 50, 52, 77
autonomy: care ethics as threat to, 182; and CHAT, 113–14, 123; relational, 191; and selfhood, 194

Babies in the Bayou (Arnosky), 156, 159
Baby Love (Walker, Rebecca), 216, 217, 218, 230
Baby Panda Is Born, A (Ostby), 156
Backfisch novels, 14, 59, 64; American, 60, 64–66, 68–70; Christian themes added, 71; contrasted with *Bildungsroman*, 60; defined, 60; differences between American and German, 71; direct address to readers, 62; German, 59, 60, 66; as transformation stories, 60; translation issues, 71
Backfischens Leiden und Freuden/ Gretchen's Joys and Sorrows (Helm), 59, 63, 66–68, 69
Backlash (Faludi), 201, 203, 216, 218; backlash culture, 219–30
Baker, Julia, 80, 92n4
Bakhtin, Mikhail, 119
Baldwin, James, 118, 126
Bank Street School, 40
Barbauld, Anna Letitia, 13, 27, 29–41; body-part game, 27, 30, 31, 32–33, 36, 37, 39, 40; conversational style, 34, 37, 38, 39, 41n4
Bardugo, Leigh, 247
Barney, Richard A., 41n2
Barrie, J. M., 170, 171, 172, 174, 175, 176, 178, 179, 180
Bassin, Donna, 4, 13, 225; "Maternal Subjectivity in the Culture of Nostalgia," 20n5, 98, 179, 225
Baumel-Schwartz, 78, 79, 92n1, 92n2
Bear Cub: At Home in the Forest (Toast), 156, 157
Benjamin, Jessica, 4, 166, 173, 177–80, 230; "The Omnipotent Mother" 20n5; on Winnicott, 173
Benz, Wolfgang, 79
Berebitsky, Julie, 6
Berenstain Bears, The, 218, 230n3
Berger, Gilda, 156, 157, 162
Berger, Melvin, 156, 157, 162
Bernardo, Joseph, 158
Bettelheim, Bruno, 8
Bilman-Maheca, Elfiede, 166
biology
  "biological fairy tales," 16–17
  biological mothers: 6, 8, 60–62, 63, 105, 186, 194, 208, 220, 221
  and definitions of motherhood, 17, 166, 166n1, 183, 185–86, 188, 190, 220; in animals, 153–157, 158, 160–62, 165; opposed to social construction views, 61, 66, 67, 69–70, 73, 105, 192, 193–94
  and gender, 147
  pseudobiology, 158
Black Feminist Thought (Collins, Patricia Hill), 64
black mothering. *See* African American mothering
Black, White, and Jewish (Walker, Rebecca), 217
Blades, Joan, 20n2

Blint, Alice, 222
blogs: *The F Bomb*, 203; *Literary Mama*, 11; "mommy bloggers," 97
blues aesthetic, 126
Bob Books, Set 1 (Maslen), 35
body-part game. *See under* Barbauld, Anna Letitia
"Bracelets, The" (Edgeworth, Maria), 29
breastfeeding, 28, 97, 134, 153
Brennan, Samantha, 182
British Children's Poetry in the Romantic Era (Ruwe), 41n1, 41n4
Brown, Margaret Wise, 99
Brown, Michael, 113, 128, 129
Brown-Wood, JaNay, 15, 99, 103–4
Brush, Lisa D., 9
Buchanan, Brad, 243
Burnett, Frances Hodgson, 56
Burney, Frances, 29
Butler, John, 156, 161
Butler, Judith, 238–39
Buzatto, Bruno A., 158
Byrne, Jenny, 164

Calling the Doves (Herrera), 15, 99, 104–6, 107
Caplan, Paula, 217
care ethics, 17, 19, 182–97; as basis for moral decision-making, 184; and biological mothering, 185; controversy, 182–83; defined, 182; distinguished from dominant psychological models, 183–84; maternal images in, 183; natural caring vs. rule-based ethics, 185; opposed to patriarchal ethics, 183, 189; and power, 183, 191; political context, 191. *See also* Gilligan, Carol; Held, Virginia; Noddings, Nel; Robinson, Fiona; Ruddick, Sara
Carlson, Chad, 31

Carroll, Lewis, 45
Catcher in the Rye, The (Salinger), 213n3
Catching Fire (Collins, Suzanne), 240–41
Champagne, Frances A., 158
Chang, Grace, 10
Chaos Walking series (Ness), 19, 235
CHAT. *See* Cultural-Historical Activity Theory
Chavkin, Wendy, 6
Chesler, Phyllis, 217
child development, 8, 28, 46, 47, 100, 114, 134, 135, 173–76, 205, 237, 241, 247
Children of Willesden Lane: Beyond the Kindertransport (Golabek and Cohen), 15, 78, 80, 82–87, 92
Children's Book Business, The (Paul), 41n1
Childtimes (Greenfield), 16, 114, 115, 116, 117, 120–23, 125–26, 127, 131n2
Chocolate War, The (Cormier), 213n3, 235
Chodorow, Nancy, 4, 8, 10, 14, 176, 177–78, 180, 222
Choldenko, Gennifer, 16, 135
Clark, Roger, 61
class
   middle: values, 36, 82, 170
   and race, 20n5, 105, 108
   stereotypes, 106, 142
   stratification, 5, 119, 126
   white middle: readers, 15; subjects, 61, 68; stereotypes, 6, 109, 204
Coats, Karen, 8, 9–10, 12, 231n6; "The Meaning of Children's Poetry," 147n1
cognitive theory, 16. *See also* conceptual blends; schemas; scripts
Cohen, Lee, 15, 78, 82–83, 85–87, 93n6
Cohen, Michelle, 41n4
Collins, Patricia Hill, 4, 14, 61, 64, 102–3; "Shifting the Center," 105, 108
Collins, Suzanne, 19, 235, 239
community: in care ethics, 182, 185, 193, 194; in CHAT, 121; imagined, 136;

importance of, 61, 62, 64, 68, 70, 73, 104, 136; interconnectedness of black, 64, 113, 117; parenting, 105; role of mother in, 104, 105; self within, 136

conceptual blends, 16, 146; defined, 133–34

Conran, Shirley, 201

conversational style of writing. *See under* Barbauld, Anna Letitia

Conversations, Introducing Poetry (Smith, Charlotte), 29

Coraline (Gaiman), 17, 146, 170–81

Cormier, Robert, 213n3, 235

Crespi, Erica J., 158

Crew, Hilary S., 9, 12, 205

Crittenden, Ann, 7

Crozat, François, 156, 161

Cultural-Historical Activity Theory (CHAT), 16, 113–31
  components of: community, 120, 121; consumption, 120, 124–25, 127; distribution, 120, 124–25, 127; division of labor, 120, 122; exchange, 120, 124, 127; objects, 120–21; rules/norms, 120–122, 123; subjects, 120, 121; tools, 120, 122–23
  defined, 114, 120
  Engeström's model of mediated action, 120–27. *See also* Engeström, Yrjö
  as transformative practice, 116, 124–25, 127

Curio, Claudia, 79

Curley, James P., 158

Dahl, Roald, 235

daughters, 11, 15, 17, 64, 116, 170, 177, 179, 205, 211–12; anger towards mother, 217, 236–37; education of, 70; as focalizers, 12, 186; and memory, 82, 83, 89; mother's influence on, 49, 50, 55, 56, 60, 66, 103, 107, 179, 209; perspectives on mothers, 186; postfeminism and, 212–13, 217; as "property," 127; relationship with mothers, 9–10, 66, 73, 80–81, 101, 118, 201–2, 205–8, 210, 212, 217, 236–37; as writers, 12, 46, 47, 50

Davey, Moyra, 10, 229

Davies, Rebecca, 41n1

Davis, Deborah, 6

Davis, Jordan, 113, 128–30

Delirium series (Oliver), 247

Der Trotzkopf (Rhoden), 59, 70

Desert Is my Mother, The (Mora), 15, 96, 99, 102–3

Dessen, Sarah, 18, 202–14; social media presence, 213n4

Dicey's Song (Voigt), 18, 216, 221, 223–25

didacticism, 15, 27, 41n3

Die Perle der Familie (Prentiss), 59, 64–66, 67, 69

Dinnerstein, Dorothy, 4

DiQuinzio, Patrice, 59

Divergent series (Roth), 146, 247

Dloniak, Stephanie M., 158, 160

Doll's House, A (Ibsen), 231n5

domesticity, 47, 51

Dorow, Sara K., 6

double consciousness, 123–24, 126

Douglas, Susan J., 19n1, 203

Dowling, Claudia Glenn, 5

Dreamland (Dessen), 207, 208

Drucker, Olga Levy, 78, 79

DuBois, W. E. B., 123–24, 126

Dudley (O'Keefe), 29

early readers, 35

Easy Introduction to the Knowledge of Nature, and Reading the Holy Scriptures (Trimmer), 14, 29, 38

Eden, Horatia K., 45

Edgeworth, Maria, 14, 27, 29, 36, 57n4

Edgeworth, Richard Lovell, 14, 36

Edin, Kathryn, 6

education: Enlightenment approaches to, 27–28; of girls, 14, 36, 47, 52, 60, 68, 70, 97, 106; and ideology, 28, 41n2; mother's role in, 15, 28, 39; othermother's role in, 65, 67, 70; power of, 28, 106; transformation through, 60
educational texts, 16, 29; primers, 30, 37–38
Ehrenreich, Barbara, 6
El Deserto Es Mi Madre (Mora), 15, 96, 99, 102–3
Electra myth, 236, 247n2
Elliott, Mary Benson, 29
Émile (Rousseau), 28
empathy, biological propensity of women toward, 186
empirical studies of mothering, 4–7
Engeström, Yrjö, 15, 115, 118, 120, 124–5; model of mediated action 120. *See also* Cultural-Historical Activity Theory
environment: and conceptual blending, 133–38, 144, 145, 146; and human development, 28, 47, 115, 116; and survival of animals, 153, 158, 159
erasure, maternal, 89, 92
essentialism, 59, 60, 61, 73, 183
ethics of care. *See* care ethics
ethnographic studies of mothering, 6
evangelical literary tradition, 64–65
Evenings at Home, in Words of One Syllable (Aikin), 35
evolutionary paradigms, 5, 17, 157–58
Ewing, Juliana, 14, 45–57

F Bomb, The (Zeilinger), 203
fairy godmothers, 48, 49
"Fairy Godmothers, The" (Gatty), 14, 46, 47, 50
fairy tales, 45, 142–45, 187, 196n3, 220, 235; formula, 48

Faith Gartney's Girlhood/ Faith Gartney's Mädchenjahre (Whitney), 59
Faludi, Susan, 18, 201, 203, 216, 218, 225, 229
family: scripts, 136, 137; values, 9, 36, 127
fantasy, 15, 16, 17, 171, 173, 174, 176, 177, 179, 180; of ideal mother/family, 17, 141, 146, 154, 174, 176, 177, 224, 229; literary genre, 17, 18, 45, 46, 160, 183, 186, 187, 193, 195, 196n3
Far to Go (Pick), 15, 78, 80, 90–91, 92
fathers, 28, 81, 82, 89, 91, 92, 206; absent, 219, 220–21, 224, 229, 231n6; and daughters, 64, 71–72, 238, 247n2; death of, 100–101, 118, 207, 208, 235, 236, 237; as economic and/or parenting partners, 7, 20n2, 105, 106, 117, 139–41, 188, 211, 229; identifying with, 234, 235, 236, 237, 239–40, 246, 247n3; missing in books, 105; neglected in scholarship, 11; patriarchal, 244, 245; as rival for mother's affection, 243; single, 223, 233–34; symbolic murder of, 235, 240, 243–44; transgender, 137
Fauconnier, Gilles, 16, 133
Feed (Anderson, M. T.), 19, 233–34
female: domestic story, 46, 50, 53; literary tradition, 47; readers, 46, 47, 53, 62, 63; writers, 45–47, 51, 53, 229, 230
femininity, as performance, 238, 240; contemporary expectations for, 204; representations of, 183, 186, 194
feminism, 4, 18, 201–2; and antifeminist messages, 218, 219; backlash to, 18, 203, 213, 216, 218, 219, 221, 222, 224, 225, 227, 228, 229, 230; and ethics of care, 182; and motherhood studies, 9; first wave, 231n5; second wave, 18, 216, 217, 218, 229, 231n5,

third wave, 216, 218. *See also* postfeminism
feminist ethics, 182, 191. *See also* care ethics
Feminist Moral Philosophy (Brennan), 182
feminist views of mothering, 4, 20n4, 59, 205–6; constructionist, 4, 20n5; psychoanalytic, 4, 8, 229
Fenwick, Eliza, 41n1
Ferguson, Missouri, 107
Fessler, Ann, 6
Fielding, Sarah, 30
First, Elsa, "Mothering, Hate, and Winnicott," 100
flower child, 222; children of, 219–20
Flower of the Family, The (Prentiss), 59, 64–66, 67, 69
focalizers: animals, 161; child, 12, 135, 219, 230; daughters, 186; granddaughters, 15, 79–80, 87
Forcey, Linda Rennie, 10
foster: home, 81, 82, 219; mothers, 64, 90, 91, 220–21
Foster, Shirley, 46
Fox, Anne L., 92n3
Fraustino, Lisa Rowe, 11, 160, 164; "The Apple of Her Eye," 97–98, 218, 230n4; "The Berenstain Bears and the Reproduction of Mothering," 230n3
Freud, Sigmund, 8; theory of gender development, 205, 237, 238, 241; theory of primal horde 243–45. *See also* Oedipus complex
Future Girl (Harris), 213n2
Fyfe, Aileen, 41n4

Gaiman, Neil, 12, 146, 170, 172, 173, 174, 176, 178, 180
Gates, Henry Louis: signifying, 123–24
Gatty, Margaret, 14, 45–51, 53–56, 57n1, 57n3
Gebhard, Ulrich, 166
Geerts, Sylvie, "Mishmash, Conceptual Blending and Adaptation in Contemporary Children's Literature writing in Dutch and English," 147n1
gender: difference, 47; expectations, 14, 46, 92; heteronormativity, 204; identity, 147n4, 237–38, 239, 247; performativity, 19, 235, 239–40, 247; roles, 138; stereotypes, 3–4, 12, 138, 142
Genlis, Madame de, 28
Gershon, Karen, 78
Gibson, Lois Rauch, "Beyond the Apron," 10
Gill, Rosalind, 204–5
Gillies, Val, 6
Gilligan, Carol, 17, 182, 183–84, 186, 196n2
Ginossar, Shlomit, 164
Girshik, Lori, 147n4
Giving Tree, The (Silverstein), 7, 15, 98, 101, 110
Gleitman, Henry, "Mother, I'd Rather Do It Myself," 42n7
Gleitman, Lila R., "Mother, I'd Rather Do It Myself," 42n7
Glenn, Evelyn Nakano, 4, 10; "Social Constructions of Mothering," 20n5, 61
Glenn, Wendy J., 202, 206, 208
Globalization of Motherhood (Chavkin and Maher), 6
Golabek, Mona, 15, 78, 82–84, 85–87, 91, 93n6
Golabek Roberts, Lisa, 84–86
"good-enough mother," 10, 17, 146, 172, 173, 176, 179; defined, 171. *See also* Winnicott, D. W.
"good mother" myth, 96–99, 101, 103, 105, 108, 109, 110, 170, 171, 174, 177, 179, 180, 217–18, 220

Göpfert, Rebekka, 79
Governess, or Little Female Academy, The (Fielding), 29, 30
Grace, Marcus, 164
Graham, Toya, 129
granddaughters: as focalizers, 15, 79–80, 87; of Kindertransportees, 88; as writers, 15, 79–80, 83
grandmothers, 83, 84, 86, 87–89, 91, 116, 117, 120, 131n2, 136–37, 144, 209, 220, 222–23, 225; great-grandmothers, 54–55, 83, 116–17, 127
Gray, Freddie, 113, 128, 130
Great Gilly Hopkins, The (Paterson), 18, 216, 219–22, 224–25
Greenfield, Eloise, 16, 114, 116, 117, 121, 126, 131n2
Greenstone, Daniel, "The Sow in the House," 11
Griffin, Susan, "Feminism and Motherhood," 222, 225
Grimm, Jacob, 235
Grimm, Wilhelm, 235
Grisha series (Bardugo), 247
Gruner, Elizabeth Rose (Libby), *Literary Mama* blog, 11
Gubar, Marah, 57n5
Gutierrez, Anna Katrina, "Metamorphosis," 147n1

habitus, 28, 40, 41n3
Hall, Suzanne, 161
Hamilton, Elizabeth, 28
Hammel, Andrea, 79
Hanley, Pam, 164
Harris, Anita, 213n2
Harris, Mark Jonathan, 81
Harrison, Allan G., 164, 165
Have a Carrot (Pearson), 11
"having it all," 201–13. *See also* "work/life balance"

Heidi (Spyri), 88
Held, Virginia, 17, 182, 185, 191
Helm, Clementine, 61, 62, 66, 67
Here and Now Story Book (Mitchell), 42n8
Herman, David, 33
Herrera, Juan Felipe, 15, 99, 105–6, 107
Hilton, Mary, 41n1
Hinton, S. E., 213n3, 235
Hirschberger, Hermann, 79, 88
His Dark Materials (Pullman): Coulter, Marisa (character), 183, 187–92
historical fiction, 229
History of Little Goody Two-Shoes, The (Newbery), 30
Hochschild, Arlie Russell, 6
Hold On to Your Music Foundation, 84, 87, 91
Holekamp, Kay E., 158, 160
Hollins University Graduate Program in Children's Literature, 9, 12
Holocaust, 78; and memory, 15, 67, 90; survivors of, 79, 87–88, 90
Holt, Kimberly Willis, 19, 216, 225–29
Homecoming (Voigt), 221
Honey, Margaret, 10, 13, 225
Hopsicker, Peter, 31
Horne, Jackie C., 11, 57n4
Hrdy, Sarah Blaffer, 5–6, 17, 153–54, 158, 160, 166n1, 166n2
Hughes, Langston, 113, 117, 125, 127, 128
Huizinga, Johan, 31, 41n5
Hunger Games, The (Collins, Suzanne), 19, 235, 236–41
Hymns in Prose for Children (Barbauld), 33

I Am a Little Panda (Crozat), 156, 161
I Came Alone (Lowesohn), 84
I Shall Wear Midnight (Pratchett), 147n5
Ibsen, Henrik, 231n5
ideal/idealized mothers. *See under* mothers

identity, 62, 65, 66, 104, 105, 107, 108, 190, 195, 223, 233, 240; communal, 61, 78; denial of Jewish, 87–89; and gender, 147n4, 238, 239, 247; maternal, 101, 138, 141, 173, 188, 190, 191, 194, 195; sexual, 100
ideology, 28, 41n2; communitarian, 16, 121, 136; domestic, 14, 51, 52, 171 Japanese, 136; of motherhood, 59, 154, 195, 219, 220, 222, 225; Victorian domestic, 51–52, 171–72
If My Mom Were a Platypus (Michels), 156, 162
Imani's Moon (Brown-Wood), 15, 99, 103–4
Impossibility of Motherhood, The (DiQuinzio), 59
In a Different Voice (Gilligan), 183–84
In Search of Our Mother's Gardens (Walker, Alice), 20n4, 217
individualism, 59, 114, 190
instincts, maternal, 129, 184, 186, 187, 188, 192, 235, 237
interdisciplinary studies, 10, 19n1
intertextuality, 33, 46, 145
invention, maternal, 90–91, 92
Is It Really Mommie Dearest? (Crew), 9

Jackson, Rosie, 226, 228
Jacobson, Heather, 6
Jenkins, Steve, 156, 162
John Locke and Children's Books in Eighteenth-Century England (Pickering), 41n3
Johnson, Angela, 16, 114, 117, 127
Johnson, Eric Michael, 5
Johnson, Joseph, 30
Jolles, Marjorie, "Going Rogue," 204
Joosse, Barbara M., 15, 99–100
Journal for the Association of Research on Mothering, 20n3
Jung, Carl, 247n2

Just, Julie, "The Parent Problem in Young Adult Lit," 11, 234–35
Just Listen (Dessen), 207

Kanner, Leo, 140
Kaplan, Maryle Mahrer, 6, 10, 13, 225
Kardon, Adam, 158
Kazden, Alan, 32, 33
Keeping the Moon (Dessen), 207
Kefalas, Maria, 6
Keller, Pamela J., 61
Kellerman, Robert, 138
Kertzer, Adrienne, 9, 161, 166n1, 248n7
Kilner, Dorothy, 30
Kilner, Mary Ann, 30
Kindertransport fiction, 84, 87, 90; maternal representations in, 15, 77, 92; mothers in, 15
Kindertransportees, 78, 81; as Holocaust survivors, 79, 87–88, 93n7; reunions, 79
Kingsley, Charles, 3
Kitchen (Yoshimoto), 16, 135, 136–39, 147n2
Knife of Never Letting Go, The (Ness), 235, 241–47
Kramer vs. Kramer, 228
Kristallnacht, 83
Kushner, Tony, 78–79

labor, domestic, 54, 55, 64, 69, 77, 81, 82, 96, 144
Lacan, Jacques, 8
Lack, David, 158, 166n2
Ladder to Learning, The (Trimmer), 35
language: as epistemological tool, 33; and mother-environment blends, 134. *See also* Barbauld, Anna Letitia: conversational style
Lardy, Philippe, 122
Lareau, Annette, 6
Larkin-Leiffers, Patricia A., 154

Lassner, Phyllis, 78, 79
Latina mothers, 100–105
Lave, Jean, 122
Lawler, Steph, 6
Lazarre, Jane, 20n4
Learning from the Left (Mickenberg), 42n8
Lee, Sung-ae, "Fairy Tale Scripts and Intercultural Conceptual Blending in Modern Korean Film and Television," 147n1
legacy, maternal, 14, 19, 47, 50, 53, 54, 55, 56, 84, 235, 246; literary, 46, 50
LeGuin, Ursula K., "The Fisherwoman's Daughter," 20n4
Lein, Laura, 6
Leiner, Katherine, 15, 99, 100–102
Lektorsky, V. P., 121
LeMasters, E. E., "Parenthood as Crisis," 170, 171
L'Engle, Madeleine, 18
Leontiev, A. N., 114
Lessons for Children (Barbauld), 13, 29–31, 34
Letters on the Elementary Principles of Education (Hamilton), 28
Leuck, Laura, 99
Leverton, Bertha, 85, 86
Lewin, Ellen, 6
life, domestic, 51, 52, 53, 146
Lion, the Witch, and the Wardrobe, The (Lewis), 145
Literary Conceptualizations of Growth (Trites), 147n1
Literary Mama blog, 11
literature
  African American, 15–16, 107, 115, 116, 121, 123–24, 126
  dystopian, 18, 19, 235, 246–47
  eighteenth-century children's, 13–14, 27, 41n3
  nineteenth-century youth, 14, 36, 45, 59, 61
  Victorian children's, 14, 17, 49
  white youth, 15, 68, 114, 121, 123; ideologies in, 115
Little Melba and Her Big Trombone (Russell-Brown), 15, 99, 107–8
Lock and Key (Dessen), 207, 211
Locke, John, 27
Logan, Kenneth A., 163
Looking Glasses and Neverlands: Lacan, Desire, and Subjectivity in Children's Literature (Coats), 12
love, 17, 66, 67, 68, 70, 73, 220
  as choice, 62
  divine, 65
  for fathers, 238
  and loss, 238–39
  maternal, 5, 7, 71, 91, 98, 102, 129, 133, 134, 140, 142, 172, 174, 179, 185, 192, 217, 224; ambivalence in, 171; as obligation, 62, 220; as sacrifice, 219, 222; unconditional, 99, 100
  for mothers, 221, 228, 229, 243
  for stepmother, 71
  romantic, 212, 236, 239, 248n5
Love You Forever (Munsch), 15, 98, 111n3
"love of employment," 14, 47–48, 53, 54, 55
Lowensohn, Shmuel, 84, 85, 86
Luria, A. R., 114

MacDonald, George, 45
Mack, Lorrie, 156, 157
Maestripieri, Dario, 158
magic realism, 136
Maher, JaneMaree, 6
Mama, Do You Love Me? (Joosse), 15, 99–100
Mama, How Long Will You Love Me? (Pignatori), 99
Mama Does the Mambo (Leiner), 15, 99, 100–102
Mama's Milk (Ross), 153, 156

Manatee Winter (Zoehfeld), 156, 157, 160, 163
manhood, 241–45
Markle, Sandra, 156, 157, 160
marriage, 14, 48, 60, 69, 212
Martin, Chia, 153, 156
Martin, Sabrina, 129
Martin, Trayvon, 113, 128–30
Marx, Karl: *Grundisse*, 124, 127; Marxist theory, 114, 120, 124, 131n3
masculinity, 238, 241; as destructive, 246; as performance, 246
Maslen, Bobby Lynn, 35
Maslen, John, 35
Maternal Theory (O'Reilly), 7
Maughan, Shannon, 98
McBath, Lucia, 129
McCarthy, William, 41n6
McCoy, Joel, 61
McFadden, Lesley, 129
McInally, Kate, "The Other Mother," 12
McKinley, Robin, 18, 183, 193–95
McRobbie, Angela, 203, 213
Mellor, Anne, 27
memoir, 10, 78, 80, 83, 84, 87, 114, 116, 130, 131n2, 216, 217. See also *Children of Willesden Lane*; *Childtimes*
memory, 15, 82, 86, 128, 134; cultural, 121; of childhood, 122, 208; loss of, 81, 84, 90, 92, 245; of mothers, 49, 78, 83; postmemory, 79, 83; repressed, 87; traumatic, 79, 80
Mending the World (Robothom), 109
mentoring, 61, 62; and unmarried women, 64, 67
metaphors, 33; embodied, 134, 140
Mezey, Nancy J., 4
Michaels, Meredith W., 19n1, 203
Michels, Dia, 156, 162
Mickenberg, Julia L., 42n8
Milton, Edith, 78

mirror, 174–77
Miss Peregrine's Home for Peculiar Children (Riggs), 88
Mitchell, Jennifer, "Of Queer Necessity," 237
Mitchell, Juliet, 237–38, 247n2
Mitchell, Lucy Sprague, 39–40, 42n8
Mommy Myth (Douglas and Michaels), 19n1, 204
"mommy wars," 7, 20n2, 97
Moody-Luther, Jacqueline, 156
Moon and More, The (Dessen), 211
Mora, Pat, 15, 96, 99, 102–3
moral development, 30, 184
Moran, Mary Jeanette, "Nancy's Ancestors," 11
More, Hannah, 27
Mother Earth, 133
mother figures, 27, 29, 41n1, 48, 49, 50, 54, 92, 134, 135, 137, 138, 196n4, 202, 206
Mother Knot, The (Lazarre), 20n4
Mother Nature, 102, 133
Mother Nature (Hrdy), 5
Mother Reader (Davey), 10
mother-environment blend, 134, 138, 142–43, 145–46
motherese, 30, 34, 37; defined, 42n7
Motherhood Manifesto (Blades and Rowe-Finkbeiner), 20n2
motherhood
  and career, 208
  ideologies of, 5–6, 16, 17, 59, 91, 97, 108–9, 154, 163–64, 221, 222, 225; biological determinism, 4, 186, 188, 190, 192; cognitive, 16, 134; constructivist, 4, 20 n. 5; psychoanalytic, 4, 8, 19, 233, 235; romanticized view of, 170; sentimentalized, 221, 224; traditional myths of, 6, 16, 96–97, 99, 101, 105, 109–10, 154, 156, 157, 159, 160, 162, 218, 224, 229

and imprisonment, 139, 140, 142, 223
and loss of self, 183; and self-sacrifice, 170–71, 174
political contexts of, 6, 183, 185, 191
refusal of, 28
representations of, 12, 135
in relation to environment, 134
studies, 4, 6–7, 20n3; and feminism, 9
See also biology: definitions of motherhood
Mothering the Self (Lawler), 6
mothering
  alternate models for, 97, 185; as distinct from biological motherhood, 69; male participation in, 185–86, 195
  communal, 59, 61, 70, 104
  as competitive activity, 204
  low status of, 185
  mainstream models for, 15, 96, 97, 99, 100, 102–5, 108, 109
  as opposed to parenting, 185–86
  reproduction of, 14
  stereotypes of, 186, 219, 227
  as unpaid labor, 7
Mothering: Ideology, Experience, and Agency (Glenn, Chang, and Forcey), 10
mothers
  archetypal, 10
  biological, 4, 8, 16–17, 60, 61, 62, 69, 70, 73, 153–54, 183, 185, 192, 193, 194, 220–21
  creative, 102
  and daughters, 9–10, 27, 38, 48, 49, 60, 73, 81, 83, 86, 87, 99, 101, 118, 201–2, 205–8, 210, 212
  dead, 70, 115, 225
  as educating heroines, 27
  and environment, 133–34
  ideal/ idealized, 3, 14, 17, 20n1, 47, 48, 50, 92, 96, 98, 171, 172, 173, 174, 181, 218, 220, 224
  identity, 101, 138, 141, 173, 188, 190, 191, 194, 195, 223
  influence: intellectual, 47, 48, 50, 60, 103, 186; on psychological development, 8, 28, 34, 46, 47, 66, 100, 134, 135, 173, 174, 205, 235, 237, 241; spiritual, 47, 50, 55
  as literary models, 14, 46, 221
  minority, 15, 96–110, 110n1, 110n2
  as mirrors, 174–76
  misrecognized, 78, 80
  moral, 27, 29, 51, 63, 184
  multidimensional, 15, 97, 103, 104, 108
  mythologized, 78, 224
  as narrators, 46, 51
  as negative models, 211
  in nonfiction, 15, 17, 107, 154–69
  as "other," 8
  and power, 8, 27, 137, 194–95
  role of, 70, 91, 172, 194, 224
  schemas, 12, 16, 137
  self-absorbed/selfish, 18–19, 175, 176, 219, 227, 228
  and sexuality, 97, 100, 101, 170
  single, 221, 223
  "smothering," 98, 139, 141
  and sons, 98, 106, 109–10, 124, 127, 128, 129
  and special needs children, 139
  strong, 102, 103, 137, 174
  as subjects, 13
  as teachers, 29, 48, 67, 102
  transsexual, 137–38
  weak, 236
  working, 207
  See also African American mothers; Latina mothers
Mothers and Others (Hrdy), 5
Mother's Journey, A (Markle), 156, 157, 160
mothers of color, 110n2. *See also* mothers: minority

Mothers, Mothering and Motherhood Across Cultural Differences (O'Reilly), 110n1
Munsch, Robert, 98, 111n3
Murdock, Catherine Gilbert, "The Adventures of Mommy Buzzkill," 11
music, 84, 85, 86, 87
My Monster Mama Loves Me So (Leuck), 99
My Mother's Voice (Kertzer), 9
Myers, Mitzi, 42n6; "Impeccable Governesses, Rational Dames, and Moral Mothers," 27; "Of Mice and Mothers," 42n6
Myths of Motherhood, The (Thurer), 4, 96–97, 101, 221

Nancy Drew series, 235
narrators: adult, 14, 62; child, 14, 50, 51, 55, 56, 57n5, 62, 101, 102, 106; daughters, 80, 90, 92, 126; granddaughters, 87; mothers, 46, 51; multiple, 118, 122; son, 225. *See also under* adolescent girls
natural caring, 185, 193. *See also* care ethics
Negra, Diane, 204, 213
"Negro Mother, The" (Hughes), 113, 117, 124, 125, 127, 128
Nelson, Marilyn, 16, 114, 121, 122–24, 126, 127, 128, 130
Nesbit, E., 56
Ness, Patrick, 19, 235
Nevers, Patricia, 166
new momism, 204
Newbery, Linda, 15, 78, 87, 88, 89
Newport, Elissa L., "Mother, I'd Rather Do It Myself," 42n7; "Motherese," 42n7
Nikolajeva, Maria, 186–87, 188
Noddings, Nel, 4, 17, 182, 184–86, 189–90, 193
nostalgia, 98, 179–80

Obstinate Maid, An (Rhoden), 59, 70
O'Connell, Paul, 166n1
Oedipus complex, 8, 19, 205, 235, 239–40, 243–45; failure of, 241; female, 237; positive, 247n2
Of Woman Born (Rich), 20n4, 172
O'Keefe, Adelaide, 29
Oliver, Lauren, 247
Olsen, Tillie, "Writer-Mothers," 20n4
101 Animal Babies (Berger), 156, 157, 162
Oppenheimer, Deborah, 81
O'Reilly, Andrea, 6–7, 9, 20n3, 110n1
Original Stories from Real Life (Wollestonecraft), 29
orphans, 48, 55, 56, 68, 78; in narrative, 18, 88, 218
Ostby, Kristin, 156
Ostertag, Julia, 154, 155, 164
Other People's Houses (Segal), 15, 77, 78, 79, 80–83, 91
othermothering, 14, 15, 59, 60, 61, 66, 72; as romance, 73; and single women, 66, 67
othermothers: adolescent girls as, 61, 63; authors as, 61–62; characters as, 63; Christian God as, 65, 71; mentors as, 63; stories as, 70, 71
Outsiders, The (Hinton), 213n3, 235

Page, Robin, 156, 162
Panda Baby (Toast), 156
Panda Bear Cub (Moody-Luther), 156
Panda Kindergarten (Ryder), 156, 159
parenting
  communal, 5, 105
  as crisis, 170–71
  eighteenth-century models, 27
  of Kindertransportees, 77, 78, 79, 81, 83, 84–85, 89–90, 92n3
  techniques, 31–33, 38–39, 40, 129
  in young adult literature, 11, 20n2, 213n3, 234–35

Parent's Assistant, The (Edgeworth), 27
Parsons, Elizabeth, "The Other Mother," 12
Paterson, Katherine, 18, 219, 221–22, 229
patriarchy, 60, 106, 127, 182–84, 189, 191, 194, 226, 237, 243–44
Paul, Lissa, 41n1
Pearson, Claudia H., 11
pedagogy: eighteenth-century rational, 27; maternal, 13–14, 27, 34, 36; modern, 30; role of play in, 30, 34
Perfect Madness (Warner), 7
Perrault, Charles, 235
Peskowitz, Miriam, 20n2
Peter and Wendy (Barrie), 17, 170–81
philosophy, feminist, 182. *See also* care ethics; thinking, maternal
photographs, 80, 86, 89, 90, 91, 92
Pick, Alison, 15, 78, 80, 90–91, 92
Pickering, Samuel F., 41n2, 42n6
picture books, 17, 97, 218
Pignatori, Anna, 99
Pilgrim's Progress, in Words of One Syllable, The (Aikin), 35
Pi-shu, the Little Panda (Butler), 156, 161
play, 30–32, 34, 41n5
Playing and Reality (Winnicott), 171, 174, 175
Plots of Enlightenment (Barney), 41n2
Poems on Various Subjects, for the Amusement of Youth (Kilner, Dorothy and Mary Ann), 30
Poovey, Mary, 53
postfeminism, 12, 13, 18, 202, 207, 208, 210, 212, 213; and class, 204; critiques of, 204–5; defined, 203–5; and gender, 213; and heteronormativity, 204; relationship to feminism, 204–5, 213; and whiteness, 204
power, 16, 115, 118; fear of maternal, 230; heterosexual models of, 61, 142; imbalance between adults and children, 17, 183

Practical Education (Edgeworth, Richard Lovell), 14, 36
Pramling, Niklas, 165
Pratchett, Terry, 16, 135, 142, 145, 147n5
Precept and Example, or a Midsummer's Holiday (Elliott), 29
pregnancy, 194–95
Prentiss, Elizabeth, 61, 64, 66, 67
Price of Motherhood, The (Crittenden), 7
Prior, Paul, 114–15
problems, domestic, 65
Psychoanalytic Approaches to Children's Literature (Rollin and West), 10
Pullman, Philip, 18
Puma Range (Armour), 156, 157, 160, 163
"Purple Jar, The" (Edgeworth, Maria), 27

queer theory, 19

Raccoon on His Own (Arnosky), 156, 157, 160
racism, 105, 106, 107, 108, 109, 127, 217
Rambles Further (Smith, Charlotte), 29
realism: contemporary, 18, 219; nineteenth-century domestic, 45
Rebecca of Sunnybrook Farm (Wiggin), 66
"refrigerator mothers," 140
rejection, maternal, 87
relational theory, 190
replacement mother: in *Dicey's Song*, 223, 225; Other Mother in *Coraline*, 173–78; Wendy in Neverland, 175, 176. *See also* Collins, Patricia Hill; othermothering; othermothers
representation, maternal, 77–78; romanticizing of, 79
Representations of Motherhood (Bassin, Honey, and Kaplan), 10, 225
Reproduction of Mothering, The (Chodorow), 14, 176; Fraustino on, 11, 230n3; Rollin on, 10
resilience, maternal, 99, 100

response priming, 30, 32
Rhoden, Emmy von, 61, 70
Rhymes for the Nursery (Taylor), 14, 36–37
Rice, Tamir, 113, 128
Rich, Adrienne, 4, 20n4, 172
Riggs, Ransom, 88
Ringrose, Jessica, 203
Robbins, Sarah, 36
Roberts, Dorothy E., "Racism and Patriarchy in the Meaning of Motherhood," 106, 109, 127
Robinson Crusoe, in Words of One Syllable (Aikin), 35
Robinson, Fiona, 17, 182, 190, 191
Robothon, Rosemarie, 109
Rollin, Lucy, 8; "The Good-Enough Mother Hubbard," 10; "The Reproduction of Mothering in *Charlotte's Web*," 10
romance, 14, 59; heterosexual, 59, 73, 211–12, 233–34; othermothering as, 73; spiritual, 59, 73
Rose, Jacqueline, 230
Rosenberger, Nancy, 138
Ross, Michael Elsohn, 153, 156
Roth, Veronica, 247
Roth, Wolff-Michael, 116, 124–25
Rousseau, Jean-Jacques, 28
Rowbotham, Judith, 46
Rowe-Finkbeiner, Kristin, 20n2
Rowling, J. K., 235
Ruddick, Sara, 4, 17, 182–86, 192, 193–94, 230; *Maternal Thinking: Toward a Politics of Peace*, 196n2, 20n4; "Thinking Mothers/Conceiving Birth," 20n5
Runaway Bunny, The (Brown), 99
Rural Walks (Smith, Charlotte), 29
Russell, Mary Harris, 187–88, 189, 190
Russell-Brown, Katheryn, 15, 99, 107–8
Rustin, Margaret, 8
Rustin, Michael, 8
Rutledge, Amelia, 188–89, 191

Ruwe, Donelle, 41n1
Ryder, Joanne, 156, 159

sacrifice, maternal, 101, 128, 170–71, 177–78, 188, 191–92, 222
Saint Anything (Dessen), 213n1
Saitō, Minako, 147n3
Salinger, J. D., 213n3
Sanders, Joe Sutliff, 11
Sanford and Merton, in Words of One Syllable (Aikin), 35
Sarah Dessen: From Burritos to Box Office (Glenn), 206
Sawers, Naarah, "The Other Mother," 12
schemas, 133, 136, 139, 141, 143, 145, 146; nurturing mother, 137
scripts, 133–46; coming-of-age, 134, 136; cultural, 139; defined, 133–34; living Earth, 134; nurturing mother, 134, 141; prison, 140
Secret Garden, The (Burnett), 56
Segal, Lore Groszmann, 15, 77, 78, 79, 80–83, 91, 92n4
Semple, Elizabeth, 35
Sexual Politics in the Enlightenment (Trouille), 28
Sherwin, Susan, 190
Shonoda, Mary-Anne, 134
Short Stories, in Words of One Syllable (Semple), 35
Show Way (Woodson), 16, 114, 115, 116–17, 121, 122, 125, 127
Shusterman, Neal, 247
Sidel, Ruth, 6
"signifying." *See* Gates, Henry Louis: signifying
Silences (Olsen), 20n4
Silverstein, Shel, 7, 97
Simmons, Elly, 104
Simons, Judy, 46
Sisterland (Newbery), 15, 78, 80, 87–90, 91, 92

Sisters & Brothers (Jenkins and Page), 156, 162

Six to Sixteen (Ewing), 14, 45–57

Slaughter, Anne-Marie, "Why Women Still Can't Have It All," 201

slavery, mothering under, 127

Sleeping Beauty, 183

Smith, Adam, 30

Smith, Charlotte, 29

Smith-Rosenberg, Carroll, 64, 69; "pseudomothering," 69

social constructions. *See* biology; feminist views of mothering; motherhood: ideologies of

Some Thoughts Concerning Education (Locke), 2

Someone Like You (Dessen), 209

sons, 7, 13, 30, 38, 109–10, 124, 129, 141, 227, 228–29; mother's influence on, 105, 106; as "property," 127; relationship with mother, 98

spaces, domestic, 45, 47, 52, 53, 62, 135, 136, 138, 183

Spencer, Herbert, 158

Spindle's End (McKinley), 18, 183, 193–95, 196n3

Spyri, Johanna, 88

Squier, Susan, 175

stand-in mother. *See* replacement mother

Stephens, John, "Mishmash, Conceptual Blending and Adaptation in Contemporary Children's Literature Written in Dutch and English," 147n1; "Schemas and Scripts," 147n1

stepmothers: fairy tale representations of, 4; in realistic fiction, 18, 202

stories, domestic, 14, 50–51, 52–53, 56; fantasy, 45; realistic, 45, 46, 47

storytelling, maternal, 80, 126

subjectivity, 13, 18, 134, 166, 173, 179; female, 203; individual, 204

Suleiman, Susan Rubin, "Writing and Motherhood," 20n4, 230

Sutton, Roger, 218

Sweanor, Linda L., 163

Swiftly Tilting Planet, A (L'Engle), 18, 193, 194–95, 196n4

Swiss Family Robinson, in Words of One Syllable, The (Aikin), 35

Taming a Tomboy (Rhoden), 59, 70

Tasker, Yvonne, 204, 213

Taylor, Ann, 14, 36–37

Taylor, Jane, 14, 36–37

Thank You, God, for Mommy (Parker), 156

That Summer (Dessen), 206–7

The New Don't Blame Mother (Caplan), 217

Theory of Moral Sentiments, The (Smith, Adam), 30

thinking, maternal, 7, 11, 19, 183, 185, 193. *See also* Ruddick, Sara

This Lullaby (Dessen), 212

This Side of Home (Watson), 118–19, 121–22, 124, 125

Thulin, Suzanne, 165

Thurer, Shari L., 4–5, 96–97, 99, 101, 221

Tiger in the Attic, The (Milton), 78

Till, Emmett, 113, 128

Till-Mobley, Mamie, 128–30

Timmerman, Nora, 154, 155, 164

Toast, Sarah, 156, 157

toddlers, 29, 32, 33

Tolson, Nancy D., 126

Tomkins, Joseph, 158

Toning the Sweep (Johnson), 16, 114, 115, 117–18, 121, 126, 127

Transgender Voices (Girshick), 147n1

trauma, 86, 90, 247n7; and childhood memory, 78

Travis, Madelyn, 79, 80

Treagust, David F., 164, 165

Treat, John Whittier, 136

Trimmer, Sarah, 14, 29, 35

Trites, Roberta Seelinger, 134, 135, 205; "Growth in Adolescent Literature," 147n1
Troester, Rosalie Riegle, 73
Trouille, Mary, 28
Truth About Forever, The (Dessen), 207, 208
Truth Behind the Mommy Wars, The (Peskowitz), 20n2
Turner, Mark, 16, 133–34

Umansky, Lauri, 9
Unwind series (Shusterman), 247

Venville, Grady J., 165
virtues, domestic, 66, 68
Voigt, Cynthia, 18, 216, 221, 223, 224, 229
Vygotsky, Lev, 16, 114, 120, 124

Walker, Alice, 4, 18, 216, 217, 229; "A Child of One's Own," 20n4, 102, 230n2; "Taking Care of the Truth: A Meditation on the Complicity of Wikipedia," 217; "A Woman Is Not a Potted Plant," 110; "A Writer Because of, Not in Spite of, Her Children," 20n4, 230n2
Walker, Carl, 166n1
Walker, Rebecca, 18, 216–18, 221, 225; "Becoming the Third Wave," 230, 230n1; "How My Mother's Fanatical Views Tore Us Apart," 217
Warne, Robin W., 158
Warner, Judith, 7
Water-Babies, The (Kingsley), 3
Watson, Renée, 16, 114, 115, 116, 118–19, 121, 124, 127
We Came as Children (Gershon), 78
We Like to Nurse (Martin), 153, 156
Wee Free Men, The (Pratchett), 16, 135, 142–46
Wenger, Etienne, 122
West, Mark I., 10

Wharton, Joanna, 42n6
When Zachary Beaver Came to Town (Holt), 19, 216, 225–29
whiteness: and mothers, 61, 106, 127; and postfeminist assumptions, 204; and Western culture, 99, 113, 170
Whitney, A. D. T., 59, 62–63, 66, 68, 69
Wigutoff, Sharon, "Junior Fiction," 218, 221
Williams, Frances, 78
Willner, Dorothy, 247n2
Winnicott, D. W., 8, 10, 17, 171, 173, 174, 175, 176, 178; Benjamin on, 20n5, 100, 173
Wolff, Ashley, 153
Wollestonecraft, Mary, 29, 41n1
Woman That Never Evolved, The (Hrdy), 5
Women and the Shaping of the Nation's Young (Hilton), 41n1
women's rights movement, 218–19, 229
women's studies, 10
Woodson, Jacqueline, 16, 114, 116–17, 121, 122, 125, 127
"work/life balance," 201, 204, 211; as impossible, 213. *See also* "having it all"
Wreath for Emmett Till, A (Nelson), 16, 114, 115, 121, 122–24, 126, 127, 128, 130
writers, male, 45
Written Maternal Authority and Eighteenth-Century Education in Britain (Davies), 41n1

Yonge, Charlotte, 47
Yoshimoto, Banana, 16, 135, 138, 147n3

Zeilinger, Julie, 203
Zoehfeld, Kathleen Weidner, 156, 157, 160, 163
Zohar, Anat, 164

Lightning Source UK Ltd.
Milton Keynes UK
UKHW01f2355290818
328029UK00002B/144/P